Relational Therapy
for Personality Disorders

WILEY SERIES IN COUPLES AND FAMILY DYNAMICS AND TREATMENT

FLORENCE W. KASLOW, SERIES EDITOR

Family Assessment: Effective Uses of Personality Tests With Couples and Families
by A. Rodney Nurse

Handbook of Relational Diagnosis and Dysfunctional Family Patterns
edited by Florence W. Kaslow

Treating the Changing Family: Handling Normative and Unusual Events
edited by Michele Harway

In-Laws: A Guide to Extended-Family Therapy
by Gloria Call Horsley

Strange Attractors: Chaos, Complexity, and the Art of Family Therapy
by Michael R. Bütz, Linda L. Chamberlain, and William G. McCown

Child-Centered Family Therapy
by Lucille L. Andreozzi

Infertility: Psychological Issues and Counseling Strategies
edited by Sandra R. Leiblum

The Self in the Family: A Classification of Personality, Criminality, and Psychopathology
by Luciano L'Abate, with the collaboration of Margaret S. Baggett

Painful Partings: Divorce and Its Aftermath
by Lita Linzer Schwartz and Florence W. Kaslow

Relationship Enhancement Family Therapy
by Barry G. Ginsberg

Ethical and Legal Issues in Professional Practice With Families
by Diane T. Marsh and Richard D. Magee

The Art of the Question: A Guide to Short-Term Question-Centered Therapy
by Marilee C. Goldberg

Relational Therapy for Personality Disorders
by Jeffrey J. Magnavita

Relational Therapy for Personality Disorders

JEFFREY J. MAGNAVITA

JOHN WILEY & SONS, INC.

New York • Chichester • Weinheim • Brisbane • Singapore • Toronto

Copyright © 2000 by John Wiley & Sons, Inc. All rights reserved.

Published simultaneously in Canada.

Library of Congress Cataloging-in-Publication Data:
Magnavita, Jeffrey J.
    Relational therapy for personality disorders/Jeffrey J. Magnavita.
        p.   cm.—(Wiley series in couples and family dynamics and treatment)
    Includes bibliographical references and index.
    ISBN 0-471-29566-3 (alk. paper)
    1. Brief psychotherapy. 2. Psychodynamic psychotherapy.
I. Title. II. Series.
RC554.M228 2000
616.89′ 14—dc21

Printed in the United States of America.
10 9 8 7 6 5 4 3 2 1

This book is dedicated to my parents, Hugo and Elsie

Finally, like the other great forces of nature—such as gravity, electricity, and the four winds—a relationship itself is invisible; its existence discerned only by observing its effects.

(Berscheid, 1999, p. 261)

Series Preface

Our ability to form strong and meaningful interpersonal bonds with romantic partners, children, parents, siblings, and other relatives is one of the key qualities that defines our humanity. These relationships shape who we are and what we become—they can be a source of great gratification of tremendous pain. Yet only in the mid-twentieth century did behavioral and social scientists really begin focusing on couples and family dynamics, and only in the last several decades have the theory and findings that emerged from studies on couples and families been used to develop effective therapeutic interventions.

We have made great progress in understanding the structure, function, and interactional patterns of couples and families—and made tremendous strides in treatment. However, it seems quite clear that both intimate partnerships and family relationships are in a period of tremendous flux. Economic factors are changing work patterns, parenting responsibilities, and relational dynamics. Modern medicine has helped lengthen the life span, giving rise to the need for transgenerational caregiving. Cohabitation, divorce, and remarriage are quite commonplace, and these social changes make it necessary for us to rethink and broaden our definition of what constitutes a family.

It is no longer enough simply to embrace the concept of the family as a system. In order to understand and effectively treat the evolving family, our theoretical formulations and clinical interventions must be informed by an understanding of ethnicity, culture, religion, gender, sexual preference, family life cycle, socioeconomic status, education, physical and mental health, values, and belief systems.

The purpose of the *Wiley Series in Couples and Family Dynamics and Treatment* is to provide a forum for cutting-edge relational and family theory, practice, and research, and also to offer an interdisciplinary venue for exploring areas that overlap several professional disciplines. Its scope is intended to be broad, diverse, and international, but all books published in this series share a common mission—to reflect on the past, offer state-of-the art information on the present, and speculate on, as well as attempt to shape, the future of the field.

Florence W. Kaslow
Florida Couples and Family Institute
Series Editor

Preface

E ven senior mental health professionals have asked me, "You don't really believe that personality-disordered patients substantially change, do you?" Theodore Millon (1990), a well-grounded empiricist and scientist, comments on this issue:

> With support and courage, human beings can be coaxed into transcending their limitations, into doing what was before considered practically impossible. No one, however, can do what is logically impossible. When personality disorders are framed through the medical model, personality change is paradigmatically impossible. Individuals who see themselves as vessels for a diseased personality should be disabused of this notion. (p. 185)

This book further advances the field of family therapy by offering practitioners and researchers a comprehensive biopsychosocial treatment model that uses a relational framework to classify and treat dysfunctional personologic systems. It is my experience that this relational framework will potentiate treatment interventions that currently exist as well as pave the way for new developments in the treatment of personality syndromes and the relationship systems that spawn them. This book capitalizes on a synergistic phase of parallel developments in classification of personality, integrative psychotherapy, research-based theoretical models of change, affective science, relational diagnosis, and psychotherapeutic approaches. This area of tremendous promise and excitement offers the hope of addressing one of the major causes of familial and societal dysfunction.

ACCELERATING THE ADVANCEMENTS: A CALL FOR COLLABORATION

A number of books already discuss treatment models that specifically focus on personality disorders. Why, then, is there a need for another book on this topic? The most fundamental need for this book has been caused by the rapid advancements in various subfields of personality and by the need to integrate this burgeoning, theoretical clinical and research material in a manner that has clinical utility. Strack and Lorr (1997) summarize their view of these changes: "The complexity of personality, and the differences in the way people view the subject matter, ensure that there will be several research lines in the next generation. Progress can be quickened by refinements in theory, the development of more assessment instruments that tap both normal and abnormal traits, and empirical studies that follow well-matched groups of normals and patients over significant periods" (p. 105). It is crucial that clinicians who daily face disorders of personality have at their fingertips the most current information on assessment, patient engagement, and treatment matching to potentiate treatment interventions. Clinicians have accumulated sufficient clinical evidence and theoretical support to present a comprehensive relational approach to the diagnosis and treatment of disorders of personality. This approach is significant for the emotional suffering that results from personality pathology and the financial ramifications of providing treatment that may or may not work.

Jeffrey J. Magnavita

Acknowledgments

I am extremely grateful to the many people who helped me create this book. Many of the ideas for this book come from the work of other clinicians, researchers, and theorists who have contributed to the development of this integrative relational model and method of treating personality disorders. I offer a special thank you to Dr. Florence Kaslow for challenging me to devise a relational diagnostic system for personality disorders and for inviting me to write this book for the Wiley Series in Couples and Family Dynamics and Treatment.

The integrative approach outlined in this book is derived from the work of many people, but especially of Dr. Theodore Millon, who developed many of the theoretical concepts and whose thinking on the subject is always at least a step ahead of the rest of us. He is generous with support and encouragement and willingly shares his passion for the field. His comments on the manuscript assured me that I was on the right path.

I also want to thank Dr. Marvin Goldfried, whose work in integrative psychotherapy has had a major influence on many theorists and clinicians. His ability to bring together various camps in the field of psychotherapy and to encourage dialogue through a common language has led to many advancements in integrative treatment. His creativity and organizational ability have shaped two organizations devoted to advancing the practice and science of psychotherapy: Society of Psychotherapy Researchers and Society for Psychotherapy Integration. Marvin's work in conceiving and editing the journal *In Session: Psychotherapy in Practice* constitutes a major contribution, bridging the clinician/researcher gap in the field. My collaboration with him in his relentless striving for clarity has sharpened my own writing and theoretical formulations.

Another important member of the psychotherapy integration movement who has been encouraging and supportive of my work is Dr. Stanley Messer, whose understanding of and commitment to the psychodynamic model were especially helpful in my first book, *Restructuring Personality Disorders: A Short-Term Dynamic Approach,* and influenced the focus of this one.

I am indebted to the pioneers in the field of short-term dynamic therapy. I would especially like to thank Dr. Habib Davanloo for his contributions to the field and for the training in individual therapy that I had the privilege of receiving from him. His intuitive knowledge of the unconscious is remarkable and his innovations are groundbreaking.

I would also like to thank Dr. Jeri Hepworth for taking the time to edit and comment on the first half of the manuscript. She was extremely generous with both her time and expertise.

My early development as a clinician was formed by my experience working at Elmcrest Psychiatric Institute in the early 1980s when systemic therapy was exploding on the clinical landscape. My experience as a clinical psychology intern and then as a staff psychologist was stimulating because of my exposure to some of the pioneers in family therapy, including Dr. Carl Whitaker and Dr. Salvatore Minuchin, who presented at workshops there. Working under the medical directors, Dr. Louis Fireman and Dr. Lane Ameen, and the director of education, Dr. Leo Berman, case conferences, seminars, and supervision afforded me the opportunity to learn and practice various modes of intensive individual and family therapy in an inpatient setting. Their dedication to training and educating their staff was far beyond what was typical at the time. I am also indebted to Dr. Anthony Ferrante, who generously invited me into his private practice and has encouraged and supported my work throughout my career. His ability to conceptualize complex cases in simple, relevant terms is a skill I continually strive to emulate. I would also like to thank Dr. Leslie Strong, one of my first instructors in family therapy, who encouraged me in this project from the start and who suggested critical reading.

My core group, Dr. William Alder, Dr. Frank Knoblauch, and Dr. Vincent Stephens, has provided a forum for me to express my ideas, often in heated debate, but always with a deep sense of acceptance and encouragement. Our monthly dinners have supported my growth as a psychotherapist in a setting that Carl Whitaker described as a "professional cuddle group" with others who believe in the value and potency of psychotherapy and share concern over its demise.

I want to thank my editor, Kelly Franklin, for her belief in the value of this book and her efforts to keep me on the path of clinical utility, so that my book will have daily relevance to those who are learning psychotherapy as well as to those who practice it. I would also like to acknowledge Karen Dorman for her meticulous copyediting of this book. Her eye for detail is much appreciated.

A heartfelt thanks is due to all attendees at my workshops and seminars. Through interaction and feedback, these individuals provided a needed antidote to the solitary task of writing and, more important, influenced my critical thinking and motivation.

Thanks to my patients for teaching me so much of what is important about the process of change, and thanks especially to those who have agreed to allow me to disguise and use their clinical material in my book.

Most important, I want to thank my wife and partner, Anne Gardner Magnavita, for her constant support, critical commentary, and deep appreciation of my life's work. Without her involvement, writing this book would not have been as exciting and enjoyable an experience. My joy in life is always sparked by my daughters, Elizabeth, Emily, and Caroline, who light the way to our future.

Contents

Chapter 1
ADVANCEMENTS AND TRENDS IN THE TREATMENT
OF PERSONALITY DISORDERS 1

Chapter 2
THEORY OF INTEGRATIVE RELATIONAL
PSYCHOTHERAPY 19

Chapter 3
DYSFUNCTIONAL PERSONOLOGIC SYSTEMS 49

Chapter 4
THEORIES, MODELS, AND TECHNIQUES
OF INTEGRATIVE RELATIONAL PSYCHOTHERAPY 71

Chapter 5
INTEGRATIVE RELATIONAL ASSESSMENT 89

Chapter 6
STAGES OF CHANGE: RESTRUCTURING
DYSFUNCTIONAL PERSONOLOGIC SYSTEMS 107

Chapter 7
INITIATING CHANGE AT SYSTEM FULCRUM POINTS 127

Chapter 8
TREATMENT MATCHING AND SELECTION FACTORS 157

Chapter 9
LANGUAGE OF THE THERAPEUTIC ALLIANCE 185

Chapter 10
TREATING THE COUPLE THROUGH THE INTEGRATIVE
RELATIONAL APPROACH 201

Chapter 11
MAXIMIZING THE THERAPEUTIC ALLIANCE IN THE
RELATIONAL MATRIX 221

Chapter 12
PREVENTION AND EARLY INTERVENTION:
USING THE RELATIONAL MATRIX 239

REFERENCES 249

AUTHOR INDEX 269

SUBJECT INDEX 273

CHAPTER 1

Advancements and Trends in the Treatment of Personality Disorders

She will not go home again, the 15-year-old runaway told her caseworker, her guidance counselor and her therapist, in no uncertain terms.

She has yanked her mother from a bar for the last time, the girl said. Undressed her for the last time because she was too drunk to put herself to bed. Taken the last blow from her grandfather. Heard the last of her grandmother's screaming, so loud that even rap music wouldn't drown it out.

"I'll go anyplace but home," said the blond, lanky teen-ager, who arrived at a runaway shelter here bruised but smiling, relieved to be at a secret location where her family could not find her. "If I have to keep running, I'll keep running. I've had enough."

(Gross, 1997, p. B1)

The same week that this article appeared in *The New York Times*, a public television special told of a six-year-old child who, apparently unprovoked, assaulted an infant and in so doing caused severe brain damage to the child ("Little criminals," 1997). A mental health professional, with all the confidence of science, revealed after his one-hour evaluation that the child was "genetically predisposed to be a murderer" and suggested that this incident was a case of a "natural born killer." The level of family pathology, only briefly mentioned in the report, included repeated

1

incidents of witnessed violence, clear neglect, and maternal substance abuse. The fact that many members of his nuclear and extended family showed evidence of personality disorder was never given attention. Instead, one expert assumed that the disorder existed within the boy; various professionals debated whether this "natural born killer" could ever be rehabilitated, while he spent six months incarcerated with teenagers and locked up every night in his cell.

These two episodes are examples of countless stories with similar themes. The common theme that they represent is dysfunctional personologic systems of a severe type. Other, less severe forms of dysfunctional personologic systems never are exposed and exist quietly and destructively for generations; each generation passes down a high incidence of different types of personality disorder.

The assertions made in this book about dysfunctional personologic families have also been observed by many novelists. Angeline Goreau (1997) writes:

> For years, I took it on faith that Tolstoy knew what he was talking about when he told us, "All happy families are alike; every unhappy family is unhappy in its own way." But on the accumulating evidence of recent memoirs, I've come around to the view that unhappy families may be more alike than we've given them credit for. (p. 5)

The complex variables that determine personality and the system in which it is configured are overwhelming without a system to organize these data. Professionals far too often work with a narrow field of variables from the broad biopsychosocial spectrum which does not necessarily take into consideration other influences at work. McGoldrick and Gerson (1985) presaged this book in their landmark book on the family genogram: "Given different family structural configurations mapped on the genogram, the clinician can tentatively predict likely personality characteristics and relational compatibility problems" (p. 5).

CASE STUDY: THE FAMILY WHO WERE HELD HOSTAGE

A neurologist treated an adolescent male for a number of years with various medications to little avail. Referrals to mental health professionals were met with defiance by the index patient and with poor treatment compliance by the family. The boy was out of control, threatening, emotionally labile, and provoking, and on occasion, he physically attacked his father and younger brother. The patient fluctuated between infantile dependency, asking his mother to pour his milk for him, for example, and grandiose demands that his material needs be immediately met. Parents were demoralized and at the end of their rope. During the family consultation, the boy made fun of previous therapists and belittled and humiliated his father in a sneering and sarcastic fashion while his mother sighed repeatedly. His younger brother was laughing but seemed terrified that his parents were being held hostage and their impotence exposed.

How does the clinician conceptualize and approach treatment in such a case? Certainly a multimodal or sequential treatment approach is required, but where does the clinician target the intervention, and where is the fulcrum point likely to result in the most substantial restructuring of this family system? This boy was exhibiting a disturbance in his personality, but there were many obvious contributing factors, such as lack of hierarchy, triangulation with parents, multigenerational patterns of abuse, and so on. School and treatment records showed a chronic pattern of behavioral disturbance, narcissistic entitlement, problems with authority, and recalcitrance. A biopsychosocial model embedded in a relational context can account for the multiple factors of genetics, temperament, attachment, parenting style, psychological structure, and ecosystem. Closer inspection revealed some interesting findings concerning the multigenerational transmission process in this family.

Family history and a genogram showed that both parents came from dysfunctional families that had a higher than normal rate of personality pathology. The mother often witnessed violent interactions, and the father was the target of a moderate degree of physical and emotional abuse. Another child, an older sibling of the index patient, was diagnosed as having a mixed antisocial/narcissistic personality and was discharged from the armed forces because of repeated difficulties. He was violent and abusive, and the younger children on occasion witnessed these explosions. The father also lost control on occasion when provoked.

Multiple members of the family were suffering from the results of these traumatic events and responded differently, depending on their personalities. Both parents seemed to have personologic disturbances, or what has been traditionally referred to as character pathology. Chronic marital disturbance was also evident. The patient was clearly caught between the parents and was distracting them from their marital conflict. This family showed features of a dysfunctional personologic system, in this case, a physically traumatizing subtype.

Dysfunctional personologic systems are organized around central pathological themes that, although unique, share certain common features that structure their interactions. These systems are based on the high likelihood of reinforcing or producing individuals that suffer from a range of personality and subsyndromal disorders. This book focuses on these families and shows how to assess, classify, engage, and ultimately restructure them.

This book works toward enhancing awareness, reducing stigma, and preventing the multigenerational transmission process.

THE PROBLEM OF PERSONALITY PATHOLOGY AND THE CHALLENGE OF FINDING NEW SOLUTIONS

A PARADIGMATIC SHIFT

In the new millennium, clinicians and researchers are faced with the challenge of finding new solutions to the treatment of disorders of personality. This area of research, theory, and clinical practice is experiencing what Sperry (1995) has aptly labeled a "paradigmatic shift." Millon (Millon & Davis, 1996), reflecting on the last 15 years, comments: "It is no understatement to describe the growth of the field of personality disorders as exponential" (p. vii). A little more than a decade has passed since the treatment of personality disorders was considered not very possible, and forms of specialized therapy have evolved or been developed with application to disorders of personality. Most clinicians as well as epidemiologists have witnessed an increase in the segment of the population that suffers from disorders of personality or character disturbances. Shapiro (1996) comments on the ubiquity of personality pathology:

> A great deal of clinical evidence now confirms that psychopathology is in fact characterological. Even the most peculiar symptoms, symptoms that seem mysterious even to their subject, are not the alien intrusions into everyday subjective life that they were once thought to be. Close observation invariably shows them to be absolutely consistent with the attitudes, the ways of thinking, and the sorts of subjective experience that are characteristic of the individual. (p. 6)

Less is known about dysfunctional personologic systems although evidence is accumulating in various branches of family therapy that provides a solid starting point for a system of classification and integrative treatment.

Even for those clinicians who do not directly treat patients with disorders of personality and dysfunctional personologic systems, an understanding of systems theory is necessary for efficient treatment of various co-morbid clinical syndromes.

BREAKTHROUGH PROBLEMS FOR PSYCHOTHERAPY

Mahrer (1997) describes a breakthrough problem as "a problem whose solution is recognized as opening the way to major advances in the field of psychotherapy" (p. 81). These central problems in the field of psychotherapy include various important formulations. Listed here are Mahrer's formulations that are relevant for my purposes:

- How can psychotherapy enable a client [*or family*] to undergo radical, in-depth, qualitative, transformational change toward what the particular client is capable of becoming?
- How can such radical, qualitative changes be accomplished quickly and effectively, even within a single session? How can such radical, qualitative, in-session changes persist and endure into the person's extratherapy world? (p. 84)

Developing effective treatments for personality disorders would certainly qualify as a breakthrough, and progress is being made on various fronts.

Bridging the Gap Between Research and Practice

In the field of mental health, psychotherapists and researchers are being called to bridge the gap that has often separated research findings from clinical practice. Goldfried and Wolfe (1996) drive home the point that was in part the impetus to write this book: "For example, the typical panic disorder patient seen in private practice would often meet criteria for other Axis I and II disorders. Yet the available treatment-efficacy research data is typically based on patients whose clinical pictures are not as complicated" (p. 1011). In fact: "It is very likely that client variables, including personality factors and comorbidity, interact in a very strong way with the effects of psychological (and pharmacological) interventions" (Barlow, 1996, p. 1055). Goldfried and Wolfe described some of the crucial issues related to making research more relevant to clinical dilemmas, some of which are:

- How to treat patients who suffer from more than one Axis I disorder, which is more typical of what the clinician faces on a daily basis.

- How to treat underlying "personality" issues and other determinants/dynamics that may be directly related to symptoms of a particular disorder. It is no longer tenable, if it ever was, to argue that these issues either do not exist or are not relevant for effective treatment (p. 1011).

And I add a third:

- How to effectively assess and treat the dysfunctional systems that engender and sustain personality pathology.

I agree with Maxmen and Ward (1995), who state that "recognizing and healing psychopathology is an everyday task for every helping professional" (p. x). I hope to inspire psychotherapists to become more effective practitioners by becoming active clinical researchers within their own practices and to see their development as a continually evolving integration of new findings and methods. This book emphasizes the *clinical utility* of the concepts, methods, and techniques that are covered here. Although efficacy findings are important to the development of the field of psychotherapy, there is danger in misuse of this information by managed care organizations. Seligman (1996) comments: "The practice of psychotherapy is now seriously threatened by predatory health schemes that welcome efficacy studies as a bedfellow for just this reason. By overlooking the questionable external validity of efficacy studies, these schemes are able to justify offering only brief and inexpensive treatment to all patients" (p. 1073). As I explain in subsequent chapters, and as all practicing clinicians who treat clinical syndromes are aware, this task is much more complex than many researchers would have clinicians believe. Seligman summarizes his conclusions concisely:

> The disinterested conclusion should be as follows: (a) If a case is simple, if a manual must be followed, if the diagnosis is made by a more experienced and better trained clinician, and if treatment must be brief, less experienced and less well-educated providers may do as well as doctoral-level specialists; (b) it seems likely that in real therapy, in which cases are complicated and more severe, no manuals are used, diagnosis as well as therapy must be done, and clinical judgment is important, more education and more experience of providers will improve outcomes; and (c) effectiveness studies of level of education and experience of providers and the cost-benefit analysis are urgently needed. (pp. 1077–1078)

The professional success of a practicing clinician is the ability to establish and maintain positive therapeutic alliances as well as the ability to demonstrate clinical effectiveness (Goldfried & Wolfe, 1996). Nowhere are these abilities more important than with patients suffering from personality pathology and their families, whose very nature often prevents easy engagement. Thus, an understanding of the techniques of motivational interviewing (Miller & Rollnick, 1991) and relapse prevention (Brownell, Marlatt, Lichtenstein & Wilson, 1986; Daley & Lis, 1995; Marlatt & Gordon, 1985) as well as a systematic review of the patient's therapeutic progress and outcome become crucial components of treatment effectiveness, continuous improvement, and quality assurance (Magnavita, 1997b).

PERSONALITY PATHOLOGY SEEN AS EXISTING WITHIN THE INDIVIDUAL

Historically, personality pathology was defined as existing within the individual; subsequently, the treatment of choice to restructure the personality was long-term, analytically oriented psychotherapy or psychoanalysis. For individuals with more serious personality pathology, psychotherapy was considered unnecessary because the primitive structure of these patients made them intolerant to derepressive psychotherapy. A patient who was not motivated for individual treatment was often labeled resistant and declared untreatable. When patients did enter individual, usually long-term, psychotherapy for characterological disturbances, the treatment was often insulated, and a sense of timelessness was engendered. Patients were discouraged from making major life decisions until analysis was completed.

Clinicians were taught not to mix modalities or risk disturbing the delicate transference neurosis and contaminating the unconscious process (Fosha, 1995). Other therapists were often not consulted, and a team approach was not considered justifiable. These standards and conditions limited the spectrum of personality-disordered patients who could be effectively treated, even if they were motivated to embark on a lengthy and costly treatment. This perspective led to a period of demoralization for many clinicians and to a feeling of frustration.

On the positive side, psychoanalytically oriented therapists have made substantial contributions to the understanding of character pathology by offering incisive descriptions that are still relevant (Millon & Davis, 1996). A number of innovative pioneers attempted to counter the trend toward longer analysis and searched for brief methods of characterological transformation. The first pioneer, Sandor Ferenczi (Ferenczi & Rank, 1925), experimented with various forms and techniques of active therapy that ran against the current of mainstream psychoanalysis. Efforts to streamline the treatment of characterological disorders evolved through a process of discovery and rediscovery by successive generations of analytically trained clinicians such as Franz Alexander (1946), Wilhelm Reich (1945), David Malan (1963), and Habib Davanloo (1980). The evolution of short-term dynamic psychotherapy has now led to a fourth generation of clinician researchers (Magnavita, 1993a), who have developed integrative forms of psychotherapy for personality disorders.

There remains a demand for even more comprehensive and integrated treatment models that capitalize on the advances in systemic theory and relational diagnosis. Although analytic workers emphasized the therapeutic relationship and considered this the prime vehicle for change, very little emphasis has been placed on the relational and systemic influences that often reinforce and complement personality styles and disorders of personality. The advancements made in the fields of family systems theory and of couple and family therapy were not meaningfully integrated with these approaches, although many clinicians out of necessity were experimenting with combined treatment approaches.

THE NEED FOR A CONCEPTUAL SHIFT

Primarily influenced by new research and a realization that the *Diagnostic and Statistical Manual* (*DSM-IV*; American Psychiatric Association [APA], 1994) limited understanding of complex clinical syndromes by minimizing the relational context and systemic dynamics, a movement to develop a diagnostic system based on the current knowledge and research from family systems was initiated (Kaslow, 1996). David Reiss (1996), in the forward of *Handbook of Relational Diagnosis and Dysfunctional Family Patterns*, describes personality disturbances as a class of "individual disorders whose evocation, course, and treatment are strongly influenced by relationship factors" (p. xi). This important conceptual shift has many implications that broaden the spectrum of individuals who can be successfully treated with a comprehensive relational approach.

One of the main assumptions that guides the approach explicated in this book was written by Florence Kaslow (1996) in her preface: "Our ability to form strong interpersonal bonds with romantic partners, children, parents, siblings, and other relations is one of the key qualities that define our humanity. These relationships shape who we are and what we become—they can be a source of great gratification or tremendous pain" (p. v). In those individuals with disorders of personality, these interpersonal attachments are invariably problematic and are a defining feature of personality pathology (Florsheim, Henry & Benjamin, 1996). Thus a relational framework allows the practitioner to select methods from a clinical toolbox that apply to each patient's interpersonal matrix and to take into consideration the multiple variables that are observed or posited by using a relational context for the biopsychosocial model.

HOW A RELATIONAL PERSPECTIVE BROADENS AND DEEPENS AN UNDERSTANDING OF PERSONALITY PATHOLOGY

The term *personality disorder* is a construct that clinicians have used to organize and classify styles and patterns of behavior that have been observed both in clinical populations and in nonclinical subjects. The study of personality has been an interest of humankind as early as the Egyptians and Greeks (Millon & Davis, 1996; Stone, 1993). In the past century, theorists and researchers have made great strides in developing systems of classification and theoretical models that explain human behavior, especially psychopathological adaptations. Various systems of classification that have been developed have theoretical validity and clinical utility (Lively, 1995). However, a relational framework applied to an understanding and treatment of personality disorders has a certain fit that broadens and deepens an understanding of personality disturbances. Some of the following reasons provide corroboration of this position:

• *Personality is formed by the relationships present from the earliest interpersonal experience and attachments.* There is abundant research and clinical evidence that the roots of personality are in the earliest maternal-infant bond and that disruption of such an attachment can cause lifelong personality disturbance (Bowlby, 1977; Florsheim et al., 1996; Greenspan, 1997). Sameroff and Emde's (1989) studies of infant development led to findings similar to those noted by systemic theorists, and as Kaslow (1996) asserts, all "individual" psychopathology has its origins in primary relationships. Maladaptive attachment styles shape the interpersonal behavior of the caregiver and begin to define the relational matrix. There is some evidence that, for example, the anxious-avoidant attachment style may develop an avoidant personality style or an avoidant personality disorder, but other types are also possible outcomes, depending on the relational matrix (Florsheim et al., 1996).

• *Personality is organized and shaped by the relationships in the interpersonal matrix that is unique to each family system.* Each family system and its patterns of interrelationships influence and form the emerging personality of the infant, toddler, preadolescent, and adolescent. The quality of attachments, the interpersonal communication, and the covert and overt rules of family functioning shape and consolidate intrapersonal structure and interpersonal structures.

• *Personality-disordered individuals consistently demonstrate disturbances in the relational matrix.* Across the board, these individuals display disturbances in their interpersonal relationships that are the most obvious manifestations of disorders of personality. The wide range of such disturbances include spousal abuse, parent-child problems, marital disturbances, problems with authority figures, sexual dysfunction, and family disturbances. Patients with personality pathology typically demonstrate interpersonal disturbances that are made apparent through repetitive maladaptive patterns in various areas such as work, home, and community.

• *Personality disordered individuals have major defenses against intimacy and closeness that interfere with the healing possibilities of human connectedness.* Individuals with disturbances of personality avoid intimate connections with the people in their daily life. The defenses that these individuals developed to protect themselves from early painful, disturbed, or nongratifying relationships are raised to prevent others from hurting or neglecting them again. Unfortunately, this relational style and defense mechanism often produces in others the problematic reaction that these individuals had originally wished to avoid (Benjamin, 1993b). Often, patients with personality disorders select a mate who is developmentally at the same level. As a result, the partners do not activate the other's personal growth.

• *The restorative or healing aspect of the therapeutic relationship is the quality of the therapeutic alliance.* Regardless of the therapeutic approach, the most important factor in predicting therapeutic change is the quality of the therapeutic relationship. The core attributes of a therapeutic relationship identified by Carl Rogers (1951)—empathy, genuineness, relatedness, and so forth—continue to account for much of the power of psychotherapy. These therapeutic conditions provide the individual or family with a healing emotional experience (Alexander & French, 1946). Much research and clinical evidence has also demonstrated that the curative aspect of all psychotherapy as well as of psychopharmacological approaches is the quality of the therapeutic relationship (Blatt, Quinlan, Zuroff, & Pilkonis, 1996).

• *The benefits of enhanced relational capacities and family support are evident in almost every current line of research.* There is a convergence of results from research on cancer survival and on recovery from medical interventions, severe mental illness, and addictions that clearly demonstrates the benefits of enhanced interpersonal capacity and reveals a connection in the recovery from physical illness or psychological disorders (Ornish, 1998; Weil, 1995). Patients with disorders of personality also fare better within a supportive and involved system.

• *Personality disturbances are reinforced and often exaggerated by cultural and family systems.* Patterns of behavior may be exaggerated or minimized by the influence of the social system that provides the context for the behavior. This influence is evident in prison populations in which the cultural conditions and systemic reinforcers exaggerate antisocial forms of personality. Evidence of this phenomenon can be seen in other social settings as well, such as a sports event at which the crowd has a temporary lapse in control and engages in violent behavior.

AN INTEGRATIVE RELATIONAL MODEL OF PERSONALITY DISORDERS

The integrative relational model presented in this book is based on a belief that disorders of personality are determined, shaped, and reinforced by a complex array of biopsychosocial factors. "General systems theory (and the biopsychosocial model) maintains that dysfunction in one system level will impact the other system levels" (Denton, 1996, p. 40). All personality pathology can be viewed in the relational context within which it is evident, whether observed in dyadic, couple, group, family, or societal systems. Nichols (1996) poses the paradox as to whether there can be personality pathology without a relationship to express and witness it, like whether the tree that falls in the woods makes a sound if no one is there to hear it. "Somebody else is required in order to fully complete transactions and express needs and desires inherent in the disorder" (p. 290). Therefore, it is my assumption, based on the accumulated clinical and research evidence, that disorders of personality are best conceptualized and treated with a comprehensive integrative relational psychotherapeutic approach that draws on various theories, methods of change, and technical interventions.

IMPORTANT MAJOR ADVANCEMENTS TO TREATING DISORDERS OF PERSONALITY AND DYSFUNCTIONAL PERSONOLOGIC SYSTEMS

A number of advancements in various related fields are fueling the paradigmatic shift that is currently evident in the field of personology and the treatment of disorders of personality. It is my hope that these new developments will further add to the field and enable clinicians to continually increase the range of patients who can be effectively helped. I summarize in the next sections some of the main advancements that are discussed in greater depth throughout the remainder of this book.

New Models of Change

Prochaska, DiClemente, and Norcross (1992) developed the transtheoretical model to explain the process of change. They formulated various stages and processes of change (precontemplation, contemplation, preparation, action, and maintenance) from an atheoretical perspective. This model has been successfully applied to addictive disorders but can be broadly applied to disorders of personality. An understanding of the processes and stages of change provides a tremendous advantage to clinicians to effectively engage and work with personality-disordered patients and their families. Instead of viewing patients and families as resistant when they do not embrace change, therapists can begin to assess readiness for change (Hanna, 1996) and determine where the individual is in the change process. In this model, change is not viewed as linear but is more like a spiral process.

Evidence of Naturally Occurring Quantum Change Episodes of Personality Transformation

Many clinicians have heard descriptions of individuals who have experienced major transformations in their lives precipitated by near death experiences from overdoses, profound spiritual awakenings, and so on. Social scientists have been loath to examine these events for fear of not being taken seriously. However, recent evidence has shown that, on occasion, individuals do experience what Miller and C'deBaca (1994) have termed *quantum change episodes*. These pioneering researchers found support for the proposition that the personality can undergo an in-depth and rapid transformation that does seem to endure. Further, these transformative experiences are, at times, naturally occurring events not precipitated by psychotherapeutic involvement such as might occur in the family life cycle (Gerson, 1995). These events need to be studied further so that these forces can be harnessed more effectively by psychotherapists.

Evolution of Integrative Psychotherapy

Integrative psychotherapy has become a popular topic of psychotherapy for researchers and clinicians (Norcross & Goldfried, 1992; Stricker & Gold, 1993). "The last two decades have witnessed the beginning of an important shift away from the prevailing climate of factionalism and parochialism among psychotherapies toward one of dialogue and rapprochement" (Safran & Messer, 1997, p. 140). This trend is, in part, shaped by the practical demands of clinical practice. Clinicians are forced to integrate approaches and techniques that produce clinical results; otherwise, their effectiveness would be limited to certain populations. Many experienced psychotherapists have developed similar skills: They learn one approach, then another; they feel disillusioned by efforts that don't consistently succeed, then they learn another, seemingly divergent, approach (Gustafson, 1986). For many clinicians working with personality disorders, this process in itself has culminated in a true blending of "disparate" approaches. Treating personality pathology requires comprehensive integration (Magnavita, 1998b). Pinsof (1995) made important conceptual advances, from a systems perspective, in synthesizing therapeutic approaches with his integrative problem-centered therapy. His conceptual framework has substantial clinical utility, and relevant aspects of his work will be touched on later in this volume. I agree with Millon, Everly, and Davis (1993), who describe the need for a comprehensive integrative approach: "It is not that integrative psychotherapies are inapplicable to more focal pathologies, but rather that these therapies are *required* for the personality disorders (whereas depression may successfully be treated either cognitively or pharmacologically); it is the very interwoven nature of the components that comprise personality disorders that makes a multifaceted and synthesized approach necessary" (p. 332).

Advancements in Briefer Forms of Treatment

By streamlining a lengthy process such as psychotherapy of personality pathology and by attempting to distill its active ingredients, therapists can learn what is essential. One positive outcome of the managed care movement was the pressure for clinicians and theorists to develop and refine effective, briefer forms of treatment for personality disorders and symptom relief (Barber et al., 1997). Guerin, Fogarty, Fay, and Kautto (1996) comment on these changes:

> Changes in the health care delivery system predicated on the demands on managed care are now demanding a form of clinical practice that focuses almost exclusively on symptom relief. Like most changes, this has both its upside and its downside. On the upside, psychiatry and psychotherapy in

particular have needed for a long time to pay more attention to the management and relief of symptoms. Managed care will force practitioners to remove the flab from psychotherapy. (p 18)

This emphasis on cost containment has led to many new developments and a rediscovery of past methods of active therapy applicable to personality or characterological disturbances (Ferenczi & Rank, 1925). Characterological analysis (Reich, 1945), short-term anxiety provoking psychotherapy (Sifneos, 1987), and intensive short-term dynamic psychotherapy (Davanloo, 1980) were evolving forms of the pioneering therapy practiced by Sandor Ferenczi wherein entrenched personality patterns were disrupted by using anxiety-arousing, defense-challenging maneuvers. Millon and Davis (1996) state: "To the credit of short-term psychotherapists, they have recognized that real change cannot be produced unless these homeostatic mechanisms are suspended, producing anxiety" (p. 13). Further, Millon and Davis also believe that building rapport, although important with the personality-disordered patient, is not enough. It is essential, for most personality-disordered patients, that the system be shaken up if change is going to occur. In many cases the homeostasis of the dysfunctional personologic system must also be disrupted if change is going to occur. Clinicians must realize when to attempt short-term interventions and when to select longer term approaches.

Advancements in Psychometric Instruments for Assessing Personality and Dysfunctional Relationships
Within the last decade, researchers have developed a number of excellent psychometric instruments that allow clinicians to accurately diagnose and identify personality pathology and dysfunctional relational patterns. In addition, relational assessment has come of age. Clinicians therefore are capable of rapidly assessing various types of personality pathology and the systems within which those pathologies exist. This technology encourages focused treatment interventions, but also allows us to monitor the effectiveness of our approach. The time-honored family genogram also has particular relevance for assessing the DPS.

Technological Advancements
Several important technological advancements have had major impact on clinical practitioners. The development of computer technology allows the average clinician access to powerful and affordable computers that are capable of rapidly scoring and interpreting complex psychological assess-

ment instruments. Affordability of audiovisual technology also allows for various innovative uses of this equipment for consultation, training and microanalysis of therapy sessions, follow-up, and patient review (Alpert, 1996; Magnavita, 1997b).

Advancements in Psychotherapy Research that Demonstrate
the Active Ingredients of Change
Lambert, Shapiro, and Bergin (1986) identified the following factors that account for improvement in psychotherapy: common factors, extratherapeutic activity, expectancy (placebo effects), and techniques. The personality-disordered patient requires that clinicians mobilize all change factors to counteract the interpersonal, intrapsychic, and systemic homeostatic mechanisms.

Advancements in Treatment-Matching Models and Technology
In the not-too-distant past, many clinicians were trained in one modality and applied this modality to most problems they encountered in clinical practice. With the technical advancements made in the field of psychotherapy and with the development of often-competing approaches, it became clear that differential therapeutics was an important concept (Frances, Clarkin, & Perry, 1984). The integrative relational model presented in this book expands on the concept of treatment matching and its emphasis on matching the modality to the disorder. The approach in this book assumes that many factors maintain the problems seen in a dysfunctional system and that the same disorder can have different underlying "problem-maintenance structures" (Pinsof, 1995, p. 26). Careful, focused systemic interventions can be delivered in various combinations, sequentially or as part of a comprehensive individualized treatment module. An understanding of how to enhance treatment is crucial in developing effective treatment plans for the patient or couple with a personality disturbance (Millon & Davis, 1996).

Advancements in the Field of Trauma Theory
Considerable conceptual advancements have been made in the understanding of the impact of major trauma on an individual's personality development and organization (van der Kolk, McFarlane, & Weisaeth, 1996). Chronic abuse leads to a fragmentation of the personality or to a failure to integrate various components, which causes severe developmental arrest (Herman, 1992). This clinically observed and research-supported observation has led to the development of specialized forms of treatment for

trauma survivors, who often have substantial personality pathology as well as post-traumatic stress disorder and various Axis I clinical syndromes. Researchers and clinicians' understanding of comorbid disorders that often coexist with personality disturbance is another advancement of the knowledge of dysfunctional systems and the types of pathology they produce.

New Attitudes Emerging Toward Personality Disorders

Along with the developments that were just listed has been a resurgence of interest in the field of personology that has slowly modified long-held attitudes and misconceptions (Magnavita, 1997c). Again, Millon (Millon & Davis, 1996) has led, in his advocacy for a new paradigm, a move to replace the restrictive medical model, proposing that the medical "paradigm itself is the enemy" (p. 185). Personality disorders are not disease entities but functional disorders of the entire biopsychosocial matrix. Millon and Davis go on to emphasize that

> The belief that personality pathologies are medical diseases, monolithically fixed and beyond remediation, should itself be viewed as a form of paradigmatic pathology, almost sufficient in and of itself to evoke self-defeating countertransference responses to personality disorder patients, and one hopefully to be remedied by supervision or self-correction. (p. 186)

In spite of these shifts in attitudes, more work on destigmatizing and educating the public as well as the professional community is essential. As was observed in the public awareness programs that were developed to destigmatize depression, both public and professional awareness needs to be addressed (Sperry, 1995; Magnavita, 1998b).

RECOMMENDATIONS FOR BROADENING THE SPECTRUM OF EFFECTIVENESS

The following recommendations emanate from an integrative relational model and can be used to broaden the spectrum of patients amenable to treatment (Magnavita, 1998b). I will elaborate on these recommendations, as well as others, throughout the remainder of this book:

- Emphasize a systemically based, relational-oriented therapeutic approach.
- Observe the clinical phenomenon from various levels of abstraction but use a biopsychosocial model as the foundation.

- Maintain a high level of therapeutic activity and engagement.
- Be flexible in sequencing, combining, and shifting approaches and modalities.
- Mobilize change patterns in various systems.
- Use theory as a springboard to creative interventions.
- Attempt a short-term approach first and shift to long term if indicated.
- Use a collaborative treatment team approach when possible.

CONCLUSIONS

Now is an exciting time for the field of personality. Major advancements have been accomplished and are moving the field of personology at a rapid pace. This book identifies a comprehensive treatment approach based on a biopsychosocial model of personality and utilizes a relational framework. Converging lines of research and clinical theory are presented to bring the most current thinking and information to clinicians and researchers and thereby to create even more momentum as well as to offer practical treatment strategies for clinicians treating those individuals struggling with disorders of personality.

CHAPTER 2

Theory of Integrative Relational Psychotherapy

Integrative relational psychotherapy has been developed for the treatment of the full spectrum of personality disorders. This chapter presents the framework for this model. The groundwork for an approach that satisfies both family systems models and personality theorists' models is clearly set out. It is no longer effective to practice psychotherapy in a one-model vacuum, whatever it may be. Family systems theorists have often taken the position that psychopathology is a function of a dysfunctional system and have ignored the developments in the field of personality, such as advancements in classification and individual treatment models. Personality theorists have tended to look myopically to the intrapsychic/intrapersonal and interpersonal matrix for an understanding of personality development and have ignored the powerful systemic forces. In fact, personality pathology as classified in *DSM* (APA, 1994) is defined as occurring *within the individual*. As Florence Kaslow (1996) writes: "Whereas in traditional psychopathology, the interest is in what symptoms tell us about the inner workings of the individual, in family systems approaches the interest is in what the symptoms tell us about the interaction among family members" (p. 7). An integrative relational model assumes that both models are necessary for understanding personality pathology and its treatment and emphasizes "a framework for organizing different specific approaches with maximal efficiency and effectiveness" (Pinsof, 1995, p. 29).

We are currently moving toward what Breunlin, Rampage, and Eovaldi (1995) describe as "a fourth stage of integration." They write: "Contemporary

family therapists are adopting a biopsychosocial perspective in which biological, psychological, relational, community, and even societal processes
are viewed as relevant to treatment. This perspective creates bridges between the tracks and their models and between family and individual therapy and social action" (p. 550).

Wynne (1996), a pioneer in family therapy, believes that current *DSM*
(APA, 1994) classification should be expanded so that greater weight is
given to the relational context of the family. Although a two-way street is
being bridged between individual and relational approaches to personality
disorder (Perlmutter, 1996), this work is in its infancy. The term *integrative*,
therefore, is used to represent an essential blending of the individual, systemic constructs and treatment paradigms. We as clinicians must utilize
both systems if we are going to effectively evolve potent forms of personologic treatment models. In particular, the integrative model detailed in this
chapter combines two theoretical advancements in family systems (Bowen,
1976; Fogarty, 1975; Guerin et al., 1996) and psychodynamics (Malan, 1963,
1976, 1979; Davanloo, 1980) that utilize triangles to explain intrapsychic,
interpersonal, and relational systems. The blending of these constructs
has considerable utility for understanding and treating the dysfunctional
personologic systems presented in the following chapter as well as the
personality-disordered individual.

Theodore Millon (Millon & Davis, 1996) provides a list of principles and
assumptions for an integrative model. For my purposes in this chapter, I
highlight three of these principles that have the greatest relevance to our
topic and that presage the field of relational dynamics and classification:

- Personality disorders are dynamic systems, not static, lifeless entities.
- Personality pathogenesis is not linear, but sequentially interactive and
  multiply distributed throughout the entire system.
- Criteria by which to assess personality pathology should be logically coordinated with the systems model itself. (p. 7)

Millon's underscoring of the systemic model in his work and Kaslow's advancement of relational diagnosis as a worthy area of research and development have set the stage for a systemically oriented model of personality.

RELATIONAL MECHANISMS IN THE
PERSONOLOGIC DYSFUNCTIONAL FAMILY SYSTEM

A number of valuable constructs have evolved from the system perspective
as well as from individual-oriented perspectives that enrich a theoretical

understanding of disorders of personality, their diagnosis, and treatment. When we as clinicians synthesize these, we increase our understanding and have access to a greater range of interventions; we also increase our access and fulcrum points. A clear conceptualization of these principles broadens the framework for subsequent interventions whether sequential or concurrent treatment modalities are used. An individual's family constellation and dynamics allow us to understand personality pathology in an organic system. "In true systemic fashion, relational therapies are designed to set into motion feedback loops that address both marital and depressive disorders that reinforce each other in a closed system" (Patterson & Lusterman, 1996, p. 56). Patterson and Lusterman's statement also holds true for disorders of personality and the systems in which they are often observed. What we have learned from an individual model allows us to work intensively with the cognitive/affective matrix of the individual that holds sacred the relational ties and experiences. This matrix is what Lorna Benjamin (1993a) refers to when she says "every psychopathology is a gift of love" (p. 1). In other words, the pathological aspects of an individual's personality often tie the person to the relational field in an attempt to gain the lost love and intimacy.

The constructs presented in the following section of this chapter are meant to be as simple as possible. I do not go into detail concerning various valuable systemic, psychodynamic, interpersonal, cognitive, and cognitive-behavioral constructs useful in conceptualizing and treating personality pathology, because such detail would require several volumes. Readers unfamiliar with this material should read the primary sources cited in the reference section and throughout this book.

ESSENTIAL SYSTEMIC CONSTRUCTS AND PRINCIPLES

THE SYSTEMIC MEANING OF STRUCTURE

"The basic unit of family structure is a *patterned sequence of behaviors*, observable in the interaction between two or more members" (Terkelsen, 1980, p. 29). Each of these patterned sequences of interaction taken as a whole represents the main structure of the system. Terkelsen (p. 30) describes the following examples of structural sequences but reminds us that there are many others as well:

- Mutual greeting sequences.
- Complaining-consoling sequences.

- Reporting-praising sequences.
- Reporting-critiquing sequences.
- Conflict-clarifying sequences.
- Conflict-resolving sequences.

Structure may also refer to the nature of relationship triangles.

Triangle/Triangulation

"A triangle is the smallest stable relationship system whether it is in the family or any other group" (Bowen, 1976, p. 76). The triangle is a three-person configuration. Guerin et al. (1996) identify four aspects of triangular structure: "(1) the fixedness and fluidity of the triangle, (2) each individual's position in the triangle, (3) the location of pain and discomfort in the triangle, and (4) the distribution of symptoms in the triangle" (p. 61). Further, they write that triangles are defenses that serve to reduce anxiety, either individually generated or within a dyadic relationship. When a two-person system becomes overwhelmed with anxiety, a third person may be brought in to diffuse the tension. This situation is most often seen in the parent-child triangle and is also common in extramarital affairs. When the parental system is overly anxious regarding conflicts that they cannot resolve, a child is pulled in and eventually may become symptomatic. In a similar fashion, too much anxiety in a couple may cause one member to seek out a third party and enter into an affair that may serve to stabilize the marital dyad. As most clinicians are aware, the child brought into therapy for emotional or behavioral problems often represents a conflict between the parents or within the extended family. Not addressing the broader issues in the dysfunctional personologic system will result in symptomatic breakouts at other times or with other family members. I see this phenomenon occurring in the new trend to treat children with antidepressant medication and ignore the personality disturbances in the parents that are feeding the child's pathology.

Guerin and his associates (1996) in their book *Working with Relationship Triangles: The One-Two-Three of Psychotherapy* remind us that triangles are not just three-person configurations but that a critical level of emotional reactivity that influences behavior must be present. They also identify various features that distinguish threesomes from triangles (Table 2.1). Guerin and associates identify three categories of triangles evident in clinical practice: (1) child- or adolescent-centered triangles, (2) marital triangles, and (3) individual dysfunction and hidden triangles. Triangles block the function of and evolution of relationships over time and impede the progressing life cycle changes. They interfere with the resolution of issues and attainment of needs. The more fixed

Table 2.1   Comparison of Threesomes and Triangles

Threesomes	Triangles
Each twosome can interact one-on-one.	Each twosome's interaction is tied to the behavior of the third person.
Each person has options for his or her behavior.	Each person is tied to reactive forms of behavior.
Each person can take "I" positions without trying to change the other two.	No one can take an "I" position without needing to change the others.
Each person can allow the other two to have their own relationship without interference.	Each person gets involved in the relationship between the other two.
Self-focus is possible and [is] the usual situation.	No self-focus in anyone, and everyone is constantly focused on the other two.

Reprinted with permission from Guerin, P. J., Fogarty, T. F., Fay, L. F., & Kautto, J. G. (1996). *Working with Relationship Triangles: The One-Two-Three of Psychotherapy.* New York: The Guilford Press.

that relationships are and the more symptoms that reside with one member of the system, the more pathological the system is. This dynamic is most evident in certain types of dysfunctional personologic systems in which there is a fixed triangulated child and evidence of chronic emotional delay.

I agree with the value that Guerin et al. (1996) place on understanding triangles, especially in light of the refractory nature of much personality pathology:

> Knowing about triangles, being familiar with how they work, and having a repertoire of interventions for exploring and resolving them are invaluable weapons in the therapist's armamentarium, no matter what the therapist's theoretical orientation. Whenever you look carefully at cases that don't respond to treatment or seem stuck, look for a triangle you haven't seen yet. Whether the treatment is systems therapy, psychodynamic therapy, medical treatment, or some combination, you'll find that defining and modifying the relationship triangles surrounding the symptom bearer or the relationship conflict are essential to therapeutic progress. (pp. 28–29)

Operating System

Just as operating systems in computers are used for organizing and managing information, operating systems in relational systems serve a similar function. Fogarty (1976) describes these operating systems between people:

The operating system defines the action, the movement, the method that people use to connect within a system. It defines the "how" of the interconnections between people. If one person is angry, does he convey it by silence, withdrawal, open fury, sarcasm, or the tone of his voice? (p. 146)

In essence, then, the operating system determines how the triangles in a dysfunctional system operate.

Differentiation

This concept, developed by Bowen (1976), represents an integration between the intellectual and emotional systems of the individual as well as between self and other. Usually, the lower the level is of emotional differentiation, the lower the level is of self-other differentiation. Fusion results when there is insufficient separation and isolation or when there is too much. If differentiation is achieved, a person can function autonomously.

Homeostasis

Homeostasis refers to the fixed nature of triangles and to the extent with which closeness and distance is regulated by individual needs for autonomy and connection (Guerin et al., 1996; Jackson, 1957, 1959). "If a change occurs in a system, other parts of the system must change or unconscious structural forces push toward reestablishment of equilibrium at the original level" (Solomon, 1996, p. 262). This model is particularly relevant to those clinicians interested in personality disturbances. The personality-disordered system attempts to reestablish the previous equilibrium that precipitated entry into therapy. For example, in the developmentally arrested family system, the parental subsystem strongly discourages individuation, and any move toward separation is undermined in the hope of keeping the nuclear system intact. Maintaining the status quo is the goal and may prevent the parental subsystem from confronting their anxiety about death, aging, or aloneness. Clinicians who are not aware of these forces often encounter major resistance when attempting to facilitate change in the personality-disordered member of the system.

Fusion/Enmeshment

Fusion makes it difficult to tell where one person ends and the other begins. It is the essential I-You relationship and the level of differentiation and emotional openness. Intense, severe fusion may cause the family system to appear as one large, undifferentiated ego mass (Fogarty, 1976) with a lack of differentiation in the members of the system. Fusion has also been termed *enmeshment* and is often evident in many of the severely dysfunctional family types.

A Defining Feature of All Dysfunctional Personologic Systems: Disturbance of Attachments and Intimacy that Results in Anxiety

Intimacy is the currency of all healthy, close interpersonal relationships and the realm in which corrective therapeutics occur. Let me then start this section with a definition of intimacy. Bradt (1980) writes: "*Intimacy* involves a caring relationship without pretense, and revelation without risk of loss or gain from one another. It is giving and receiving, an exchange that enhances because it facilitates the awareness of selves, of their differences and sameness" (p. 126).

One of the main assumptions of an integrative relational model is that all people seek intimacy and closeness (Fogarty, 1976). Intimacy in the integrative relational model, in fact, is a primary drive, whereas in a classic psychodynamic model, sexual and aggressive drives are primary. The family system, then, is the crucible for personality development, and intimacy is the transformative element that shapes the biopsychosocial ingredients. The intimate attachments one experiences in childhood provide the crucible for both "healthy" and "disordered" personality development. The dysfunctional family system frustrates or substitutes—through inappropriate sexual contact or narcissistic use—the craving for intimacy. To some degree, all the dysfunctional systems outlined in the following chapter disrupt or prevent the development of close relationships with significant figures. Either there is too much—fusion—or too little—abandonment.

As humans, we all continually balance the conflicting forces of attachment longings and healthy separation of self. Each type of personality disorder has a particular style of managing and regulating intimacy levels when they become too threatening. The passive-aggressive individual becomes noncompliant, the histrionic makes a scene, the obsessive-compulsive gets lost in the details, and so on; each style has its own characteristic relational and defensive responses. The various substitutes for true intimacy and closeness only serve to further derail the system in an endless attempt to overcorrect for the deficits. One of the main tasks of the therapist is to deal with the approach/avoidance paradox (Magnavita, 1997b). The individual attempts to make intimate attachments, but this attempt activates triangles and defensive structures developed to protect the self from a reactivation of the painful affects associated with the early relational matrix. For the patient suffering from personality pathology, this defense system creates obstacles in the process of emotional growth and development as well as in the establishment of a therapeutic relationship.

Firestone (1997) describes relational difficulties that ensue when a couple has personality pathology. "In their coupling, conflict develops because people strive to maintain their defenses while, at the same time, they wish to hold on to their initial feelings of closeness and affection" (p. 95). After the honeymoon phase of the relationship, many of these individuals encounter severe relational disturbances. Firestone notes that another sign of the deterioration of intimacy between the couple is a lack of direct eye contact. Eye contact is often one of the most common and pervasive signs noted by marital and individual therapists who work with personality pathology.

SYSTEMIC AND PSYCHODYNAMIC CONSTRUCTS

The blending of two substances, such as two different metals, may result in an amalgam that is stronger and more durable than either of the two components. Ackerman (1958), a pioneer in family therapy, was one of the first workers to comprehensively blend psychodynamic and systemic concepts to broaden the scope of therapy. More than four decades ago he wrote:

> Each family tends to be characterized by typical foci of anxiety and conflict. These foci come sharply into view when the family relations fail to meet the emotional expectations of its members. Sometimes the patterns of anxiety and conflict are well established and stable, sometimes erratic and shifting in their expression. In one such pattern, the main conflict is contained and reflected in the personality of a particular family member; the personality of this member becomes, so to say, the dramatic expression of the pattern of stress that characterizes the particular family group. (p. 105)

I also have found that blending certain psychodynamic and systemic constructs creates a stronger amalgam for the process of psychotherapy with the personality-disordered patient and the dysfunctional personologic system. The following three constructs, all representing triangular configurations, are simple, clinically relevant, and once mastered, excellent for beginning as well as seasoned clinicians to conceptualize and guide treatment interventions. These constructs are triangle of conflict, triangle of persons, and triangle of relations (Figure 2.1).

1. *Triangle of conflict.* The triangle of conflict is a psychodynamic concept that depicts intrapersonal structure and dynamic interaction among impulse/feeling, anxiety, and defense. Painful feelings that threaten to emerge give rise to anxiety, which is warded off by defensive

TRIANGLE OF CONFLICT

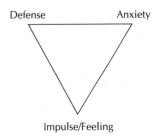

Defense   Anxiety

Impulse/Feeling

TRIANGLE OF PERSONS

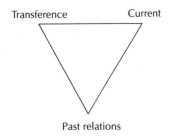

Transference   Current

Past relations

TRIANGLE OF RELATIONS

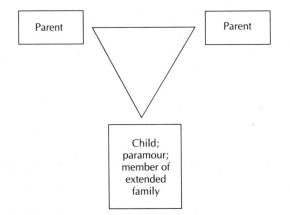

Parent   Parent

Child; paramour; member of extended family

Figure 2.1 Three triangles: conflict, persons, and relations.

mechanisms. Particularly relevant to the personality-disordered patient is that feelings are not accessible and that defenses either overcontrol or undercontrol the anxiety (see Figure 2.1).

2. *Triangle of persons.* The triangle of persons is psychodynamically derived, yet incorporates interpersonal operations (Benjamin, 1993b) and cognitive operations (Early Maladaptive Schema; Young, 1990). This triangular construct depicts the parallels between relationships and the tendency to reenact past relationships (traumatic injuries) in both current relationships and the transference relationship (see Figure 2.1).

3. *Triangle of relations.* The triangle of relations, a systemic construct called Relationship Triangles by Guerin et al. (1996), portrays the triangular relationships present in dysfunctional human interactions.

This triangle can be used to depict any combination of interlocking triangles or subsystems. Clinicians are concerned with the most common condition, wherein a dysfunctional dyad transmits the interpersonal anxiety through a third person, often a child who becomes symptomatic, or through an affair. Triangles serve at least three functions: "(1) containment of tension, (2) displacement of conflict and (3) avoidance of intimacy in the dyadic relationship" (p. 98).

Blending the Constructs

As I have previously stated, individual models of personality stress what happens in the intrapersonal and interpersonal matrix of the personality-disordered patient. The systemic model explains the field within the system that manifests itself in individual dysfunction or symptomatic behavior. Clinicians, using these three constructs that were just described, can understand personality disturbances as an interlocking array of feedback loops that generate and maintain disorders of personality, often through successive generations.

CASE STUDY

The patient is the youngest of three children and the only daughter. She is in a physically/sexually traumatizing dysfunctional personologic system. Her father, a highly authoritarian man, is domineering and controlling to an excessive degree (narcissistic type). Her mother, on the other hand, is submissive and compliant and caters to every whim of her husband to keep the peace (avoidant type). The mother might also be described as enabling in that she does not intervene to protect the patient but instead tries to soothe the father, who is chronically irritable and frustrated. There is little emotional intimacy or physical affection between the couple or with the children. The parents have limited capacity to directly express their emotions and needs. Both have significant abandonment fears based on early experiences of neglect and abuse (triangle of persons). When tension mounts between the couple, the father becomes overly harsh and critical of the patient (triangle of relationship). She reacts to this treatment by becoming angry, but she is fearful of expressing her anger and so instead defends against the treatment by passively responding; she introjectively accepts the criticism but becomes overwhelmed with fear and anxiety that floods her psychic system (triangle of conflict). This display of "weakness" by his daughter causes the father to explode with verbal abuse and, on occasion, physical abuse. The patient is in a double bind; regardless of how she reacts, she will be mistreated. She has become the family scapegoat, in part because she reminds him of his mother, who was abusive and whom she physically resembles. As a result of the chronic family dysfunction, the patient has a fragile defense system that shudders and crumbles under almost any life stressor. She would be placed on the borderline spectrum. This chronic intermittent pattern only temporarily ceases when the daughter marries and leaves home. Unfortunately, the relational matrix that she carries with her plants the seeds of these difficulties in the next generation.

ANXIETY AND THE PERSONOLOGIC SYSTEM

The personologic system is referred to as the total complex interplay among the biopsychosocial variants as they exist in the relational system. An understanding of how anxiety manifests itself is central to the task of working with the personality-disordered system. Bowen (1976) addresses this issue of anxiety as it manifests itself in the individual as well as the family system:

> All organisms are reasonably adaptable to acute anxiety. The organism has built-in mechanisms to deal with short bursts of anxiety. It is sustained or chronic anxiety that is most useful in determining the differentiation of self. If anxiety is sufficiently low, almost any organism can appear normal in the sense that it is symptom free. When anxiety increases and remains chronic for a certain period, the organism develops tension, either within itself or in the relationship system, and the tension results in symptoms or dysfunctions or sickness. The tension may result in physiological symptoms cr physical illness, in emotional dysfunction, in social illness characterized by impulsiveness or withdrawal, or by social misbehavior. (p. 65)

We can also see that Bowen is describing what are currently termed *personality disorders* and *dysfunctional systems*. Understanding the concept of anxiety and its various individual and system forms is basic to effective treatment of personality pathology.

INDIVIDUAL AND SYSTEMIC ROOTS OF ANXIETY

Anxiety has many roots and is best conceptualized as a multiple pathway phenomenon. Anxiety can be experienced consciously, as anxiety—tightness in the chest, sweaty palms, dry mouth, jitteriness, need to urinate, palpitations, and so forth. Or it can be channeled into various somatic forms, such as backache, asthma, chronic pain, gastrointestinal upsets, and so forth. Anxiety can also be channeled into defensive constellations such as reaction formation or idealization. In addition, anxiety can also be channeled into relational interactions such as occur in a pattern of scapegoating and triangulation.

All theoretical systems that attempt to explain psychopathology require an understanding of anxiety and its roots as well as how it is channeled or externalized into the larger system, contained in the individual defense system, or absorbed by the physiological system. Thus, anxiety can take various pathways. A stress-diathesis model explains how every individual has a particular channel of vulnerability and when stresses will channel the anxiety in a certain direction.

Types of Anxiety

Existential Anxiety

Most psychodynamic and family systems theorists ignore the concept of existential anxiety (Frankl, 1959; Yalom, 1980). This basic anxiety is present in all humans whether we defend against it or not. The primary root of this anxiety is related to our mortality, an issue that is often avoided. Firestone (1997) believes that existential anxiety creates an important aspect of developmental psychopathology. Individuals who are overly defended do so at the cost of more effective and fuller emotional experience. Existential anxiety represents a certain level of pain that all humans are aware of. For the dysfunctional personologic system as well as for all human beings, the denial of this pain leads to greater emotional blockage. Death anxiety is aroused at almost every normal developmental transition, which leads to greater separation and developmental progression. In the dysfunctional personologic system, aging and mortality may be threatening to the narcissistic formation of the parental figures who communicate that nothing has changed.

Conflictual Anxiety

Conflictual anxiety is the traditional concept of anxiety as viewed by psychodynamic theorists. It pertains to the tension among intrapsychic agencies: id-ego-superego. Conflict anxiety is the essential tension between impulses and societal restrictions. This type of anxiety is amplified by early disrupted attachments and developmental injuries. In situations in which greater levels of systemic and individual protection are required to manage these warded-off feelings, there is an increased level of dysfunction. Thus, defensive functioning and homeostatic mechanisms are employed to a greater degree than in the normal system.

Systemic Anxiety

Systemic anxiety is the anxiety stimulated within a system when threatened externally or from within. The flow of anxiety can occur along vertical and horizontal dimensions (Bowen, 1978). *Vertical anxiety* involves generations of unresolved feelings that accumulate, and great energy is required to maintain these feelings at a repressed level. This repression occurs primarily through emotional triangling (McGoldrick & Gerson, 1985). The system often organizes around the personality disorder in a manner similar to the manner in which a family may organize around a new addition (Perlmutter, 1996). These dynamics often create chronic anxiety and tension that is defended by characteristic defenses in a perpetual feedback loop. "It is important to remember that the essence of a triangle is to lower anxiety in the individual and tension in the twosome by shifting to the discussion of a third person or an issue" (Guerin et al., 1996, p. 49) and "believe that dyadic instability is tied to people's conflicting needs for autonomy and connection" (p. 86). In one case, for example, a woman whose husband was involved in an ongoing affair ignored the signs of her husband's infidelity and instead shifted her focus to her adolescent son's sex life; she became preoccupied with his dating, an activity that the son continually made her aware of. This change in focus shifted the anxiety between the parental subsystem. *Horizontal anxiety* results from current external stressors, such as coping with misfortunes and transitions in the family life cycle (McGoldrick & Gerson).

THE IMPORTANCE OF HOW ANXIETY IS MANAGED

How anxiety is regulated has major implications for work with personality-disordered systems and individuals, on both an intrapersonal level and a systemic level. Anxiety is often excessively regulated by maintaining a homeostatic balance in fixed triangular constellations or rigid defense systems. "If, over the span of time, conflict and anxiety exceed the integrative resources that the individual can mobilize within his family group, the process of disorganization and disablement spread to invade a progressively widening segment of adaptation" (Ackerman, 1958, pp. 105–106). Thus, normal anxiety related to family life cycle challenges and developmental transitions are not met and managed effectively. Anxiety that ensues from closeness/distance struggles or balance of power issues are regulated by homeostatic mechanisms (Hoffman, 1980). Thus for example, in a Somatic Dysfunctional Personologic System, a couple with personologic issues affecting their intimacy and closeness needs may systemically transmit their separation anxiety to an asthmatic child, who then realigns the couple subsystem to care for the child.

Disruptive family events may also result in overwhelming anxiety that cannot be effectively managed by the nuclear or extended family. The therapeutic task often necessitates increasing and decreasing anxiety at key points to break the homeostatic balance and free up individual development. This task is probably one of the most vexing and challenging aspects of working with the dysfunctional personologic system. If anxiety is pushed too high, many negative results can occur. However, if anxiety is kept at the maximal level of tolerance, more rapid and in-depth changes can be engendered.

Regulation and monitoring of anxiety is the art of conducting psychotherapy for many personality disorders (Magnavita, 1997b; McCullough Vaillant, 1997). "The processes of regulation and balancing of emotion and impulse, the neutralization of anxiety, are functions partly of individual personality, partly of role adaptation to the family group" (Ackerman, 1958, p. 109). When there is a breakdown in anxiety regulation, symptoms develop, and over extended periods of time or via the multigenerational transition process, personality disorders emerge and appear in successive generations. The constructs presented in this book enable the skilled clinician to map out and intervene at the most appropriate time with just the right level of potency that will accelerate the developmental processes both within the individual and the family system.

A BIOPSYCHOSOCIAL MODEL IN THE RELATIONAL FIELD

Personality development is an extraordinarily complex process that does not lend itself to simplistic or reductionistic explanations. Therefore, personality disturbance is neither interpersonal, intrapsychic, biological, cognitive, societal, or developmental in etiology; rather, all these factors contribute to personality. Guerin et al. (1996) state: "It is a simple enough step to move from thinking about the biological predispositions and psychological trauma of individuals to the tension and conflict in their relationships" (p. 20).

One premise of this book is that the etiology and pathogenesis of disorders of personality is best conceptualized by a biopsychosocial model (Engel, 1977, 1980) or more aptly by a biopsychosocial process in a relational context. "The biopsychosocial model conceptualizes nature as arranged on a hierarchical continuum ranging from molecules, through individuals, to families, to societies" (Denton, 1996, p. 40). The adoption of the biopsychosocial model has advanced the understanding of many disorders and has enhanced treatment effectiveness. This advancement is most evident in the field of psychoactive substance disorders in which the incorporation of the biopsychosocial model has generated a more sophisticated understanding of the complex variables that influence addictive processes (Zucker & Lisansky Gomberg, 1986). Researchers and theorists have also been proponents of applying this model to personality disorders (Paris, 1994; Sperry, 1995; Tyrer, 1988).

The following section of this chapter presents a biopsychosocial model of personality that provides the underpinnings for the integrative relational framework presented in this book. This model is applicable both to normal and disordered personality development and will be used to guide the treatment interventions that are now available as well as future developments for treating personality pathology. This model also has major implications for prevention, which is probably the best way to eradicate most forms of personality pathology.

A biopsychosocial model can serve as a foundation for various other useful theories. Millon with Davis (1996) in their comprehensive text *Disorders of Personality DSM-IV and Beyond* summarized personality theories. They present five prominent groupings that represent variations of psychodynamic, cognitive, interpersonal, statistical, and neurobiological models of personality, which are generally consistent with a biopsychosocial model. In fact, the authors state that a comprehensive scientific explanation of personality is "based in evolutionary tasks that are applicable to every living organism as a biopsychosocial system" (p. 9). Millon and Davis describe the evolutionary model:

Personality and psychopathology develop as a result of the interplay of organismic and environmental forces; such interactions start at the time of conception and continue throughout life. Individuals with similar biological potentials emerge with different personalities and clinical syndromes depending on the experiences to which they were exposed. . . . The theory asserted further that the interaction between biological and psychological factors was not unidirectional such that biological determinants always precede and influence the course of learning and experience; the order of effects can be reversed, especially in the early stages of development. (p. 66)

THE BIOPSYCHOSOCIAL MATRIX

The biopsychosocial matrix allows theorists to organize the broad array of variables or contributing factors that are responsible for seeding, sprouting, and stunting personality growth. This organization then allows a more focused treatment program. Variables can be organized into three factors that contribute to the development and trajectory of disordered personality: biological, psychological, and social factors. Figure 2.2 shows how personality development can be influenced by the biopsychosocial factors.

BIOLOGICAL FACTORS

Genetics

Biological variables such as genetic endowments and biological dispositions set the parameters for personality. "Clinicians since Hippocrates have posited that biological and chemical elements undergird temperament and psychic pathology (Lively, 1995, p. 23). Cloninger (1986, 1987) has presented a neurobiological schema of personality. He proposed three neurobiologically based, heritable personality predispositions—reward dependence, harm avoidance, and novelty seeking—and links these to various neurotransmitter action mechanisms. These personality dispositions are hypothetically related to later personality organization. Joseph (1997) suggests specific pharmacological strategies for each personality disorder. However, Livesley comments: "Not only are there sound reasons to approach neurobiological speculations with a measure of skepticism, given the tenuous nature of our knowledge concerning the complexities of neurochemical interaction; hesitation must also be expressed concerning the hypothesis that proposes direct parallels between neurobiological and behavior-emotion systems" (p. 24). Kramer (1993) has observed profound changes in personality in certain depressed spectrum individuals treated with Prozac. Underlying biological deficiencies are presupposed when the response appears so miraculous.

One of the clinically most productive aspects for understanding the biological factors has to do with the common co-occurrence of Axis I disorders, such as anxiety and depression, that may be effectively treated with

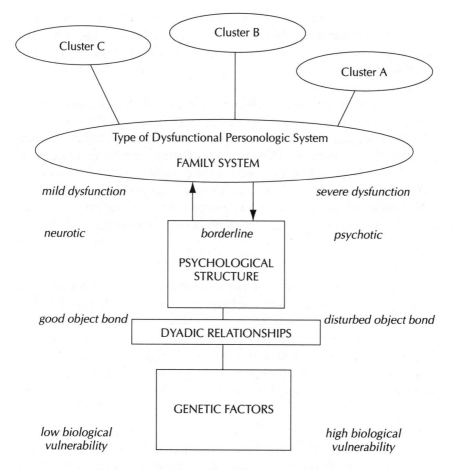

Figure 2.2 Biopsychosocial and relational matrix.

pharmacotherapy (Soloff, 1997). This issue requires careful consideration and is discussed in Chapter 8.

Probably the most apparent manifestation of underlying biological predispositions in the personality-disordered individual is a history of temperamental variation. There continues to be debate as to whether temperament is innate (Greenspan, 1997). Greenspan states: "Newborn babies do not exhibit innate traits of temperament such as introversion or extroversion" (p. 139). Rather, he proposes that newborns display various levels of physical sensitivity, reactivity, and motor problems. He then categorizes five different patterns of "reactivity, processing, and sequencing" and describes "the ways they can be exacerbated or turned into strengths by different styles of interaction between caregiver and child" (p. 144). Greenspan's five different patterns are the active, aggressive pattern (antisocial); the highly sensitive pattern; the inner-focused or self-absorbed pattern; the strong-willed pattern; and the difficulties with attention pattern.

However, most researchers and child developmental specialists believe that temperamental variation can be observed in infants (Buss & Plomin, 1975, 1984; Kagan, 1994; Thomas & Chess, 1977). An understanding of temperament has tremendous clinical utility. Temperamental traits exhibited by the infant exert a strong influence on the caregiver and set in motion personality development. A responsive caretaker can maximize developmental potential. On the other hand, an unresponsive caretaker can set into motion a developmental sequence that later permits personality pathology.

Other Biological Factors
Other biological predispositions may also have an effect on personality development. Body morphology has been identified as having an influence on personality development. Learning disabilities, attention deficit disorders, schizophrenia, and bipolar disorder all have a genetic component and may influence the development of personality. Highly aggressive, attention deficit hyperactive males, for example, may be more likely to receive a diagnosis of antisocial personality (Lynam, 1998).

Temperamental Styles
Buss and Plomin (1975, 1984) have suggested three temperamental variants: activity, emotionality, and sociability. Thomas and Chess (1977) rate temperamental variation with a broader array of factors. Kernberg (1996) also believes that temperament as well as character are crucial to personality development. He defines temperament as "the constitutionally given and largely genetically determined, inborn disposition to particular reactions to environmental stimuli, particularly to the intensity, rhythm, and thresholds of affective responses" (p. 109). He believes that, with regard to the etiology of personality disturbance, the affective aspects of temperament are fundamental in importance.

Attachment Styles
Attachment styles are the interaction between temperamental features and the caregiver's interpersonal style. Thus, systemic factors and relational

dynamics begin to form and shape attachment styles at birth. A good match will enhance development, and a poor one will contribute to developmental difficulties. Florsheim et al. (1996) list and summarize various categories of attachment (Table 2.2). Potential problems emerge from these attachment styles that will certainly contribute to adult personality pathology.

Whether described as temperamental variations, patterns of reaction, or attachment styles, these differences become the initial stage of the developmental processes that turn the infant into a fully developed person with unique personality attributes. Millon and Davis (1996) comment on the importance of this interaction between biological dispositions and parenting styles:

> First, the biological dispositions of the maturing individual are important because they strengthen the probability that certain kinds of behavior will be learned. Second, it is clear that early temperamental dispositions evoke counter-reactions from others that accentuate these initial tendencies; that is, a child's biological endowment shapes not only his behavior but that of his parents as well. The reciprocal interplay of temperamental dispositions and parental reactions has only now begun to be explored. It may be one of the most fruitful spheres of research concerning the etiology of psychopathology. (p. 67)

Developmental Processes

Developmental processes are crucial yet often overlooked variables in the biopsychosocial matrix. Greenspan (1997) describes this "dance of development": "With the birth of each child, a unique set of inborn characteristics begins its lifelong dance with an equally distinctive sequence of experiences" (p. 137). He delineates the following levels of development that "may be thought of as the mind's deepest structural components, supporting all later development, just as the massive piers and girders at a skyscraper's base allow the top floors to reach the clouds" (p. 43).

- First level: making sense of sensations.
- Second level: intimacy and relating.
- Third level: buds of intentionality.
- Fourth level: purpose and interaction.
- Fifth level: images, ideas, and symbols.

Development is progressive and based in part on mastery of the issues of each stage. Each patient with personality pathology will have at the various levels developmental issues that were compromised.

Table 2.2   Classifications of Attachment

Attachment Type	Description
Child to Parent	
Secure attachment	This child is confident that the parent figure will be responsive, available, comforting, and protective, particularly under distressful circumstances. This assurance enables the securely attached child to explore the environment and test his or her developing abilities (Ainsworth et al., 1978).
Anxious-ambivalent attachment	This child is uncertain whether the parent will be responsive, available, or protective when needed. Anxious-resistant children tend to be clingy, greatly distressed by separation, and often fearful of their environments. This pattern is associated with inconsistency in parental availability and threats of abandonment (Ainsworth et al., 1978).
Anxious-avoidant attachment	This child has no confidence that the parent will be responsive, caring, or protective and expects to be ignored or rebuffed. Such a child will attempt to live life without the love and support of others. Conflicts regarding dependency needs are hidden (Ainsworth et al., 1978; Bowlby, 1988).
Disorganized/disoriented attachment	This child behaves erratically and inconsistently, often sending opposing messages at the same time. These children appear confused and engage in "incomplete or undirected movements or expression" (Main & Solomon, 1990, p. 122). These children were often found to be victims of abuse/neglect or their parental figure was grossly preoccupied with own problems (Crittendon, 1988; Main & Solomon, 1990).
Adult to Adult	
Secure attachment	The secure person has a positive view of self and others, a moderate to high level of intimacy and autonomy, and a moderate to low level of dependency (Bartholomew & Horowitz, 1991).

(Continued)

Table 2.2   *(Continued)*

Attachment Type	Description
Adult to Adult	
Preoccupied attach-ment	An interpersonally preoccupied person strives for self-acceptance "by gaining the acceptance of valued others" (Bartholomew & Horowitz, 1991, p. 227). Experience is characterized by a sense of unworthiness juxtaposed against a positive view of others.
Dismissive attachment	A dismissive person has a positive view of self and a negative view of others (Bartholomew & Horowitz, 1991; Main & Goldwyn, 1985). A dismissive person protects the self against disappointment by "avoiding close rela-tionships and maintaining a sense of independence and invulnerability" (Bartholomew & Horowitz, 1991, p. 227).
Fearful-avoidant	A fearful-avoidant person has a negative attachment view of self and others and anticipates betrayal, rejec-tion, and criticism. Such a person is likely to protect him- or herself from rejection or attack by avoiding involve-ment with others (Bartholomew & Horowitz, 1991).
Compulsive self-reliant	A compulsive, self-reliant person avoids turning to oth-ers for comfort, attachment support, or affection and places a high premium on self-sufficiency. However, this form of avoidance is motivated by a counterdependent need to be self-sufficient, rather than by outright disdain for others (Bowlby, 1977; West & Sheldon, 1988).
Compulsive caregiving	A compulsive caregiver insists on taking the caretaker role in all relationships, never allowing others to recipro-cate. These people's own needs are met by caring for others, thus they insist on providing help whether it is requested or not. Attachment is associated with feelings of self-sacrifice and self-neglect (Bowlby, 1977; West & Sheldon, 1988).
Compulsive care-seeking	A compulsive care seeker experiences a constant need to confirm the availability and responsiveness of attach-ment figures. These people have a heightened sense of vulnerability to loss, they tend to define their attachment in terms of receiving care, and feel unequipped to take responsibility for themselves (West & Sheldon, 1988).

(Continued)

Table 2.2   (*Continued*)

Attachment Type	Description
Adult to Adult	
Angry-withdrawn attachment	An angry withdrawn person is likely to react to responsiveness and unavailability with anger and defensiveness (West & Sheldon, 1988).
Obsessive-compulsive personality	An obsessive-compulsive personality style is characterized by excessive differentiation and a rigid adherence to a vision of how things should be. Such a person regards relationships as secondary to work and productivity, and prefers not to discuss problems and feelings with others (Pilkonis, 1988).
Lack of interpersonal sensitivity	An interpersonally insensitive person is unaffected by external feedback, is oblivious to the effect of his or her actions on others, tends to engage in antisocial behavior without guilt or remorse, and resents being held back by external demands (Pilkonis, 1988).

PSYCHOLOGICAL FACTORS

As can be anticipated from the previous discussion, the psychological factors emerge from the biological factors, and personality is shaped by the parent-child relationships and concomitant mastery of developmental sequences. The mind becomes increasingly structuralized as a result of the affective stimulation from primary intimate relationships.

Intrapersonal Structures

The cognitive/affective matrix mediates impulses, consolidates object representations, and regulates emotional expression. When compromised, this intrapersonal organization forms defensive structures, which are prominent in patients with personality pathology.

Affective Matrix   Greenspan (1997), based on new research, contends that affective development provides the basic architecture of the mind. Kernberg

(1996) believes that "affects, in short, are both the building blocks of the drives and the signals of activation of drives" (p. 115), which places emotion in the context of the interpersonal or object representation system. Affective development occurs when an individual learns to experience, express, and regulate basic emotions. Affective development is stimulated by the intimate attachments that are provided and nurtured by the caregiver. In patients with disorders of personality, emotional regulation is problematic. Goleman (1994) suggests that overall emotional intelligence is low. In an extreme form, such as in an alexithymic patient, the ability to experience emotions is severely impaired, and a disconnection between the cognitive and affective domain is evident. Other patients demonstrate emotional dysregulation as well, in which they experience overwhelming affect states, such as in borderline pathology. The affective matrix includes the *defensive system* that has developed to regulate and modulate emotions and protect the individual from anxiety. The defensive structure primarily protects the individual from two major sources of pain: interpersonal and existential (Firestone, 1997).

Interpersonal:
Deprivation, rejection, and overt or covert aggression on the part of the parents, family members, and significant others, particularly during the formative years.

Existential:
Basic existential problems of aloneness, aging, illness, death, and other facts of existence that have a negative effect on a person's life experience: social pressure, racism, crime, economic fluctuations, political tyranny, and the threat of nuclear holocaust. (p. 16)

Cognitive Matrix   The cognitive matrix includes the thoughts, attitudes, and beliefs that form cognitive structures and schematic representations. These schema become the filter through which interpersonal and affective experiences are processed. Interpersonal behavior and affective processes are shaped in a circular process and are consolidated over time, often guiding behavioral reactions at a preconscious level. These cognitive representations are internalized aspects of the parent-child relationship described by Firestone (1997) as the voice. Usually preconscious, the voice can result in a powerful release of affect, which reduces the anxiety and tension caused by the suppressed emotions.

SOCIAL FACTORS

Interpersonal Matrix
The interpersonal matrix is composed of the attachments and relationships that serve as the vehicle for the unfolding of the personality or self. The basic needs for intimacy, connection, and validation are core requirements for healthy development. When these basic needs are insufficient, as in the case of faulty caretaking or external circumstances, developmental sequences are delayed, derailed, or completely arrested, and the intrapersonal structures are structurally deficient or unformed.

Systemic Factors
The systemic factors consider the broader relationships and systems. These factors include the dynamic interplay in the marital, family, and extended family systems in which the developmental processes unfold and are shaped. Surely there is a relation between psychoneurotic personality and the occurrence of conflict in family relations (Horney, 1937). And this relation is a circular one. "Conflict in family relations often preceded the emergence of psychoneurotic symptoms, and, at a later point in time, further conflict in family relations influences the fate of these symptoms or plays a role in the induction of new ones" (Ackerman, 1958, p. 108). In the development of disorders of personality, marital and family dysfunction are often evident in preceding generations and create powerful relational models. Certain personality styles may develop as preferred adaptations. For example, enmeshed families are likely to discourage individuation at critical periods and reinforce dependent or avoidant styles (Olson, 1996). Disengaged families create a different set of dynamics, and other types of personality pathology will be reinforced, such as schizoid or paranoid.

Cultural/Societal Factors
Patient lives are contextualized within a cultural background (Messer & Woolfolk, in press). Cultural and societal factors are of tremendous importance in creating the social matrix that engenders personality pathology. Messer and Woolfolk (in press) remind us that between psychotherapy and culture there exists a reciprocal influence. Psychotherapy itself promotes customs and values. Although cultural factors do exert an influence on personality and how it is assessed, some researchers believe there are commonalities cross culturally, which is suggestive of a universal set of dimensions (McCrae & Costa, 1997). McCrae and Costa state "that the struc-

ture of individual differences in personality is uniform across several cultures and may in fact be universal" (p. 509). In some cultures, certain personality types may be favored and adaptive, such as passive or dependent types in women or aggressive, macho types in men.

BEYOND A MULTIPERSPECTIVE VIEW: A GENERAL SYSTEM MODEL

Understanding various levels of personality pathology provides a multiperspective view of the contributing factors that influence and maintain personality disturbances (Parker, 1997). However, a biopsychosocial formulation goes beyond a multiperspective view. The various ways, or lenses, that are used to view contributing factors to disordered personality should not be thought of as discrete entities but rather as a complex synergistic interplay of multiple factors. "General systems theory (and the biopsychosocial model) maintains that the dysfunction in one system level will impact the other system level" (Denton, 1996, p. 40). I agree with McGoldrick and Gerson (1985), who wrote: "A basic assumption made here is that problems and symptoms reflect a system's adaptation to its total context at a given moment in time. The adaptive efforts of members of the system reverberate throughout many levels of a system—from the biological to the intrapsychic to the interpersonal, i.e., nuclear and extended family, community, culture and beyond" (p. 5). We as theorists and clinicians therefore compromise our understanding of personality disturbances when we limit ourselves to using only one or two lenses. For example, a clinician who views a patient with a personality disturbance only through an intrapsychic lens will severely limit his or her understanding and will narrow the case formulation as well as compromise treatment efficacy. Another clinician who approaches the same pathology with multiple lenses and understands the interplay of various systems will have a much broader and more comprehensive framework with which to understand and ultimately treat the patient.

ASPECTS AND ASSUMPTIONS OF A BIOPSYCHOSOCIAL MODEL OF PERSONALITY PATHOLOGY

Any model of human behavior, and especially one that attempts to contend with the complex syndromes seen in the personality disorders, makes certain assumptions that need to be stated.

- *Disorders of personality are multidetermined.* This model assumes that no single genetic, biological, or psychosocial cause will be discovered that accounts for the spectrum of personality pathologies. An understanding of personality comes from an understanding of the interplay within a relational field among the biopsychosocial factors.
- *Personality is organic and, even in the most rigid system, malleable.* Personality is a construct that attempts to categorize and explain a living organic system that is in continual biological, social, and psychological flux. Any attempt to describe, classify, measure, and so forth will necessarily fall short, because the system is continually changing.
- *Personality disorders represent a maladaptive developmental sequence that has become entrenched or arrested.* The epigenetic principle states that development proceeds from a relatively undifferentiated state to higher and more complex forms of differentiation and maturity. Personality pathology represents a developmental discontinuity arising from the biopsychosocial matrix that limits developmental progression.
- *A comprehensive understanding of personality disorders demands an understanding of general systems theory, which best captures the organic process called personality.* Clinicians can move beyond a multiperspective approach when we incorporate general systems theory into the equation. This integration allows us to understand the reciprocal and synergistic processes that occur both within the individual and among individuals and the larger context.

HOW THE RELATIONAL BIOPSYCHOSOCIAL MODEL AIDS IN ASSESSMENT AND CASE CONCEPTUALIZATION

Most clinicians, even if not consciously aware of the biopsychosocial matrix, consider the unique combination of factors that make each human and his or her personality truly unique. So how do we as clinicians use this model to broaden our understanding of personality disturbances? We use it to assist us in our case conceptualization and keep us mindful of the complexity of interactive factors that relate internally in closed loops as well as in complex systemic feedback processes. The model also enables us to select treatment interventions that will maximize the systemic influence. Let us go to the following case.

CASE STUDY: THE PASSIVE-DEPENDENT PERSONALITY

The 42-year-old patient requested consultation to discuss his marital problems, which had been of going on for more than 20 years. He described a marital relationship that provided very little emotional satisfaction or companionship (interpersonal factors). In the interview, the patient appeared very hesitant, with a prominent stutter (interpersonal factors). In fact, it was later noted that every time he tried to suppress angry feelings, his stuttering was activated (intrapsychic factors–affective matrix). When he did stutter, no one in his family ever commented one way or the other. He had stuttered since starting a new school at age 7. His parents never sought evaluation or help. The patient wondered if he was worthwhile or acceptable enough to have another relationship if he divorced and worried that he might disturb or kill his aging father with the news of his divorce (intrapersonal factors–cognitive matrix). The patient's wife alternately mocked him or told him he was indeed the "crazy" one for entering therapy, and she refused to attend any individual or couples sessions, though he repeatedly asked her.

The patient had always responded with a passive style to his wife's demands and attempts to control him (interpersonal factor), a pattern that was also evident at work. He repeatedly was taken advantage of as he tried to please others. Although one of the best in his specialty in his company, he did not advance as far as he might because of his lack of confidence.

Developmentally, the patient had been a shy, inhibited child whose stuttering and lack of confidence created a sense of loneliness, social isolation, and feelings of worthlessness (genetic factors). He developed a pattern of attempting to elicit affection and approval by pleasing and doing for his parents, especially for his father, a "quiet king." As a teenager, the patient drove his father places, "like a chauffeur." The son never complained but tried to do more for his father, who rarely gave him affection, love, or guidance. Whenever there was a problem in the family, his father required the family to kneel and pray together, after which no discussion was tolerated.

Whenever the patient made a move toward separating from his wife, his father would react with guilt-inducing behavior. On one occasion when the patient left his wife, he went to live with his parents. Even though he described to them the kind of emotional abuse he suffered in his marriage, his father commanded him to return. The son did as his father ordered. The patient seemed trapped in a system that was in a state of homeostasis. All the significant figures in his life were invested in his staying with his wife regardless of how miserable the two were and had been for years. His parents seemed troubled when he did not follow their script, and his wife told him he couldn't make it without her. This systemic expectation created more anger, anxiety, and fear in the patient, which he suppressed, causing him to stutter more and avoid his wife when possible (systemic factors).

AN ORGANIC PROCESS

This patient's difficulties are driven and maintained by a complex array of interconnected variables (indicated in parentheses). Breaking these variables down into substrates demonstrates the various domains that contribute to the total personality organization. These factors do not exist in an isolated fashion but interrelate in a synergistic manner. There is a fluidity in all personality pathology as the systems interrelate; assessment as a static picture can only approximate the personality and relational system.

QUESTIONS ON HOW TO PROCEED

In this case, the clinician has many available paths for intervention. How does the clinician select from the array of treatment methodologies and formats? What are the diagnostic considerations? Does the clinician attempt marital therapy to stabilize the marriage? How should the clinician deal with the fact that his wife refuses therapy? Is individual therapy recommended to overcome the limitations of the defensive structure? Is group therapy recommended to build social skills and enhance interpersonal functioning? Is this patient considered untreatable because of the long-standing nature of his personality pathology? Does the therapist recommend cognitive therapy to restructure faulty schema? Is psychoanalytic therapy suggested to address developmental and structural defects? Is experiential therapy the best way to help the patient contact his emotions? The questions of appropriate treatment matching are critical. Most clinicians would suggest the approach that they are most comfortable with, but is adhering to familiarity the best way to proceed?

Most workers in the field of personality disorders would recommend an integrative approach (Frances, 1987; Millon & Davis, 1996; Stone, 1993). But how does the biopsychosocial matrix translate to an integrative treatment approach?

What Is Required of the Clinician Who Wants to Conduct Treatment?   At this point, a caveat is important. Clinicians who plan to undertake intensive psychotherapy with patients who have disorders of personality need a broad-based clinical and theoretical background before proceeding. Millon and Davis (1996) describe what is required:

> Obviously, a tremendous amount of knowledge, both about the nature of the patient's disorders and about diverse modes of intervention, is required to perform personologic therapy. To maximize this synergism requires that the therapist be a little like a jazz soloist. Not only should the professional be fully versed in the various musical keys, (i.e., in techniques of psychotherapy that span all personologic domains), he or she should be prepared to respond

to subtle fluctuations in the patient's thoughts, actions, and emotions, any of which could take the composition in a wide variety of directions, and integrate these with the overall plan of therapy *as it evolves.* After the instruments have been packed away and the band goes home, a retrospective account of the entire process should reveal a level of thematic continuity and logical order commensurate with that which would have existed had all relevant constraints been known in advance. (pp. 211–212)

In addition to basic knowledge in mental health and sufficient clinical experience, clinicians should have a broadly based and sound knowledge of the following areas:

- Psychopathology and abnormal psychology.
- Developmental psychology.
- Current theories of disorders of personality.
- Systems of classification of personality—individual and relational.
- Principles of assessment and procedures.
- Current approaches to treating personality disorders.
- Psychoactive substance abuse disorders.
- Comorbid disorders and their treatment.
- Long-term and short-term treatment models and the benefits and disadvantages of each.
- Treatment selection and matching methods.
- Psychopharmacological methods.
- Principles of integrative psychotherapy.

CONCLUSIONS

This chapter presents an integrated relational model of psychotherapy that synthesizes constructs from systemic and individual models. The complexity of variables that make up personality requires clinicians and researchers to adopt a model that considers all the known major factors that reflect this organic process. A biopsychosocial model encourages clinicians to broaden their perspective. When the clinician introduces and emphasizes the model's relational components and uses them as the framework, the biopsychosocial model can reflect the person and system in an organic fashion. Using a relational framework provides the clinician with the type of flexible organic model with which to mend defects in the biopsychosocial and relational matrix. In the following chapter, I expand my discussion by elaborating on the various types of dysfunctional personologic systems.

CHAPTER 3

Dysfunctional Personologic Systems

Over the course of many years of working with personality-disordered patients and dysfunctional families and systems, I have observed a pattern among certain dysfunctional systems that produces widespread personality pathology in their members. This pattern has often been a multigenerational phenomenon documented by a thorough history and genogram. I define this dysfunctional personologic system as follows:

- A dysfunctional family system in which a preponderance of individuals suffer from personality pathology, often observable over generations.
- A lineage of certain types of personality pathology associated with central family themes, dynamics, and triangles.

Although there is clearly great variation, some families indicate a lineage of certain types of personality pathology in successive generations that were associated with central family themes and dynamics. This chapter presents my system of classifying the dysfunctional personologic system and identifying various subtypes encountered in my clinical work and through the clinical observations of others. The goal is to offer clinical utility to the practitioner and future direction for researchers.

THE RELATIONAL MATRIX—THE CRUCIBLE FOR PERSONALITY DEVELOPMENT

Personality is shaped and very often maintained by the relational matrix in which it exists. Nearly two decades ago in a now-classic book, *The Family Life Cycle: A Framework for Family Therapy* (Carter & McGoldrick, 1980), Terkelsen in a theoretical chapter presaged the basic tenet of this model: "To be sure, family-level changes impact on all members, leading to changes in personality structure" (p. 24). Modifying personality structure was mentioned no more, but this statement showed great insight. The family is the original context from which an individual's perception of self and others is formed. A common element of all personality pathology that until recently has been virtually overlooked is a dysfunctional family system (Kaslow, 1996). A patient with a disordered personality has inevitably been exposed to destructive family patterns that have exaggerated from the biopsychosocial matrix certain temperamental predispositions, styles, and reactions.

In one of the few books on this topic, Donaldson-Pressman and Pressman (1994) describe how emotional abuse and neglect can exist in either covert or overt forms, in what they term the narcissistic family system. "In the narcissistic family system the responsibility for the meeting of emotional needs becomes skewed—instead of resting with the parents, the responsibility shifts to the child. The child becomes inappropriately responsible for meeting parental needs and in so doing is deprived of opportunities for necessary experimentation and growth" (pp. 12–13). This reversal of the parent-child relational subsystem is a central element of the dysfunctional personologic system. All the variations of personality pathology, from the less disturbed variants such as dependent and avoidant to the more severe such as borderline or schizotypal, share a similar crucible—the dysfunctional family system.

THE DYSFUNCTIONAL FAMILY SYSTEM

In dysfunctional family systems, the emotional, social, developmental, and security needs of the members are compromised, or the system falls short of sufficiently meeting certain needs. "A *family* is a small social system made up of individuals related to each other by reason of strong reciprocal affections and loyalties, and comprising a permanent household (or cluster of households) that persists over years and decades" (Terkelsen, 1980, p. 23).

Members enter when they are born, adopted, and marry, and only through death do they leave; even then they are often carried in symbolic unconscious and conscious form through successive generations.

"Good-enough," or functional, families provide sufficient holding, nurturing, affirmation, curiosity, and support. In contrast, in dysfunctional families, "the relationships take on qualities like hate, guilt and retribution; the ambiance is disjunctive" (Terkelsen, 1980, p. 26). "In many families where individuals manifest severe personal problems, the members have a striking lack of curiosity about one another" (Shapiro & Carr, 1991, p. 11). The dysfunctional family believes that it possesses more power than is actual (Carter & McGoldrick, 1980). Dysfunctional family members may ignore the reality of children growing and leaving; they may pretend a child is not married and that there has been no change of status with the married adult-child. These attitudes are a reflection of the rigidity and often deep-seated denial of death anxiety that is aroused in individual and family transitions.

Within this crucible of the family system there exist infinite variations that account for the individual differences observed in humankind. However, certain distinguishing features are evident in these families.

Personality Disorders as an Adaptive Response to a Dysfunctional Family System

One of the main assumptions of a relational approach is that all personality pathology, regardless of the form or variation, is an adaptive reaction to various levels of chronic emotional neglect or abuse along with severe communication disturbances that exist within a dysfunctional family system. Unfortunately, the personality configuration of the patient with a disorder of personality loses whatever adaptive value it had when the person leaves the system, or the system changes. There is a tendency to re-create the relational matrix that originally led to the personality disorder, thus reinforcing and consolidating the disorder and leading to multigenerational transmission. "Relational attitudes in their affective-programmatic structuring contain the blue prints of the person's actions" (Boszormenyi-Nagy & Spark, 1973, pp. 14–15). In a landmark longitudinal study of personality and family development in context, researchers found that despite strong generational differences, "it can also be confirmed clearly that parental childrearing behavior is handed down from one generation to the next"

(Schneewind & Ruppert, 1998, p. 151), which the researchers believe is evidence of intergenerational transfer. This intergenerational transfer of parenting styles is a significant factor that has been virtually overlooked in the field of personality but is crucial to a systemic understanding. This factor also points the way to preventive measures that can be incorporated to ameliorate this societal problem. One of the points that Schneewind and Rupert emphasize is the pattern of specific relationships, or of structure, in the relational matrix:

> Current parent-child relations can be predicted, to a notable extent, on the basis of the parental childrearing style assessed 16 years before. This produces specific patterns of relations, depending on the relationship aspect in question: The more competent and confident parents were in dealing with their children in 1976, the greater the interpersonal closeness perceived by parents and children 16 years later. Loving attention on the part of the parents prepares the ground for positive communication between parents and their adult children. A high measure of parental protection in childhood and adolescence predicts a controlling attitude in later parent-child relations. Strong conflict in the relationship between parents and their adult sons and daughters has its antecedents in an increased tendency toward parental anger and less confidence in rearing their children. (p. 186)

There is little question that the results of neglect, abuse, deprivation, and medical and psychiatric disorders will affect the course of individual and family development. Brody (1998a), in an article in *The New York Times*, writes: "Depression is a family affair, in more ways than one. Not only does depression in one family member affect everyone else, depression in one or both parents greatly increases the risk that their children will also become depressed or develop other emotional disorders" (p. F7). Lidz (1973) commented: "As the family is a true small group in which the actions of any member affect all, its members must find reciprocally interrelating roles or the personality of one or more members will become distorted"(p. 19).

LIMITATIONS OF CURRENT MODELS

Although current theoretical formulations concerning personality pathology—most notably interpersonal (Benjamin, 1993b), cognitive (Beck & Freeman, 1990) and psychodynamic (Magnavita, 1997b; McCullough Vaillant, 1997; Stader, 1996)—have emphasized the interpersonal processes and dynamic mechanisms, little attention has been placed on a systemic relational perspective. We as clinicians understand much of how personality pathology is developed and maintained interpersonally, primarily as these transactions occur in a dyad, but we have less understanding of how it is engendered systemically. We are beginning to identify the various factors that contribute to personality pathology—from the biopsychosocial model— but how the system shapes these elements is an aspect that has been virtually overlooked. As Perlmutter (1996) wrote: "The biopsychosocial model needs strengthening, and family therapy provides a pragmatic knowledge base for integrating the 'social' part of the model" (p. 2). It is important to define what is meant by a *system*, because this construct is at the heart of integrative relational psychotherapy.

Definition of System
Bowen (1976) describes a system as "any relationship with balancing forces and counterforces in constant operation" and wrote that "the notion of *dynamics* is simply not adequate to describe the idea of a *system*" (p. 62). A system is greater than the sum of the individual parts. Even if clinicians had a complete understanding of the variables in the biopsychosocial matrix, they would miss something without an understanding of how the interacting parts affect the whole. The assumption is that it is impossible to reduce personality to any of the biopsychosocial variables because it is the interplay of these factors that defines the personality.

Although there are varieties of family systems that require further classification and research, observation of family systems in clinical practice and the personality configurations associated with them offer a useful starting point.

ISSUES OF CLASSIFICATION AND DIAGNOSIS

"Until recently not much value has been placed on relational problems and even less on diagnosis" (Denton, 1996, p. 37). Clinical evidence suggests that a variety of family systems spawn personality pathology. Many of these systems will be recognizable to clinicians who conduct therapy with a personality-disordered population. These systems will also be recognized by therapists who work in the fields of addiction, child abuse, and trauma. Some dysfunctional systems are severe by their very definition and are almost always going to produce severe personality pathology such as those seen in the Cluster A Personality Disorders (schizotypal, schizoid, and paranoid) in *DSM-IV* (APA, 1994). Others may exist on a continuum; thus, one system within the category may produce personality disorders and other strong personality traits that may not constitute full-blown disorders. Three common patterns have been observed in families: functional, midrange, and dysfunctional (Lewis, Beaver, Gossett, & Phillips, 1976). Sound empirical research may help determine which systems are likely to promote various classes of psychopathology. However, clinical evidence shows that dysfunctional families are more likely to be associated with various forms of personality pathology than are the midrange or functional families. Systems that generate personality pathology are by their nature dysfunctional and have certain common features. These include:

- Impermeable or weak external boundaries that separate the family system from others.
- Poor boundaries among family members.
- Disturbed levels of communication and overreliance on primitive defenses.
- Reversal of the parent-child relationship.
- Need for family to revolve around narcissistic parent.
- Poor emotional differentiation and regulation.
- Emotional malnourishment.
- Financial instability.
- Multigenerational transmission effects.

IMPERMEABLE OR WEAK EXTERNAL BOUNDARIES

Dysfunctional family systems have external boundary problems. They most often have impermeable boundaries that separate them from other systems and individuals that may potentially threaten the family homeostasis. This impermeability can be observed in *family secrets* (Imber-Black, 1993), which is the unspoken or spoken directive to keep the abuse, neglect, and so on from being acknowledged by anyone outside the system (Donaldson-Pressman & Pressman, 1994). Impermeable boundaries often serve to isolate children and adolescents from social contacts outside the nuclear family. In this manner outside influence is kept to a minimum so that family cohesion is maintained. This impermeable boundary leads to a closed system that increases family isolation and hinders socialization.

Other dysfunctional systems may exhibit very weak external boundaries. People may come and go or be absorbed into the family with no consideration for the effects on the other family members. These families may take in boarders, acquaintances, or foster children with such fluidity that it is hard for an individual to know which members define the "family." These "members" can sometimes contribute to the abuse of other family members.

POOR BOUNDARIES WITHIN THE FAMILY SYSTEM

Dysfunctional systems have boundary problems within the family. Poor or semipermeable boundaries among members of the system may be evident. In extreme cases, as in psychotically organized systems, poor boundaries may become manifest as fusion or symbiotic attachments in which it is difficult to determine where one individual ends and the other begins. In these cases, it is as if two or more individuals share the same identity. In one *severe* case, a hospitalized adolescent and her parents all three were grossly overweight and seemed to have no awareness emotionally or physically of where one ended and one started. They talked as if they were one entity, and they seemed fused in their physical relations, sitting practically on top of one another, sleeping in the same bed, and having incestual involvement. On the opposite end of the continuum is the situation in which the boundaries within the family are so impermeable that family members are emotionally isolated and abandoned by other members.

DISTURBED LEVELS OF COMMUNICATION

Dysfunctional family systems are noteworthy in their communication disturbances. The use of low-level or primitive defenses predominate (Magnavita, 1997b). Especially under conditions of stress, there is a regression to primitive defenses such as projection, blaming, externalization, and acting-out.

Members of the family may expect others to be capable of reading their emotions and thoughts without the need to express them. Because emotional differentiation (Bowen, 1976) is often so poor, there is an inability to identify and express feelings directly. Defensive operations often take the place of healthier emotional communication. For example, in a lower functioning family, an adult who is angry may display the affect behaviorally—going to a bar to drink and not telling anyone—which can engender further anger in the spouse, who now feels abandoned and anxious. Marital and family therapists observe endless variations of these destructive communication patterns. A common couple phenomenon during conflict is the chain reaction in which the wife's primitive defensive reaction, such as projecting onto her husband that he will abandon her, triggers a primitive defensive reaction in her husband, such as screaming and threatening to walk out; this regressive downward spiral often culminates in verbal or physical abuse.

REVERSAL OF PARENT-CHILD RELATIONSHIP

Another common feature is the reversal of the parent-child relationship. In the dysfunctional family system, the child serves to meet the physical or emotional needs of the unhealthy parent(s). A child may be required overtly or covertly to assume an inappropriate level of responsibility or level of care for younger siblings or a disabled grandparent or parent. Thus, clinicians encounter situations, for example, in which an eight-year-old child nurses a bedridden grandparent while parents work, or an eight-year-old child takes care of younger siblings, cooks, cleans, and so on. This phenomenon is not limited to lower socioeconomic level families. Even well-educated, financially affluent families can be observed inappropriately leaving young children home to care for others. I have noticed a trend in some dual career couples to leave their children home alone from very young ages or to expect older siblings to care for younger ones. The result is often sibling abuse, which emerges out of the frustration and rage inherent in such a situation.

NEED FOR FAMILY TO REVOLVE AROUND NARCISSISTIC PARENT

Often there is a need in the dysfunctional system for the entire family to hold up the character structure of a parent. The narcissistic system may require other members to serve, to flatter, and to bolster the family member who has the narcissistic inflated self in order to prevent the eventual collapse of that person into the depressed self. For example, a teacher may require that dinner be served at precisely 5:30 every night because his schedule and his job are so important. When his expectations are not met, he goes into a narcissistic rage and leaves in a depressed state. His wife decides she should comply to "keep the peace."

POOR EMOTIONAL DIFFERENTIATION AND REGULATION

Dysfunctional systems can also exhibit a lack of emotional differentiation as well as poor emotional regulation. Often family members show a lack of emotional control and primitive episodes of emotional dyscontrol or, conversely, severe emotional dampening in which emotional expression is not tolerated. Various members of the family may be at opposite ends of the spectrum of emotional regulation. One member may be extremely passive and prone to withdrawal, and the other may be emotionally overreactive and prone to explosive discharge of affect. These styles may complement one another and form the bases for successive cycles of reenactment of earlier relational disturbances. Emotions are often covered by moods (Perlmutter, 1996) that predominate while direct emotional expression is discouraged and viewed as too threatening. Family members may have catastrophic fears that if they tell another member of the family how they truly feel, that person may die or leave.

EMOTIONAL MALNOURISHMENT

Another phenomenon observed with emotionally disturbed individuals and their families is emotional malnourishment. This is the tendency to avoid primary emotional responding and processing. This lack of emotional expression and communication leads to a state of emotional malnutrition and craving. In her work with eating-disordered individuals, Maine (1991) has termed this emotional deprivation when it occurs in the context of an emotional absent paternal figure *father hunger*. Screaming at one another in some families has been equated with anger, almost as if the screaming and loss of control—a regressive defense—is really the emotion. This lack of differentiation between defenses and emotions is ubiquitous.

FINANCIAL INSTABILITY

One sign that is overlooked in the psychological literature is financial instability across the socioeconomic spectrum. The Freudian adage that for most people money is a more uncomfortable topic than sex is evident in clinical practice.

MULTIGENERATIONAL TRANSMISSION EFFECTS

Each generation of dysfunctional personologic systems show the effects *"of an endless chain of influence linking the developmental experience of each generation to that of its immediate and distant ancestors"* (Terkelsen, 1980, p. 43). Although Terkelsen was not specifically writing about the dysfunctional personologic system in the same sense that it is being presented in this book, his concept of multigenerational transmission effects are clearly evident in clinical work.

CASE STUDY: THE MAN WITH CHRONIC PAIN

The 30-year-old patient suffered from years of chronic pain related to severe emotional/physical abuse from a physically/sexually traumatizing dysfunctional family system. The patient's father repeatedly set up situations that would test the patient's courage, such as making him fight a physically larger neighbor, but that would result in humiliation and anger. The patient's mother was physically abusive. During the course of his treatment, the patient learned of an incident that occurred during the war when his grandfather was in a heated battle. The grandfather's platoon was charging the enemy in what seemed like a suicidal attack. The soldier in front of the grandfather was killed when he moved forward. The grandfather was next to go and resisted, seeing that death was inevitable. His commander pointed a revolver at him and declared, "you will either get it in the front or the back, you choose," at which point the grandfather moved forward and was severely wounded.

According to the family story, the grandfather never overcame his sense that he was a coward and went to his grave with this shame. He was described as an irritable man who frequently lost his temper with his children. The patient's father seemed to absorb this shame; he reacted with abuse and humiliation to any sense of vulnerability or weakness in his son. When the patient at age 17 joined the armed forces, he had a severe emotional breakdown in boot camp that was triggered by the abuse of the drill sergeant. He was ashamed of his weakness and feared the disapproval of his father for his cowardice. This incident resulted in a psychotic episode and a hospitalization that was followed by a period of destructive events that nearly resulted in the patient's death.

The multigenerational impacts in the dysfunctional personologic system offer the clinician a window into the power of unresolved issues from previous generations. These events are not only unconsciously transmitted but affect the adequate functioning of the parental subsystem to the point of creating another generation of personologic disturbance.

Individual Variation in the Dysfunctional Personologic System

The clinical diagnostician must be mindful of the factors that can mitigate damage from any dysfunctional personologic systems. Even the most pathological families contain certain individuals who seem to have "normal" personalities and to have made good adjustments. At times, the pathological dynamic forces within a family system have a strong valence to one particular family member: One member may be idealized, and one or more members devalued and abused. Some of the following factors can prevent the development of personality pathology in even the most severely dysfunctional family systems.

Mitigating Factors
1. Positive relationships with members of extended family such as an aunt, uncle, or grandparent.
2. Positive attachment to a member of the nonfamilial community such as a coach, teacher, police officer, or community worker.
3. Sibling position—sometimes an older sibling can provide a positive attachment to a younger one, mitigating the pathological impact of the larger system.
4. A degree of resilience wherein the individual has special attributes to draw upon such as intelligence, physical strength, or special talents or abilities.
5. A high level of intellectual ability, which gives the person access to educational experiences and knowledge that strengthens the ego.
6. A certain quality, such as a likeness to a parent or grandparent, that insulates the individual from blatant forms of abuse.
7. A family system that focuses its pathology on one member but spares another, i.e., one sibling is "good" and the other is "bad."

CLASSIFICATION OF DYSFUNCTIONAL PERSONOLOGIC FAMILY SYSTEMS

In the following system of classifying dysfunctional personologic family systems, the adjective *dysfunctional* indicates that forces within the family have reached a level at which the family is no longer in the midrange level of functioning but has become truly dysfunctional—that is, members of the family are *chronically* no longer having their developmental needs appropriately satisfied—and various members either have or are in danger of developing a disorder of personality. In these systems, clinical observation indicates that the family's adaptation is centered on one or more of the following themes reflected in the subtypes. Unlike the functional family that may be destabilized and then restructured to a new configuration during times of challenge, the dysfunctional system is chronically influenced by these dynamic themes that mute many other aspects of their functioning and adaptation.

SUBTYPES

- The Addictive Dysfunctional Personologic System (AdcDps).
- The Narcissistic Dysfunctional Personologic System (NarDps).
- The Covertly Narcissistic Dysfunctional Personologic System (CNrDps).
- The Psychotic Dysfunctional Personologic System (PscDps).
- The Developmentally Arrested Dysfunctional Personologic System (DevDps).
- The Physically/Sexually Traumatizing Dysfunctional Personologic System (TraDps).
- The Depressigenic Dysfunctional Personologic System (DepDps).
- The Chronically Medically Ill Dysfunctional Personologic System (MedDps).
- The Paranoid Dysfunctional Personologic System (ParDps).
- The Somatic Dysfunctional Personologic System (SomDps).

DEGREE OF PATHOLOGY

Although the level of pathology in any dysfunctional family system exists on a continuum, certain subtypes of dysfunctional personologic systems, because of their central organizing features, are more likely to represent severe forms of pathology or to exist in less virulent forms (see Table 3.1).

This classification should be used only as a rough guideline, because other factors can magnify or reduce the level of pathology present in a system. Also, combinations of these types are likely and can magnify the pathology exponentially. For example, in a system that is organized at a psychotic level of interaction, the presence of chronic addictive processes will likely increase the pathology and potential for abuse.

ELABORATION OF SUBTYPES

In the following sections, the ten subtypes of dysfunctional personologic systems are elaborated; where indicated, various personality disorders that

Table 3.1 Types of Dysfunctional Personologic
Family Systems and Level of Pathology

The Psychotic System	Severe pathology
The Physically/Sexually Traumatizing System	Severe pathology
The Paranoid System	Severe pathology
The Addictive System	Moderate to severe pathology
The Narcissistic System	Moderate to severe pathology
The Depressigenic System	Moderate pathology
The Chronically Medically Ill System	Lower pathology
The Covertly Narcissistic System	Lower pathology
The Developmentally Arrested System	Lower pathology
The Somatic System	Lower pathology

are likely to emerge from these systems are listed. These general guidelines are clinical markers and encourage empirical validation. A rule of thumb is that the more severe the level of family dysfunction is and the fewer mitigating variables there are, the greater the likelihood is of more severe forms of personality pathology.

The Addictive Dysfunctional Personologic System
The addictive dysfunctional personologic system (AdcDps) is probably one of the more commonly observed dysfunctional systems encountered by medical and mental health professionals. When severe, the addictive process, whether to alcohol, drugs, or gambling, takes precedence over the emotional and security needs of the family, and the family adapts to the addictive process. Much has been written about these families and the types of syndromes spawned, such as codependency.

Addictive systems produce a variety of personality pathologies as well, with a wide range of disturbances. Variables that affect the development of personality pathology include stage of addictive process, number of children, developmental period when addiction develops, and number of members actively using. Although not all addictive systems promulgate personality disorders, research reflects the high rate of comorbidity between substance use disorders and personality disorders (Tyrer, Gunderson, Lyons, & Tohen, 1997). Because substance use disorders can exaggerate or mimic personality disorders, careful evaluation of these comorbid conditions is in order (see Chapter 8).

Personality Disorders Likely to Develop:
- Antisocial personality disorder.
- Dependent personality disorder.
- Borderline personality disorder.

The Narcissistic Dysfunctional Personologic System

The narcissistic dysfunctional personologic system (NarDps) is fairly common in clinical practice and readily evident to the astute observer (Donaldson-Pressman & Pressman, 1994). These families almost immediately engender countertransference reactions in the therapist. Berkowitz, Shapiro, Zinner, and Shapiro (1974) comment on their work:

> In our studies of families of adolescents with severe disturbances in self-esteem, we find in the parents of these adolescents a narcissistic vulnerability similar to that of their adolescent offspring. Moreover, we find that family transactions are frequently orientated towards the parents' efforts to protect and maintain their tenuous self-esteem in ways which have important consequences for the development of narcissism in the adolescent. These parents' attempts to maintain their narcissistic equilibrium dominate their relationship to a maturing child throughout his development. (p. 353)

There is a blatant use of the children to pay tribute to the narcissistic parent or parents. One parent may indeed behave as if he or she were a king or queen and may expect other family members to constantly acquiesce to his or her needs and demands. Children are valued for how their accomplishments reflect on the parents. Even though every attempt may be made to give the child access to the best schools and experiences, there is a basic level of emotional neglect or overindulgence. The parental subsystem may contain two highly achievement-oriented individuals who continually place their needs above those of their children. It is not uncommon to find that children in these systems are essentially left alone from a very early age with little parental or adult supervision. Often an older sibling is placed in charge of younger ones, and all exhibit anger over the parental abandonment.

Personality Disorders Likely to Develop:
- Schizoid personality disorder.
- Passive-aggressive personality disorder.
- Narcissistic personality disorder.
- Depressive personality disorder.
- Avoidant personality disorder.

The Covertly Narcissistic Dysfunctional Personologic System

The covertly narcissistic dysfunctional personologic system (CNrDps) places the parental needs foremost, but the parents pretend to be agents of their children's development (Donaldson-Pressman & Pressman, 1994). Even when there is true concern for the welfare of the children, emotional deficiencies in the parents place the children in the untenable position of parenting their parents. These patterns are subtle in their narcissistic emotional use of the children. Miller (1983) describes these family constellations in her writings. The child or adult often truly believes that he or she was raised in a loving, healthy family and is unaware of the family deficiencies. One way to differentiate this system from the overt type is that these families generally do not elicit countertransference reactions in the clinician. The clinician may feel puzzled or confused: Things look good, so why are members of the family suffering?

Personality Disorders Likely to Develop:
- Avoidant personality disorder.
- Schizoid personality disorder.
- Obsessive-compulsive personality disorder.
- Histrionic personality disorder.

The Psychotic Dysfunctional Personologic System

The psychotic dysfunctional personologic system (PscDps) is easily identifiable by the mental health professional. In these systems, physical and psychological care of the children is jeopardized by major untreated psychiatric disturbances such as schizophrenia or bipolar disorder, often with coexisting personality disturbance, in one or both parents. An "intergenerational spiral" may occur when a child or adolescent suffers from major psychiatric disorder, as described by Doane and Diamond (1994):

> Our observations of the similarity across generations regarding disturbed, damaged, or negative attachments led us to speculate that perhaps the stresses involved in dealing with the psychiatrically impaired child activate preexisting internal problems of the parent and involve disappointments and burdens experienced with his or her own parents. The ill child then may serve as a catalyst for reactivating old "unfinished business" for the parent. The theme of intergenerational transmission of risk factors through processes of projection and expression of negative affect is central within disconnected families. (p. 106)

Skynner (1976) observed that "families containing schizophrenic members, for example, appear to have excessively permeable boundaries between the individuals which comprise them" (p. 6). Bowen (1976) calls these permeable boundaries "undifferentiated ego mass" (p. 69). Often there is also a lack of clearly defined boundaries between generations. These families may experience periods of severe abuse and emotional/physical abandonment but they also have periods of positive attachment, particularly if one parent is not disturbed or is in a state of remission. When one parent is disturbed and the other is sadistic or psychopathic, severe personality pathology is evident in some of the children. Mitigating factors such as extended family support are very important in immunizing the children in these systems.

Personality Disorders Likely to Develop:
- Borderline personality disorder.
- Schizotypal personality disorder.
- Paranoid personality disorder.
- Antisocial personality disorder.

The Developmentally Arrested Dysfunctional Personologic System
The developmentally arrested dysfunctional personologic system (DevDps) thwarts individuation and maturation of the members, with evidence of a severe lack of autonomy in family members (Bowen, 1976). These families often have one or more adult children living at home and floundering in terms of career development and outside relationships. I have treated systems in which two or three adult children continue to live at home and function developmentally like adolescents. There is an intolerance for differences and moves toward autonomy are met with subterfuge. In this dysfunctional family subtype, the parental subsystem is often genuinely interested in the development of their children and puzzled about why their children fail to establish themselves independently. However, strong emotional needs on the part of the parents continually undermine the separation-individuation process. There may be an unhappy marriage that lacks emotional intimacy and that is only held together by an empty commitment. These couples often say they are staying together for the children. Severe dependence is fostered, but at the same time the children are episodically attacked for this very dependency, thus further confusing them. These are families in which the children never leave, or leave but then fail at establishing themselves and come home defeated and more needy and depressed. The offspring may be alternately indulged and then denied basic emotional support, guidance, and financial assistance.

Personality Disorders Likely to Develop:
- Avoidant personality disorder.
- Dependent personality disorder.
- Histrionic personality disorder.
- Schizoid personality disorder.

The Physically/Sexually Traumatizing Dysfunctional Personologic System
Because of a variety of factors (see Pearlman & Saakvitne, 1995), the physically/sexually traumatizing dysfunctional personologic system (TraDps) may exist unnoticed for decades or throughout generations. There is ample evidence that suggests these systems spawn personality disorders as well as various other severe pathologies (Trepper & Niedner, 1996). Often the members are bound by intense feelings of filial loyalty. The level of abuse is often unimaginable by those who have not been exposed to such systems. Children are viewed as objects for parental manipulation and forced into child prostitution, pornography, and ritualized sexual abuse. Severe abuse and torture often predominate the interactions.

Psychopathic (Evil Subtype) Charney (1996) and Peck (1983) discuss a variant, or subtype, of this system—doing harm to others in family relationships. In some variants in which the abuse is extreme, evil is predominant. This type of family system is probably not as uncommon as is believed but no statistics or research document its prevalence. The main feature of this system includes an utter disregard for and even enjoyment in the suffering of others.

The Incompetent Subtype Charney (1996) discusses "Disorders of Incompetence, Vulnerability, and Personal Weakness" (p. 481). In this subtype, which has many variations, the harm done to others is unwitting or unconscious. Often individual members of this system fulfill the criteria for narcissistic and antisocial personality disorders, in which domination and control are defining aspects of the behavioral repertoire of the individual. Substantial progress has been made in explicating the couples dynamics evident in these systems.

Couples Dynamics Couples relationships in these systems are often characterized by sadomasochistic interactions (Glickauf-Hughes, 1996). Often both members of the couple are suffering from severe personality pathology such as borderline, malignant narcissism, or schizoid type. Glickauf-Hughes suggests some of the following features of these couples:

- Pathological jealousy and possessiveness.
- Fragile self-esteem.
- Frequent relationship breakups (and reconciliations).
- Hostile-dependent behavior.
- Power struggles.
- Intermittent loving and abusive behavior.
- Victim-persecutor dynamics.
- Distancer-pursuer dynamics.
- Frequent and extreme blaming.
- Problems with boundaries and limits.
- Explosive fights.

These systems are the most likely to result in severe personality pathology as well as in various other comorbid conditions such as drug and alcohol addiction, dissociative disorders, and mood disorders.

The Profile of Batterers   Another common element present in the physically/ sexually traumatizing dysfunctional personologic system is battering— physical aggression used to intimidate, control, and subjugate another person. In an extensive study of batterers, Jacobson and Gottman (1998) identified two profiles: Pit Bulls and Cobras. Pit Bulls metabolize anger in a slow burn, constantly building until the explosion. Cobras are calm and show evidence of less physiological arousal but more likely to display violence outside the family and are more severely prone to violence than are other batterers. They are also more likely to have a diagnosis of antisocial personality disorder, whereas the Pit Bulls are more likely to have dependent personality disorders. Cobras come from more violent and chaotic family backgrounds. It is common for women who are raised in these systems to seek out abusive relationships.

Personality Disorders Likely to Develop:
- Borderline personality disorder.
- Antisocial personality disorder.
- Narcissistic personality disorder.
- Sadistic personality disorder.
- Histrionic personality disorder.

The Depressigenic Dysfunctional Personologic System
The depressigenic dysfunctional personologic system (DepDps) is one in which the depletion of the parental system is so severe that there are not

enough emotional supplies to meet the children's needs. "The interpersonal burdens inherent in living with a depressed partner can increase the nondepressed partner's susceptibility to depression" (Gollan, Gortner, & Jacobson, 1996, p. 328). "It is not at all easy to live with and love a person who is chronically depressed. Stress, conflicts, arguments and misunderstandings are far more common in close relationships with depressed people, and depression and the sexual problems that usually accompany depression are the main reasons couples seek marital counseling" (Brody, 1998b, F9). Often there is a history of severe untreated affective disorders that disables the parental subsystem and can be observed in previous generations when family history is taken. Children often become caretakers and act in a parentified manner. Partial support for this diagnostic category is provided by the epidemiological findings of a high degree of comorbidity between depression and personality disorders (Tyrer et al., 1997).

Personality Disorders Likely to Develop:
- Depressive personality disorder.
- Schizoid personality disorder.
- Avoidant personality disorder.
- Obsessive-compulsive personality disorder.
- Avoidant personality disorder.

The Chronically Medically Ill Dysfunctional Personologic System
In the chronically medically ill dysfunctional personologic system (Med-Dps), the medical illness is a central organizing feature. "The chronic illness of an individual affects the entire system in which he or she exists (McDaniel et al., 1992). For example, not only does an individual have cancer, the entire family system does" (Barth, 1996, p. 496). The relational impact of chronic disorders such as arthritis, cancer, or diabetes can shape the entire system and thus influence the personality development of the members. Often one member of the family inordinately assumes the role of the caretaker and sacrifices other members of the family in the process.

Personality Disorders Likely to Develop:
- Dependent personality disorder.
- Avoidant personality disorder.
- Obsessive-compulsive personality disorder.
- Narcissistic personality disorder.

The Paranoid Dysfunctional Personologic System
In the paranoid dysfunctional personologic system (ParDps), there is a clear us versus them position. Here the term *paranoid* is not being used in the sense that there is a discrete paranoid personality, although there may be, but rather the term refers to the stance taken by the family, which is so distrusting that outsiders are never to be trusted. The message is that the only people who can be counted on are family members. Cultural factors may strongly influence these systems, as in the case of a newly immigrated family who do not yet know the language or the expectations of the dominant culture. Assimilation of first-generation children into the dominant culture may bring these unnoticed dynamics to the surface and may result in significant family distress when an individual openly attempts to break away.

Personality Disorders Likely to Develop:
- Paranoid personality disorder.
- Obsessive-compulsive personality disorder.
- Avoidant personality disorder.
- Schizoid personality disorder.

The Somatic Dysfunctional Personologic System
In the somatic dysfunctional personologic system (SomDps), the entire system is organized around one or more somatic individuals. These families have parental subsystems wherein almost all the needs and emotions of one or both parents are expressed in somatic terms. Various psychophysiological and psychosomatic disorders are characteristic of these families, including ulcerative colitis, asthma, migraine headaches, and chronic unremitting back pain as well as others. The main issue is that the entire family adopts a communication style and is organized around this often endless litany of somatic ailments that disrupt the family.

Personality Disorders Likely to Develop:
- Depressive personality disorder.
- Avoidant personality disorder.
- Obsessive-compulsive personality disorder.
- Passive-aggressive personality disorder.

Blends of Dysfunctional Personologic Systems
Like any system of classifying complex phenomenon, this system has overlap and blends. In fact, blends may be the most common clinical presenta-

tion. But identifying a significant theme or subtype allows clinicians to focus attention and to make focal interventions. The degree of overlap requires empirical research and clear criteria for diagnosing each subtype, which at this stage of development is premature. However, clinicians should be alert to the possibility that certain subtypes, based on clinical observation, are likely to covary. For example, the AdcDps and the TraDps are likely to be evident in the same system. Chronic addictive processes often fuel deterioration in the family system, which leads to a greater incidence of abuse and neglect.

Generational Shifting of the Type of Dysfunctional Personologic System Although no research evidence exists, clinical observation reveals that dysfunctional personologic systems show generational shifts in category or type. For example, in the case study titled "Man with Chronic Pain," the patient's nuclear system was the TraDps but he was clearly creating a system that was SomDps. His chronic pain was becoming the focus of his life, and his family system began to revolve around his pain. Other patients who have been raised in a TraDps organize their own family along the lines of the CNrDps. This situation often exhibits material overindulgence of the children but a covert emotional neglect. This neglect may result not from maliciousness but from severe narcissistic wounds that parents try to heal by using the children to vicariously experience what they wished they had received.

Other Features That Can Be Observed From the Clinical Landscape The clinical landscape of the dysfunctional personologic system also has a number of other common features. These features, not diagnostic alone, offer useful clinical corroboration, and point toward more careful assessment. Such clinical signposts include the following:

- *Negative reactions at holidays.* Individuals who have grown up in dysfunctional personologic systems may have very strong unexplained negative reactions during holidays. Although stressful for many people, holidays often result in exacerbation of individual and family problems. Individuals may recall parental neglect, abuse, or intense conflict. The actual experiences may be forgotten, but the emotional sequela—depression, emptiness, and so on—remains, often further confusing the individual. The media attention to holiday depression does not address the dramatic impact that dysfunctional systems have on their members years later.

- *Dramatically inconsistent public versus family persona.* Another feature I have often observed is the perception offered by family members that someone, often a parent, is highly esteemed in the community but mistreats family members at home. These individuals often have a well-constructed false self that is used to create a public image. The result is that other family members often feel that their perceptions are distorted, and they are confused. One patient from a CNrDps questioned her experience with the following statement: "How he treats me can't be that bad; he is a deacon in the church."

- *Family rationalizations.* Family rationalizations are used to explain and minimize dysfunctional patterns. Family members may make comments such as "Everyone's family is messed up" or "All families are dysfunctional." These defenses serve to mitigate the emotional pain but do no service to suffering family members. In some families past traumatic events are turned into humorous stories that are retold and laughed at; for example, one family told the story of how their father got drunk every Christmas and passed out. The content of the stories is often troubling to the listener.

- *Numerous family members with evidence of low self-esteem.* Signs of low self-esteem in various members of the family may be another indication of a chronic pattern of dysfunction.

- *A level of chronic misery.* In many types of dysfunctional systems there often exists a chronic state of misery and suffering that seems to go on unabated. This state may engender strong countertransference feelings of hopelessness or impotence.

CONCLUSIONS

This chapter presents a relational system of classification of dysfunctional personologic systems, various features of which have been observed and reported by systemically oriented clinical researchers and theorists. This classification system represents an initial attempt to organize the clinical phenomena observed by clinicians who work with personality-disordered systems. An awareness of these systems will increase the clinical utility of the practitioner treating and preventing personality disorders.

CHAPTER 4

Theories, Models, and Techniques of Integrative Relational Psychotherapy

Contemporary theories of personality, including psychoanalytic (Kernberg, 1996), cognitive (Beck & Freeman, 1990) and interpersonal (Benjamin, 1993b), focus primarily on the cognitive/affective and interpersonal matrix of the individual. Clarkin and Lenzenweger's (1996) book, *Major Theories of Personality Disorder*, makes no mention of a relational/systemic model. This omission is not an oversight but a reflection of the view of personality pathology in the context of an individual or perhaps dyadic process but not in systemic context. This book's relational approach encompasses these individual perspectives, the dysfunctional personologic system, and also an ecological system.

The clinical treatment of the personality disorders benefits from the integration of these conceptual models. At times the clinician must focus on the intrapsychic operation, and later a flexible integrative framework can be the scaffolding of this relational approach. This chapter reviews some essential contemporary theories and adds the relational components of the model to describe an integrative relational approach.

CONTEMPORARY THEORIES OF PERSONALITY

Each of the major contemporary theories of personality are enhanced when the systemic perspective is added. Although categorical distinctions are somewhat arbitrary, for heuristic purposes it is useful to examine the domains of various theoretical models. The following theories tend to emphasize the unique domains:

- Psychoanalytic—Affective Domain.
- Cognitive—Cognitive Domain.
- Interpersonal—Interpersonal-Dyadic Domain.
- Systemic—Relational Domain.

Figure 4.1 demonstrates how the three domains can be placed in a systemic relational context.

PSYCHOANALYTIC THEORY

Psychoanalytic models of personality began with Freud's publication of *Character and Anal Eroticism* (1908/1925). Although psychoanalysis originally attended to symptoms, symptom neurosis became separated from character neurosis and became labeled as personality disorder when the *DSM* began classification. Character neurosis represented more entrenched forms of psychopathology. Various analytic workers including Deutsch (1965), Fenichel (1945), and Reich (1945) expanded upon this field of investigation with developments that still have strong conceptual and clinical utility. Otto Kernberg (1996) is probably the most active voice of contemporary psychoanalytic theory of personality disorders. In his conceptualization Kernberg believes that personality is codetermined by temperament

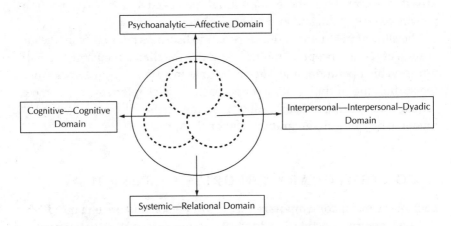

Figure 4.1   Overlap in theoretical domains in systemic context.

and character. Temperament refers to innate or inborn biological dispositions such as affective reactivity, and character becomes the behavioral manifestations of an individual's ego functions.

Structural concepts and developmental processes are based on the internalization of object relations (dyadic interactions with significant others). Personality is assessed by the ego functions (impulse control, affective regulation, psychological mindedness, motivation) and character traits (passive, dependent, obsessional, hysterical). Well-functioning personality is characterized by:

1. Integrated concept of self and others.
2. Ego strength—capacity for affect and impulse control and capacity for sublimation into work and values.
3. Mature superego—a sense of personal responsibility, commitment to standards, and so forth.
4. Appropriate management of sexual and libidinal drive—full expression of needs and ability to establish and maintain commitments.

The basic criteria for severe personality pathology is aggressive affect expression and for less severe personality pathology—neurotic character as Horney (1937) and Shapiro (1965) refer to it—is libido, or sexual expression.

Psychoanalytic theory also distinguishes between *deficit* and *conflict* pathology. Deficit pathology is more severe and reflects the lack of basic trust and biological vulnerability that make it difficult to develop a stable self-structure, in other words, the ability to trust, form attachments, regulate impulses, and so forth. Conflict pathology, in contrast, has more to do with the feelings that emerge from triangular relationships or oedipal struggles. Most personality-disordered individuals have a mixture of both deficit and conflict pathology. For an excellent contemporary presentation of this topic, readers should review McCullough Vaillant's (1997) clear review. Although these concepts have not been applied to families, they are nevertheless useful. Families that manifest more signs of deficit pathology are generally lower functioning, and there is more danger of detrimental effects on the offspring as well as intergenerational transmission of destructive patterns.

Cognitive Theory

The cognitive theory of personality is the newest of the contemporary models and expands on the pioneering work of Beck, Rush, Shaw, and Emery

(1979) in treating depression. The cognitive model, essentially an information-processing model of psychopathology (Pretzer & Beck, 1996), incorporates three components:

1. Automatic thoughts (beliefs and assumptions) shape and elicit emotional and behavioral responses; these are organized into structures called *schema*.
2. Interpersonal strategies are based on schema and can be distorted and reinforcing in the personality-disordered individual.
3. Misinterpretation of events leads to cognitive distortions.

The cognitive theory has produced schema for personality disorders that represent the intrapsychic cognitive matrix used to process information and to respond (Beck & Freeman, 1990; Young & Gluhoski, 1996).

Cognitive theory offers a powerful lens for viewing the belief system of personality-disordered individuals. Schema are developed in the setting of dysfunctional personologic systems and are often transmitted from one generation to the next through modeling and internalization. Thus, clinicians often see signs of low self-esteem and faulty self-concepts/ representations transmitted verbally from parent to child. These vocalizations, often subliminal, can be elicited as a powerful way to begin to restructure these detrimental beliefs that influence behavior and negative emotional reactions.

Linehan (1993) has developed a cognitive-behavioral model expressly for the treatment of the borderline personality disorder, especially those patients with parasuicidal behavior. This approach is an integrative model that draws from behavioral, cognitive, psychoanalytic, and strategic modalities.

INTERPERSONAL THEORY

Interpersonal theory's greatest proponent is Benjamin, who has continued in the tradition of Sullivan (1953) to emphasize the interpersonal processes that shape and maintain personality disturbance. Interpersonal theory underscores both the attachment process and the process of differentiation that occur in humans. Unlike the cognitive and psychoanalytic conceptualizations, this theory focuses on the interpersonal matrix that so strongly influences the maintenance of personality pathology. Benjamin (1993b) has developed a coding system for the scientific study of interpersonal processes, termed Structural Analysis of Social Behavior (SASB), which she has applied to the study of personality disorders. Benjamin's system is a blend that "recognizes the interplay of cognitive, affective, and interpersonal dimensions in her effort to articulate the fundamental qualities of each of the personality disorders" (Millon & Davis, 1996, p. 57). Various interpersonal styles of interacting can be observed and coded using this system.

INTEGRATIVE THEORY

Probably the most systematically conceived integrative theory of "personologic therapy" has been presented by Millon (1990, p. 165). He states that the "crossover point" among the various aspects of the biopsychosocial matrix is the person—"the only organically linked system in the psychological domain" (p. 165). Therefore, the therapy is personologic for the personality-disordered individual. He suggests coordinated strategies of methods and technical interventions that are designed to optimize treatment potency. Millon's integrative approach emanates from his evolutionary model of personality, which emphasizes three polar domains: pleasure/pain; passive/active; and other/self. The goal, then, of treatment is to orchestrate a better balance between the polarities. Millon suggests "catalytic sequences" (p. 167) and "potentiating pairings" (p. 167), which are therapeutic arrangements and timed interventions that promote polarity balances.

SYSTEMIC THEORY

Applying systems theory to our study of personality disorders is in its infancy. However, a number of trends have made the timing right for this integrative leap. Advancements in our understanding of family systems theory are finding broad application to various psychological and medical conditions (Kaslow, 1996; Mikesell, Lusterman, & McDaniel, 1995). Mikesell et al. broadly define *systems therapy* as follows:

> the comprehensive set of interventions for treating the family, including individuals, couples, nuclear families, families of origin, medical systems, and other larger contexts (such as school and work), and the cultural and ethnic contexts in which these are embedded. At any particular time, a unique feature of systems therapy is that it gives the therapist a paradigm from which to

view multiple causes of contexts of behavior. Consequently, it provides one of the most comprehensive models for the development of interventions and one of the most promising models for change. (p. xv)

This perspective has particular utility when applied to the treatment of personality disorders for a number of reasons.

- *An understanding of the dysfunctional personologic system enables health professionals to identify sources of potential personality pathology that might otherwise be overlooked.* For example, a child was referred for treatment by his parents with vague complaints about his performance in school. A family evaluation revealed a SomDps. The father, who appeared unkempt and depressed, disclosed that he had been suffering from chronic back pain for 12 years and was unemployed. He was focusing all his energy on his only child, whom he wanted to be a success. This focus was creating a high degree of anxiety in the boy.
- *Having such broad-based points of access to the dysfunctional personologic system affords the clinician the opportunity for creative engagement of the personality-disordered system and individual.* In the case just described, the father was suffering from long-standing personality pathology, and the system was accommodating to his disturbance protectively. Significant distress in the couple subsystem was not being addressed.
- *A broad-based systemic approach encourages integrative approaches to the treatment of personality disorders rather than single perspective interventions.* Single perspective interventions may be quite powerful with the right patient at the right time. Personologic disorders are too complex to consistently yield any single approach. A broadly based systems approach encourages clinicians to seek out the best treatment match possible and to refrain from a myopic perspective.
- *A systemic model is an umbrella for integrative approaches.* Most therapists who work extensively with dysfunctional personologic systems and individuals by necessity tend to be pragmatic and eclectically use various theories and techniques. A systemic model is an umbrella for the various models and approaches.

ADOPTING AN INTEGRATIVE ORIENTATION

THE RELEVANCE AND TYPES OF INTEGRATION

Many experienced psychotherapists have evolved along similar developmental trajectories. They learn one approach, feel disillusioned by efforts that are only partially effective, and then learn another, seemingly divergent, approach (see Gustafson, 1986). For many clinicians, this process has culminated in a true blending of disparate approaches in the development of a formal model that attempts theoretical integration or in an intuitive blend of approaches that is never formally explicated. For others, this process has entailed using technology from divergent approaches to attain beneficial results, or technical eclecticism. Still another form of integration is identifying and incorporating the common elements that cut across theoretical orientations and that attribute change to common factors (Norcross & Newman, 1992). Many clinicians at some point have followed all three paths toward integration in the service of trying to enhance clinical outcome. In sum, all three types of integration are central to this model

Theoretical Integration
Wachtel and McKinney (1992) rejected the assumption that among theoretical orientations there is a fundamental incompatibility. In reality, the major schools of psychotherapy deal with the expressed domains of the other. Thus, there is no incompatibility among cognitive, interpersonal, psychoanalytic, or systems theory, even though each system has a certain emphasis.

Technical Eclecticism
Technical eclecticism has often been discredited as being a collection of disparate techniques that do not necessarily follow a theoretical orientation and is, without guiding principles, dangerous. However, technical eclecticism can also be informed. Selection of techniques from various persuasions can be done carefully and with guiding principles. In many ways, clinicians find less risk in staying with a circumscribed, prescribed set of technical interventions as well as with a therapeutic stance, but they miss the flexibility to blend technical interventions in a new amalgam. Although overlooked for many years, Sandor Ferenczi presaged the development of technical eclecticism. William Rachman (1997) has facilitated recognition of Ferenczi's work, which has been repressed for decades (see Rachman for a history of this unfortunate occurrence). Ferenczi's advances are compatible with the model of integrative relational psychotherapy.

Ferenczi's Technical Developments
- Time-extended sessions of two-hour duration.
- Heightened emotional experiencing in the here and now and the flexible use of time limits.

- Confrontation of resistances.
- Elasticity of the therapeutic situation; employment of different modes of activity.
- A holistic approach to the human condition—a reuniting of the emotional, intellectual, physical, and interpersonal.
- Responsibility for the therapeutic relationship—a partnership in the joint struggle to achieve a breakthrough.
- Willingness to give advice, develop activities, and directly encourage and suggest avenues for potential growth.
- An emphasis on empathic attunement.
- An active method.
- The use of contertransference to understand and guide the process.
- Judicious use of therapist self-disclosure related to countertransference reactions. (Rachman, 1997, pp. 164–165)

Ferenczi believed that character neurosis, or personologic disturbance as we currently refer to it, in the form of "parental psychopathology—narcissism, rage, empathic failure, sadism, perversion—are considered the locus for trauma (not the child's internal process of oedipal fantasy)" (Rachman, 1997, p. 318). Human psychopathology at its roots can be attributed to three broad categories. Ferenczi identified the first two, traumatic experiences and empathic failures on the part of the parental figures. He also seemed to be on the verge of discovering the impact of relational psychodynamics that occur in family system as another root of personologic disturbance. The failure of personality-disordered individuals to metabolize overwhelming affects caused by these early experiences results in symptom complexes, which, when severe, lead to personality disorder. Ferenczi believed that the therapist should be dedicated toward healing and cure. He did not blame patients for their lack of improvement; instead he believed that if the patient did not respond to treatment, the therapist should examine his or her technique and countertransference issues. This attitude was a refreshing change from the typical stance of describing the patient as "treatment resistant."

Ferenczi also presaged our current understanding of trauma theory. He recognized not only physical and sexual abuse but also emotional abuse as factors central in the development of personality pathology. He was on the vanguard for presenting cases for scrutiny by giving an indication of the actual words exchanged between patient and therapist. This presentation was unusual for the early twentieth century, a time when cases were presented in the form of clinical summaries rather than transcripts of dialogue.

He rejected the role of the therapist as the blank screen and instead proposed a highly engaged therapeutic stance to provide the core conditions or common factors for personologic growth.

Common Factors
Techniques aside, evidence suggests that most improvement comes when a good-quality therapeutic relationship provides the core conditions that facilitate change. These core conditions include therapist characteristics such as warmth, unconditional positive regard, care, and acceptance. Although these conditions have been described by Carl Rogers (1957) as the only ones necessary for change, it is unlikely that these characteristics alone will result in personologic change in a patient. Alper (1992) presents the ideals that clinicians should strive for (the first four listed here), and I add some of my own:

1. Therapeutic personality, which includes warmth.
2. Empathic imagination, which is the ability to objectively see another's experience through one's own eyes.
3. Kindness.
4. Clinical sensibility and artistry—"the technique that cannot be taught, is more important than the technique that can be taught" (Alper, 1992, p. 196).
5. A belief in the inherent healing capacities of the human psyche and body.
6. An ability to tolerate the uncertainty, vulnerability, and ambiguity of oneself and of the healing relational matrix.
7. A continuous desire to evolve as a human being and healer.
8. Flexibility and consistency.

These elements are the foundation of the effective therapeutic alliance that allows the patient to experience the hope of mastering difficulties and engaging in personologic change.

OTHER WELL-ESTABLISHED GROWTH FACTORS

Elements of personologic change that are not subsumed under the categories in the previous section are also important aspects of personologic change. These elements include extratherapeutic factors and expectancy or placebo effects.

Extratherapeutic factors often contribute significantly to the change process. Clinicians do not have to be reminded that the amount of time a patient spends with therapists is very limited compared with out-of-session time. Extratherapeutic factors include environmental variables such as social support or fortuitous events (Lambert, 1992). Therapists may attempt to mobilize these factors in an ecosystem by encouraging someone to go to school, join a community organization, and or enhance relationships.

Expectancy (placebo effect) is the credibility that the individual or system attributes to the treatment approach, therapist, or institution that stimulates the natural healing process. This factor may be called hope and is an overlooked aspect of the treatment experience. In fact, disregard for the potency of this factor may in fact lead to negative treatment expectations and poor outcome (Weil, 1995). Therapists who are confident in their abilities and their approach inspire greater confidence and hope in those they treat.

CORE TECHNIQUES OF FAMILY SYSTEMS INTERVENTIONS

Incorporating an integrative relational approach to the treatment of personality pathology substantially broadens the range of interventions available to the clinician. The spectrum of interventions possible make it easier to more precisely match the treatment to the needs, degree of pathology, and stage of change that each system or individual presents. Therapists can capitalize on "differential treatment effectiveness," which, although more an art than a science (Frances et al., 1984), is nevertheless a step in the direction of more effective treatment planning. Treatment matching is covered in greater depth in Chapter 8. In this section, the core treatment interventions are reviewed. Seaburn, Landau-Stanton, and Horowitz (1995) concisely list the following three core techniques in family therapy:

1. Here and now interventions.
2. Transgenerational interventions.
3. Ecosystem approaches.

The authors identify several here and now interventions that are common to many styles of family therapy: reenactment and enactment, reframing/positive connotation/noble ascription and symptom prescription, restructuring the family in session, defining the problem and establishing goals and action plans, family psychoeducation, and therapist's use of self with the family. Transgenerational interventions include genogram development, trips home, inviting extended family into therapy, and symbolic inclusion of family of origin. Ecosystemic approaches (Auerswald, 1968) view the family embedded in the context of various biopsychosocial systems and interventions. Other unique technical interventions and techniques are utilized. One original technique is network sessions, which may involve large numbers of members of the ecosystem (Rueveni, 1975). For my purposes, I have organized the interventions into five somewhat different categories: (1) multigenerational interventions, (2) psychoeducational interventions, (3) family restructuring, (4) corrective emotional experiencing, and (5) ecosystem interventions.

CATEGORIES OF CORE TECHNIQUES

Multigenerational Interventions
Systems theorists and family therapists have stressed the concept of the transmission of emotional conflicts through successive generations. Relevant for the field of personality disorders is the strong evidence that personality pathology is transmitted from generation to generation in a complex process that involves genetics, modeling, communication, and systemic reinforcement. One advantage of the relational model is that regardless of the initial point of contact the clinician has with the dysfunctional personologic family system, he or she can observe the process of multigenerational transmission and can then intervene at the most appropriate level of contact (the most accessible fulcrum point).

Multigenerational intervention expands the reference point to include the past two generations and assesses how the family system over the generations has dealt with emotional conflict, reared children, and established new subsystems. The therapist identifies resources from various generations to resolve the emotional and developmental fixations that are assumed to be the foundation of personality disturbance.

Family Psychoeducational Interventions
A psychoeducational model has been applied to various medical and psychosocial disorders with the primary focus on schizophrenia (Miklowitz, 1995). Although promising, this model has not been applied to the treatment of personality. A psychoeducational approach can educate family members about personality disturbance and can help change attitudes that

are destructive to the process of recovery. Processes that reinforce certain personality pathology—such as the enabling that often occurs with dependent and avoidant personality disorders—can be explained, and changes can be encouraged. Family members may be provided with reading material. Educating the individual and the family also allows for the discussion of diagnostic labeling. The pros and cons of diagnostic labeling are discussed in Chapter 5. However, through the use of metaphors, psychoeducation can be done without ascribing a pathological label. For example, a narcissistic individual can be described as someone who is thin-skinned and sensitive to criticism. I explore the issue of therapeutic metaphors in more depth in Chapter 9. The goals of psychoeducation are to change attitudes, increase awareness, illuminate new response patterns, increase understanding, and set realistic expectations.

Restructuring
The goal of most systemic interventions, whether overtly or covertly expressed, is to alter the basic structure of the dysfunctional personologic system. The basic structural organization of the family is observed through the repetitive relational dynamics and patterns of communication observed during assessment and treatment. The most common structural relationship evident in the family system, discussed in Chapter 3, is the triangular relationship often comprised of a conflicted marital relationship and an enmeshed child.

In one case, for example, parents, who both suffered from personality disturbance, brought their symptomatic son to treatment because he would not comply with parental expectations concerning academic achievement. There was obvious dysfunction in the marital subsystem. The father had been unemployed and was depressed, whereas the mother was a career-driven individual who carried the weight of the whole family. Significant rage in the parental subsystem was never overtly addressed; instead all energy was directed toward the son, who was overwhelmed with anxiety and could not concentrate.

In this case, restructuring the system entails detriangulating the child from the parental subsystem, which can be achieved through various strategies such as strengthening the parental subsystem or seeing the parents alone. Within sessions, blocking maneuvers can halt the scapegoating of the child; these maneuvers will increase anxiety within the couple and will help them address this anxiety and their underlying, unexpressed emotion. Alternatively, the parents can discuss their plan to resolve the problem and to create a boundary between the parental and child subsystem.

Another, more traditional method of restructuring the dysfunctional personologic system is to modify the personality of one or more members of the system in the hope of mobilizing the growth of the system. This approach to treating personality disorders has been described in my previous book, *Restructuring Personality Disorders: A Short-Term Dynamic Approach* (Magnavita, 1997b), and a similar approach is discussed by McCullough Vaillant (1997) in her book, *Changing Character: Short-Term Anxiety-Regulating Psychotherapy for Restructuring Defenses, Affects, and Attachments.* In clinical work with personality-disordered patients, McCullough Vaillant and I have observed a powerful phenomenon: when one member of a couple or family experiences a transformational course of psychotherapy, that person's enhanced capacities provide a developmental boost to the others. This improvement is especially observed when a key member of a system receives effective personologic treatment. Unfortunately, the opposite reaction can also be observed, which is what prompted me to write this book. Occasionally, I would observe after a successful course of treatment a calcification of the significant other that often resulted in divorce. The divorce may have been inevitable for many reasons, but I was perplexed by why some systems moved forward in their healthy development and others showed deterioration. Far better outcomes were seen in cases that involved successful sequential treatment of individuals followed by an additional course of couples treatment.

Corrective Emotional Experiencing
The concept of the corrective emotional experience (Alexander & French, 1946) has been a mainstay in the understanding of one of the curative ingredients in psychotherapy. This concept, when applied to the dysfunctional personologic system, emphasizes the here and now interactions in the relational matrix. The corrective emotional experience is the activation and experience of the relational matrix within the session, in a safe and healing environment so that feelings can be experienced and metabolized and deeper intimacy can be experienced. The following techniques are used to facilitate a here and now corrective emotional experience:

- Active emotional engagement is encouraged.
- Relational patterns are allowed to emerge and tension allowed to build before the therapist intervenes.
- Defense systems of various members of the system are clarified and challenged.
- Homeostatic balance may be disrupted.

- The therapist uses himself or herself actively.
- Family rules are identified and challenged.
- Affective communication is modeled.

Ecosystem Intervention

Ecosystem interventions involve, alter, or strengthen the areas that make up a family or individual ecosystem. Traditional, psychoanalytically oriented therapists often felt that ecosystem intervention was not appropriate because it might corrupt the therapeutic field. Interventions in the ecosystem often have very immediate and powerful results. A 24-year-old man with an avoidant personality disorder and comorbid agoraphobia lived with his parents in a DevDps. He was encouraged to enter a career rehabilitation program offered by the state, and after three months, he was employed for the first time since he graduated from high school. This step greatly improved his self-esteem. The impact on his parents was mixed; they were pleased but seemed to fight more. The marital issues are often exposed during such interventions and can be addressed when the time is right.

PROCESS ISSUES

- *Flexible movement from the micro level to the macro level to the systemic level of defense and communication.* The therapist must be adept at fluid movement from the macro level of dynamics within the system to the micro level of the intrapsychic dynamics. The three triangles—triangle of conflict, triangle of persons, and triangle of relations—can serve to orient the clinician and provide a gauge for deepening the therapeutic process and for continually restructuring the relational matrix as well as the individual's cognitive/affective and interpersonal matrix. However, clinicians will find that moving from one realm to another—maintaining an eye on the therapeutic alliance while increasing the depth of feeling, contact, and intimacy—is no small task; it requires great attention to process and a trust in one's own unconscious process. As Linehan (1993) and Josephs (1997) emphasize, efficient psychotherapy with the personality-disordered individual as well as with the personologic system is more like a dialectic process than a linear one.
- *Maintaining the level of anxiety most conducive to emotional growth and defense restructuring.* One of the crucial learnings from short-term dynamic therapists like Davanloo (1980, 1990) and Sifneos (1987) is their courageous use of anxiety at just the right level of tolerance to activate

the therapeutic process (Magnavita, 1997a). We as clinicians shy away from anxiety-provoking interventions for many reasons, not the least of which is our own anxiety about the emotions that exist underneath. Millon and Davis (1996) comment: "To the credit of the short-term psychotherapists, they have recognized that real change cannot be produced unless these homeostatic mechanisms are suspended, producing anxiety" (p. 13).

SYSTEMIC ANXIETY MANAGEMENT AND REGULATION

One advantage to incorporating a systemic model in the treatment of personality disorders is the flexibility that is afforded in terms of anxiety management and regulation. McCullough Vaillant (1997) has stressed the importance of anxiety-regulating therapy, reminding clinicians that the goal of treatment is not to provoke undue anxiety in the patient or, in this case, the system. Too much anxiety is likely to create iatrogenic disturbance—caused by the treatment. Conducting effective therapy with the dysfunctional personologic system is not a matter of crudely generating anxiety; it requires a sophisticated understanding of the variants of anxiety, of how the individual and the systems regulate anxiety, and of how to therapeutically mobilize as well as reduce anxiety. What is often overlooked is how to systemically shift the anxiety from one subsystem to another or from one individual to another.

Shifting Anxiety to Another Member of the System

One characteristic of many dysfunctionl personologic systems is that anxiety often resides in one member of the family in a way that is less threatening to the homeostasis. A good example is the patient with an ego-syntonic personality in which the defense system is like a coat of armor protecting the patient against intimacy and internal anxiety (Reich, 1945). The patient becomes identified with his or her defenses, as if this defensive structure represented the patient's "true self" or identity. The ego-syntonic personality is one of the most resistant to therapeutic engagement precisely because such patients see the problem as existing outside themselves, or externalized. Many of these patients exhibit what I have termed the Popeye Syndrome—"I am who I am." Reich (1945) identified this problem in his work: "For the neurotic character traits a reason is often put forward which would immediately be rejected as absurd if it were applied to symptoms, such as: 'He just is that way'—with its implication that he was born so, that this 'happens to be' his character, which cannot be altered" (p. 133). So the ego-syntonicity then serves as a type of resistance to the process of change and to the treatment process itself.

The typical ego-syntonic patient enters therapy reluctantly and has a litany of complaints: Everyone in his or her life orbit is deficient, problematic, and not good enough. This individual is not aware of the destructive nature of his or her personality, or more accurately, defensive style. Commonly in these cases, other members of the system are experiencing anxiety but the ego-syntonic individual is in no distress. A first step in restructuring the system is to shift the anxiety to the ego-syntonic personality. This shift can be accomplished in a variety of ways; the methods depend on the various factors that have led the system or individual in treatment. A direct elaboration of the ego-syntonic individual's defense system can rapidly increase anxiety so that destructive personality patterns and effects on the members of the system can be explored. This action can be highly emotionally arousing, and the clinician should be trained in individual defense analysis as well as systems interventions before proceeding.

Shifting Anxiety From One Subsystem to Another
Shifting anxiety from one subsystem to another is a commonly recognized procedure that many therapists utilize, especially those who treat children systemically. The most common occurrence is when a child is brought to the clinician because of symptomatic outbreaks or chronic behavior disturbances. The clinician assesses that the family is dysfunctional and that the symptom bearer is holding the anxiety for the dysfunctional personologic system. The clinician may invite the parental subsystem in for consultation in a nonthreatening manner, for example, to emphasize improved parenting. The goal would be to direct the couple to their relational dynamics and to engage them in couple therapy. Another clinician might more rapidly intervene and reframe the problem in some way that underscores the disturbance in the marital relational matrix. Issues can then be identified and an assessment made.

Increasing Anxiety Tolerance Within the System by Exploring Catastrophic Fears
Anxiety is generated by a disequilibrium of the family's homeostatic mechanism. Focusing on conflictual material in the family session and encouraging emotional expression in a direct manner is highly threatening to the dysfunctional personologic system. Whitaker (Whitaker & Keith, 1980), in what has been termed *Symbolic-Experiential Family Therapy*, was noted for

his ability and willingness to explore the family's unconscious process and expose their fears of, for example, going crazy, divorce, murderous impulses, incestual feelings, and so forth. This type of deep family interpretation is similar to the type used by Sifneos (1987) in his text *Short-Term Dynamic Psychotherapy: Evaluation and Technique.* Exploring these unconscious issues openly can increase anxiety tolerance and enhance open communication by making even the most frightening revelations nonthreatening. The therapist provides the holding environment that serves as the crucible or container so these affects and unconscious elements can be tolerated and metabolized.

CLINICAL GUIDELINES WHEN SYSTEMICALLY SHIFTING AND REGULATING ANXIETY

In dysfunctional personologic systems, homeostatic mechanisms operate to contain anxiety or displace it in a way that is not as threatening to the system or a particular subsystem. Exposing destructive relational or individual behavioral patterns often goes against the covert family agreement to conceal problems.

Dysfunctional Personologic Systems With Deficit Pathology
Systems that primarily suffer from deficit pathology usually need to have the system stabilized and anxiety lessened. Highly impaired systems often suffer from biological vulnerabilities, and members need to have their most pressing needs attended to. Attempting to address generations of personality pathology without an awareness of the basic needs is likely to be fruitless.

Dysfunctional Personologic Systems With Conflict Pathology
Systems that are suffering from conflict pathology may better tolerate anxiety and thus can be dealt with more rapidly. These systems do not have major developmental psychopathology; they are struggling more with competitive issues and misalliances that do not require major relational restructuring.

Normalizing the Anxiety Associated With Change
The emergence of anxiety generated from systemic restructuring or from individual change can be highly disconcerting. Anxiety aroused from structural shifts is often primitive and frightening, creating a sense of

dread, apprehensiveness, and panic. Individuals may report a fear of going crazy or going out of control, perhaps suicidal, homicidal, or catatonic. Although these dysphoric states are often an inevitable aspect of change, they often represent activation of the unconscious process and are indicative of a growth phase. The therapist must be alert to these states and be able to normalize and understand that these experiences are a part of the process of growth.

TREATMENT GOALS

General treatment goals that are based on an integrative relational model include:

1. Improved communication.
2. Enhanced emotional capacity.
3. Creation of functional family hierarchies.
4. Development of higher order defenses.
5. Enhanced capacity for intimacy.
6. Improved problem-solving capacity.
7. Greater tolerance for anxiety without compromising family functions.

CONCLUSIONS

The management and regulation of anxiety is a central task in restructuring the dysfunctional personologic system. Combining major theoretical models and blending treatment techniques allows for both a micro level and macro level approach. Comprehensive assessment and treatment requires that the affective, cognitive, interpersonal, and relational components be addressed.

CHAPTER 5

Integrative Relational Assessment

Denton (1996) summarizes 40 years of family research and concludes that how a family interacts is definitely associated with the level of individual and family functions but that no relational diagnosis is uniquely associated with specific disorders. In other words, a specific dysfunctional personologic system will produce a variety of personality disturbances and clinical syndromes. How, then, do therapists go about making assessments that have clinical utility? This chapter addresses these issues and offers guidelines based on current accumulated clinical and research knowledge.

THE RELEVANCE OF ASSESSMENT AND DIAGNOSTIC LABELS

The limitations and advantages of conducting assessment, especially the aspect of diagnosing, is an ongoing debate in the field of psychotherapy but is even more controversial for the field of family therapy (Olson, 1996). Polemics aside, most clinicians conduct a formal or informal assessment before formulating treatment strategies, and assessment is an ongoing aspect of clinical practice. The main danger in the assessment process of personality disturbance is the use of diagnostic labeling that creates a limiting construct from which it may become difficult to escape. In fact, Gergen, Hoffman, and Anderson (1996) suggest that diagnosing is disastrous; these authors espouse the avoidance of diagnostic systems. Gergen et al. discuss the harmfulness of "psychiatric hate speech" (p. 108), or what I have described as the pejorative use of labels (Magnavita, 1997b). This pejorative use is especially relevant in the field of personality assessment, where the disorders themselves are considered stable and difficult to alter. Part of the problem is that many therapists in the field believe that personality is immutable and that being labeled with a personality disorder is to be written off. In fact, the result of *DSM* and the labeling of personality pathology has resulted in renewed research and clinical focus on these disturbances. Fortunately, the belief that personality is inalterable is eroding, and new advancements in the field are being proposed (Magnavita, 1998a, 1998b). With this caveat, I can reiterate Millon's (Millon & Davis, 1996) principle, which is also a paradox: Personality disorders are not truly diagnosable, and yet we as clinicians can and must conduct an assessment in order to more effectively structure our interventions.

Naming or labeling anything—especially variants of human behavior in a professional context, that is, patient or client and doctor or clinician—involves the exercise of power. Labeling and classifying is an essential element of science (Barlow, 1996). Some of the negative association involves not labeling but that which is labeled. The label *cancer* arouses feeling in most everyone. Changing the name to something else does not reduce the associated reactions that people have to this label. This power to label can be used to limit or add to our understanding of that which we label. Certain important aspects of this process mitigate against the insensitive or iatrogenic use of labels.

USING CLINICAL JUDGMENT

The medical or legal authority to diagnose is provided to groups that have attained a high level of knowledge and professional experience. The power to diagnose mental disorders entails mastery of a substantial body of knowledge as well as development of the judgment necessary to apply this knowledge. Avoiding diagnostic knowledge and current theoretical and research findings can be misguided and damaging. Underdiagnosing can lead to malpractice problems, the misapplication of treatment, and unwarranted suffering. The clinician also has the power to underemphasize labels and to explain the difficulties that therapists have with current diagnostic systems so that patients don't feel constrained or trapped by diagnostic labels. One caveat before proceeding: Those therapists not trained in the appropriate bodies of clinical or psychological knowledge or without the legal authority should refrain from diagnosing psychological disturbances, especially personality pathology, because the misinformed use of these labels can be damaging.

CLASSIFICATION SYSTEMS FOR PERSONALITY DISORDERS

Various systems of classification are used for the study of personality. Because each system level in the biopsychosocial model represents a dynamic whole, it is understandable that there are unique methods of studying and understanding each level. Perlmutter (1996) emphasizes an important point:

> There is no sharp distinction between normal and disordered when it comes to personality. Everyone has some repetitive, habitual ways of behaving, and almost everyone could be at risk of being labeled "personality disordered," especially during times of crisis or imbalance. Awareness of the family context of the disorders also introduces a degree of "relativism" to the criteria for personality disorder. (pp. 326–327)

With this point in mind, I can proceed to review current systems of classification. Classification of disorders specific to each system level are needed, and numerous proposals for family classifications have been offered (Denton, 1996). The current major systems include categorical, dimensional, structural, cognitive, interpersonal, and relational. Each of these systems offers a somewhat different perspective of personality, and each has various methods of assessing personality. The clinician working with the personality-disordered individual should have knowledge of the major systems of classification and in-depth knowledge of at least two systems, preferably more. Otherwise, case conceptualization and treatment interventions will be one-dimensional. Next, I briefly describe each of the major systems and some of their strengths and limitations.

CATEGORICAL CLASSIFICATION OF PERSONALITY

The categorical system, represented by the *DSM* (APA, 1994), reflects a major advancement in the classification of mental disorders (Lively, 1995). Each personality disorder is distinguished by seven or eight observable criteria that, if met, indicate the presence of a personality disorder. This system is the main one in use in field of psychiatry and is necessary for all insurance reimbursement.

The *strengths* of categorical classification are: It is easy to use; it offers operationalized criteria; it is the best fit for some personality disorders, such as antisocial personality disorder; it suggests other characteristics to look for (Millon and Davis, 1996); and it provides a standard reference for mental health professionals.

Its *limitations* are: It has no underlying theory to hold it together; its behavioral descriptions are based on eight or nine criteria; disagreement still exists regarding core nature of personality disorders (Clark, Lively, & Morey, 1997); it works best with discrete categories, yet a high degree of overlap exists; the most commonly diagnosed personality disorder is "Not Otherwise Specified"; lack of convergent and discriminant validity remain problematic; and the yes or no diagnostic categories do not account for subsyndromal variants that require intervention (Weston & Arkowitz-Weston, 1998).

DIMENSIONAL CLASSIFICATION OF PERSONALITY

The dimensional system of classification evolved from the study of normal personality and is based on factor analytic approaches that distill the essential constructs that best represent variations in personality. Personality is rated on these underlying traits, or dimensions, and personality disorders are diagnosed when a predominance of maladaptive traits or exaggerated traits occur. The five-factor model (Costa & McCrae, 1992) has identified the following dimensions: neuroticism, extraversion, openness, agreeableness, and conscientiousness.

The *strengths* of dimensional classification are: Its psychometric perspective offers increased reliability; it accounts for both standard disorders and variants; it can differentiate threshold and subthreshold variants; it does not miss important variants; and it is valuable as a psychoeducational vehicle.

Its *limitations* are: Its face validity may be questionable because data is often derived from normal personality studies; its cutoff scores may be arbitrarily assigned; it relies heavily on self-report, which may be biased; and most models do not fully describe or predict personality disorders (Ball, Tennen, Poling, Kranzler, & Rounsaville, 1997).

STRUCTURAL CLASSIFICATION OF PERSONALITY

The structural system is based on psychoanalytic diagnostic formulations derived from generations of case material. This system relies on psychoanalytically observed character types and on the structural integrity of the intrapsychic system (McWilliams, 1994). Although esoteric to the nondynamically informed clinician, structural classification offers rich clinical formulations. This system assumes that the same behavior or patterns can have divergent unconscious dynamics.

The *strengths* of structural classification are: It is clinically relevant, that is, it directly informs treatment planning; it can be assessed with a structural interview; it accounts for individual differences; it attempts to understand what is beneath behavior; and it provides a broad-based functional appraisal of strengths and deficits.

Its *limitations* are: It takes longer to master; it relies on clinical interview and is not suitable for screening; it is not as well validated through research as other classification systems are; and its theoretical model is not integrative.

COGNITIVE CLASSIFICATION OF PERSONALITY

The cognitive model examines personality structure through an assessment of cognitive schema, the organization of an individual's assumptions and beliefs. These schema are unique for each personality disorder; they provide a useful method for showing various configurations of personality disorders that are easy for patients to understand. The schema are usually not in the patient's awareness, but they strongly influence emotional reactions and repetitive maladaptive behavior. By listening to the patient's internalized voice, the therapist can assess the cognitive structure of the personality-disordered patient.

The *strengths* of cognitive classification are: It has tremendous psychoeducational value; it is easy to use; it provides a nonthreatening method for establishing a diagnostic formulation; and it directly informs the treatment.

Its *limitations* are: It is rather narrow in focus; it may be too simplistic for clinicians to solely rely on; and it doesn't address structural configuration.

INTERPERSONAL CLASSIFICATION OF PERSONALITY

The interpersonal system of classifying personality bases the assessment on the interpersonal matrix with special emphasis on the reciprocal processes that occur between individuals. These interpersonal tendencies can be observed with significant others as well as with therapists and are reflected in transference/countertransference processes.

The *strengths* of interpersonal classification are: It provides a rich source of data for understanding and classifying personality; it highlights complementarity of interpersonal process; and it takes advantage of the here and now interactions.

Its *limitations* are: It offers a somewhat narrow spectrum of personality; and it ignores the intrapsychic organization and structure.

RELATIONAL CLASSIFICATION OF PERSONALITY

The attempt to develop a diagnostic system based on relational diagnosis has emerged in part from the discontent with *DSM* from systemic theorists and family therapists (Kaslow, 1996). The relational system views personality pathology as existing within a complex biopsychosocial system, not exclusively within the individual. As presented in Chapter 4, relational diagnosis attempts to characterize the variety of *dysfunctional personologic systems* that spawn personality disorders and that often result in multigenerational transmission.

The *strengths* of relational classification are: It has clinical relevance; it encourages a much broader perspective; it gives credence to the systemic factors that are in operation; it suggests various channels for intervention; it has strong implications for intervention; it provides increased validity from informants; and it emphasizes the impact on others, which is a Schneiderian definition of personality (Tyrer, 1995).

Its *limitations* are: It is still in the process of development; it has a limited research base; the conflicting roles of the clinician may be problematic; and it has few well-established psychometric instruments.

COMBINING CLASSIFICATIONS: MULTISYSTEM ASSESSMENT OF PERSONALITY PATHOLOGY

Because each of the systems described in the previous section has various strengths and limitations, the use of a multisystem assessment approach seems preferable to strict adherence to any one system. "There exist *interactions* between these levels, but the levels also function independently of each other. We should continue to try to understand these connective links but appreciate at the same time that it is unlikely that we will find simple, 'linear' linkages between what goes on *within* and *between* people" (Denton, 1996, p. 42). Clinicians may find it easier to know and be proficient with one system, but the constraint of a single viewpoint is that important data may be missed. Comprehensive assessment utilizes various systems, placing them in the relational matrix to provide a broader perspective. A combined approach to diagnosis and classification is probably the most utilitarian for clinical practice and is also best for research protocols if used flexibly:

- Use the *categorical approach* to establish a rough diagnostic formulation and to complete insurance forms.
- Use a *dimensional approach* to corroborate impressions and to evaluate threshold and subthreshold variants.
- Use a *structural approach* to formulate a more precise treatment strategy.
- Use a *cognitive approach* to elicit pertinent schema.
- Use an *interpersonal approach* to validate the effect that the personality style has on others; this effect is especially evident in transference and countertransference.
- Use a *relational approach* to engage the broader system and to intervene at fulcrum points.

ADDING RELATIONAL DIAGNOSTIC TAXONOMY TO *DSM* FORMULATIONS

Frances et al., (1984) suggested adding an Axis VI that emphasizes relational disorders to *DSM*'s multiaxial system. Adding relational information to *DSM* in any form will certainly broaden formal diagnostic taxonomy. A comprehensive diagnostic formulation for personality pathology considers the type of dysfunctional personologic system. An individual patient might then be assessed using all six Axes.

CASE STUDY: THE SEVERELY ABUSED 28-YEAR-OLD MALE

The patient is a 28-year-old male who entered therapy with a variety of complaints. The patient had been subjected from an early age to severe abuse from his father. His father seemed to have strong psychopathic/sadistic characteristics and seemed to enjoy the terror and humiliation he subjected his son to in the course of chronic physical and sexual abuse. The mother seemed to have characteristics of a borderline personality with a significant history for alcohol abuse or dependence.

The patient showed signs of severe dissociative phenomenon and had various aspects to his personality. The following diagnosis was considered:

Axis I: Dissociative disorder and Post-traumatic stress disorder.
Axis II: Borderline personality disorder.
Axis III: None.
Axis IV: Problems with primary support.
Axis V: Global assessment of functioning scale—50 serious symptoms.
Axis VI: Physically traumatizing dysfunctional personologic system—
             psychopathic subtype.

Assessing the Relational Matrix

Further diagnostic precision can be added through the use of various dimensional models such as the family circumplex model developed by Olson (1996). The following three factors are assessed: family cohesion, flexibility, and communication.

Family Cohesion
There are four levels of cohesion: disengaged (very low), separated (low to moderate), connected (moderate to high), and enmeshed (very high). A high level of cohesion indicates high consensus and a lack of differentiation and autonomy. At the other end of the continuum, low cohesion reflects weak commitment and attachments. The middle levels indicate emotional closeness with independence.

Family Flexibility
There are four levels of flexibility: rigid (very low), structured (low to moderate), flexible (moderate to high), and chaotic (very high). These levels refer to the amount of flexibility in the executive leadership and to role flexibility in the system. Unbalanced systems tend to be chaotic or rigid. Systems that have too little control are characterized by disorganization, and those with too much control exhibit repression. Systems with moderate levels of flexibility tend to be more adaptive in response to the demands of changing roles and challenges.

Family Communication
The ability to listen, express emotions, respect, provide empathy, and so forth are useful skills and domains that facilitate family and interpersonal

communications. Communication skills are rated as positive or negative, but a more formal scale is not included.

DEVELOPMENTAL STAGES

As each phase of the family developmental process unfolds in well-functioning, adaptive families, a shift will occur. For example, as the children become more autonomous, family cohesion will loosen and the style of communication will shift from parent/child to adult/adult.

CASE STUDY: FURTHER ASSESSMENT OF THE 28-YEAR-OLD SEVERELY ABUSED MALE

When therapy began, the patient resided with his parents. Although the family was not seen, it was clear from assessment that the family system was highly disturbed. The patient's father, now declining, seemed isolated and withdrawn. The parents, although divorced, were living together for financial reasons. They discouraged their son from moving out because they felt he would not survive. The other siblings had established separate households. The patient's mother seemed enmeshed with him and undermined any attempt at separation. The patient felt responsible for the well-being of his parents, and there was hostility in their mutual dependence. The patient was himself fearful that his parents' projections were well founded and that if he left he would have to assume an independent life, of which he was fearful. He enjoyed the position of power he had in his family and was frightened of asserting himself with peers in the outside world. The relational triangle was very stable and impervious to attempts by other family members to destabilize this system.

Relational Assessment

1. Family cohesion—very high, i.e., enmeshed.
2. Family flexibility—rigid.
3. Family communication—poor.

This family system was *highly toxic* to the patient's growth and development, and his response was to accept his crippled position. The fact that the patient continued to reside with his parents was crucial to the maintenance of the personality disturbance as well as the dissociative phenomenon. A relational assessment provided important information for understanding the active factors in the relational matrix and for developing the treatment plan and implementing treatment strategies.

ASSESSMENT METHODS

Clinicians have a somewhat paradoxical task when assessing and diagnosing personality that includes subthreshold, threshold, and full-blown manifestations of disordered personality. This chapter has depicted a number of useful systems of classification and their strengths and limitations. Psychometric and clinical assessment procedures can also assist in this endeavor. Clinicians tend to have strong biases; they often learn one assessment method, master it, and stop there. It is surprising to discover how many experienced clinicians, for example, do not use psychometric instruments and rely solely on clinical interviewing techniques. In addition to formal assessment, clinical intuition and experience often are crucial to early detection of personality pathology. Certain red flags are seen often at the onset of treatment.

The Red Flags of Personality Disorders and Dysfunctional Personologic Systems

Often, experienced clinicians use clinical intuition to alert themselves to the presence of personality disorders in individuals that would warrant further exploration to rule out presence and type of dysfunctional personologic system. These indices should only be considered guidelines:

- Patients with numerous previous therapeutic experiences, especially unproductive ones.
- Patients who have unremitting Axis I disorders in spite of treatment attempts.
- Patients who engender immediate countertransference reactions.
- Patients who have immediate transference reactions.
- Patients who have severe interpersonal difficulties that are repetitive.
- Patients with chronic suicidal preoccupation.
- Patients who don't respond to short-term treatment interventions or who get worse.
- Patients who are irresponsible in upholding their treatment contract; for example, they cancel sessions, or come late.
- Patients with highly diffuse initial complaints or presenting problems.
- Patients with a family history of chronic medical/psychiatric disturbance.

Additionally, the following signs are often indicative of a dysfunctional personologic system in a family:

- Identified patient is the least disturbed in the system.
- Strong negative countertransference feelings after experiencing family process.
- Severely malignant style of communication.
- Chronic dysfunction in a large percentage of family members.
- Evidence of severe scapegoating.
- Severe degree of fusion/enmeshment among family members.
- Obvious severe pattern of emotional, physical or sexual abuse or neglect.
- Diagnosed personality disorders in multiple family members.

CATEGORIES OF ASSESSMENT PROCEDURES

Traditionally, assessment in individual treatment has focused primarily on the individual in the context of the therapeutic relationship. The most common assessment procedure remains the clinical interview and history that is completed by a clinician trained in psychopathology, psychodynamics and developmental theory, and systems theory. A second, less frequently used form of assessment is psychometric assessment. Psychometric assessment originated in academic psychology, spurred on by increasing needs for valid research instruments. A family history and Genogram are also vital to a multiple level assessment.

CLINICAL INTERVIEWING

The clinical interview and history remain the mainstay of diagnostic formulation of personality pathology as well as of clinical syndromes. For the beginning clinician, a number of excellent sources cover assessment, such as Maxmen and Ward's book, *Essential Psychopathology and Its Treatment* (1995).

Structural Interviewing
More advanced practitioners can facilitate a rapid diagnosis by using the structural interview pioneered by Kernberg (1984), who emphasizes long-term psychoanalytic psychotherapy for severe personality disorders, and Davanloo (1980), who pioneered a form of intensive short-term dynamic psychotherapy for characterological disorders. The structural interview is a method that uses anxiety-arousing questions and clarifications, defensive challenges and confrontations, and transference interpretations to observe the manifestations of the intrapsychic system (how anxiety is tolerated,

how defensive structure is connected to feelings). For example, a patient presenting with features of a passive-aggressive personality might, during the initial diagnostic interview, reveal a tendency to place blame for personal failures on those around him or her while taking a passive stance in most areas of life. During the interview, the clinician might point out the patient's passive style of responding as he or she waits for the clinician to take charge. This challenge to the defense system increases anxiety and defensive reactions. The patient might then become sarcastic or defiant—a characteristic of this personality. Another patient might begin to project in a primitive manner that the clinician is out to get him or her—a potentially paranoid trait. Thus, by modulating the degree of anxiety present in the process, the clinician observes reactions that can guide the diagnostic process.

Structural interviewing with the personality-disordered patient requires substantial training and experience and should not be undertaken without proper training. However, this significant technical advancement is well worth the effort to learn. Structural interviewing can be conducted less rapidly; interested readers may find McWilliams's (1994) work an excellent source for examples of interviews that assess personality organization and structure.

PSYCHOLOGICAL TESTS

Psychometric instruments used to assess and classify personality based on statistical techniques have allowed for the development of scientific research but are also valuable aids to the clinician. The most well-known and widely used instruments are the Millon Clinical Multiaxial Inventory-III (MCMI-III) and Minnesota Multiphasic Personality Inventory (MMPI) (Millon & Davis, 1996). A variety of other useful instruments are comprehensively reviewed by Millon and Davis. These instruments offer the clinician the opportunity to corroborate clinical impressions and rapidly formulate hypotheses.

Projective techniques are traditional forms of psychological testing used to assess personality and can be quite effective in the hands of a qualified examiner. The best known of these techniques are the Rorschach Inkblot Test and Thematic Apperception Test but there are many others. In the hands of an experienced examiner, these instruments provide a picture of the deep structure of an individual and overall level of ego functions as well as personality characteristics and traits. Unfortunately, fewer clinicians are being trained in evaluation through the use of projective techniques.

Family History and Genogram — A Personologic Emphasis

Family history and genogram are essential assessment procedures for accurately describing dysfunctional personologic systems. "The family is the primary and, except in rare instances, the most powerful system to which a person belongs" (McGoldrick & Gerson, 1985, p. 5). The genogram developed by Bowen as part of his systems theory "provides a graphic picture of family structure and emotional process over time" (Carter & McGoldrick, 1980, p. xxiii). A genogram is a visual map that allows the clinician to rapidly identify generational themes and interaction patterns (McGoldrick & Gerson). As I have stated earlier, families repeat themselves in a multigenerational transmission process. With modification, a genogram can reveal personality disorders that may not otherwise come to the surface in a standard interview.

In addition to making the standard inquiries about ages, marriages, births, deaths, illnesses, divorces and so forth, when taking a family history and genogram, the clinician should attempt to attain a personality profile of related family members to determine whether there is evidence of multigenerational transmission and dysfunctional patterns. Patients are generally not used to describing personality features of other members, so the clinician needs to use careful questions to elicit the intergenerational information and relational dynamics. Such questions include:

1. How would you describe your mother, father, grandfather, brother?
2. What was his or her personality like?
3. Did his or her personality contain any traits that you admired or wished you could change?
4. Do you know of any history of emotional, physical, or sexual abuse in any branch of your family?
5. Whom do you most admire and why?
6. Whom in the family are you most like in terms of your personality?

Other family information, including education, occupation, job stability, or number of marriages, can be assessed for indirect effects on personologic functioning. If, for example, a parent was never employed for more than a few months at a time or if the parent frequently moved from one location to another, the clinician might consider the possibility of antisocial pathology as a contributing factor to family dysfunction.

The interviewer should look for themes of enmeshment/fusion as well as disengagement. The tendency toward management of anxiety through triangular relations should be noted. Roles of individual members should be noted and explored. Labels such as the *black sheep* of the family, the *family hero,* and so forth often have implications for various types of personality disorders. The black sheep may be antisocial; the hero may be obsessive-compulsive or narcissistically predisposed.

McGoldrick and Gerson (1985) recommend that the following four areas of functioning be explored: (1) serious problems—psychological and physical; (2) work history—job changes, income level; (3) drug and alcohol history—attempts to cope with; and (4) trouble with the law—arrests. When interpreting a genogram, the interviewer should also note basic family structure (intact, single parent, remarried family), sibling constellations (birth order, sex, years apart), pattern repetition across generations, and life cycle events. Those readers not familiar with conducting a family genogram are encouraged to study the McGoldrick and Gerson (1985) book, *Genograms in Family Assessment.*

MULTIPLE LEVEL ASSESSMENT

Synder, Cavell, Heffer, and Mangrum (1995) have developed a "multifaceted, multilevel approach" (p. 163) to marital and family assessment that is also valid for assessing the dysfunctional personologic system. They conceptualize the following five levels of assessment: "(a) individuals, (b) dyads, (c) nuclear families, (d) extended families and related systems interfacing with the immediate family, and (e) community and cultural systems" (p. 164). Within each subsystem, they identify five domains: "(a) cognitive; (b) affective; (c) communication and interpersonal; (d) structural and developmental; and (e) control, sanctions, and related behavioral domains" (p. 165). Each subsystem may be assessed across the five domains using various assessment techniques (see Figure 5.1). This model, applied to personality disturbance, is useful to assess the presence and type of dysfunctional personologic system in families of origin. Individual personality disorders may also be assessed by viewing the individuals microscopically. Adopting a systemic perspective to the assessment of the relational matrix is a powerful addition to traditional personality assessment.

Couple Relational Assessment

A number of clinical researchers have observed the coexistence of personality in the relational matrix of many couples who seek conjoint treatment. Clinicians have regularly observed a tendency for patients with certain personality disorders to form partnerships that are very resistant to intervention. People

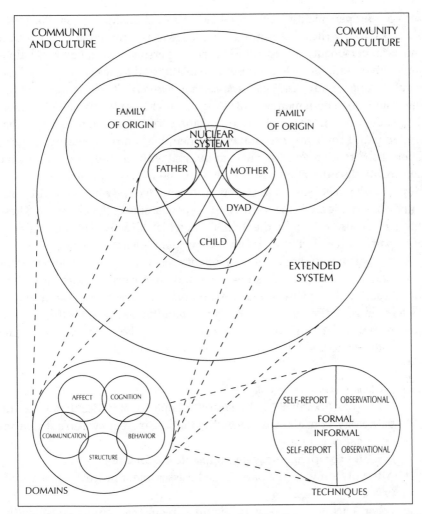

Figure 5.1 Conceptual model for assessing families from a systems perspective. The model presents five system levels including: (a) individuals, (b) dyads, (c) the nuclear family, (d) the extended family system, and (e) the community and cultural systems. Each system level may be assessed across five overlapping domains: (a) cognitive; (b) affective; (c) communication and interpersonal; (d) structural and developmental; and (e) control, sanctions, and related behavioral domains. Information across domains may be gathered using multiple assessment strategies, including both formal and informal self-report and observational techniques. From *Integrating Family Therapy: Handbook of Family Psychology and Systems Theory* (p. 166), by Mikesell, Lusterman and McDaniel, eds. 1995, Washington, DC: American Psychological Association. Copyright © 1995 by the American Psychological Association. Reprinted with permission.

with certain personality traits may tend to attract others with similar traits. Nichols (1996) writes, for example, that it seems common that patients with antisocial personality disorder and histrionic personality establish a relationship with one another. He proposes two relational diagnoses: *Antisocial Relational Disorder* and *Histrionic Relationship Disorder*. These diagnoses are suggested when both members of a couple suffer from the personality disorder. There are numerous other combinations of personologic couples that tend to pair. People are also drawn together by a complementarity of traits. Clinical observation reveals that an individual with an obsessive-compulsive personality disorder often mates with someone who has a histrionic personality disorder. The obsessive is drawn to the affectively charged histrionic and the histrionic seeks the security and predictability of the obsessive. These pairings are also evident in the AdcDps, in which an active substance abuser often pairs with an individual with codependent issues (Williams, 1996).

These pairings do not create personality disorder, but they tend to reinforce and consolidate preexisting traits and characteristics that have their foundation in the dysfunctional personologic systems that these individuals have lived in. Personality is not a fixed entity; because it is to some degree responsive to the context, it can certainly be exaggerated in one particular relational matrix or minimized in another.

Guide to Clinical Assessment of Couples
- When one member of the couple manifests significant personality pathology, consider the possibility that the mate may also suffer from personality pathology.
- Look for complementary and opposite combinations.
- Attempt to engage the partner in the assessment process when appropriate.
- When encountering severe disturbance in the couple, consider the possibility of personality disturbance in one or both partners.

Assessment Procedures   Many instruments are used to assess various aspects of the couple relationship. One of the best methods is to experience and observe the process and dynamics of the couple in their relationship. This method is the mainstay of couple assessment; its basics are addressed in Chapter 10. A series of conjoint and individual sessions can clarify diagnostic issues and reveal a tremendous amount about the interactional patterns in operation.

Family Process Relational Assessment

Family process assessment of personality pathology is a relatively new phenomenon because systems therapists traditionally disparaged diagnosis as being antisystemic. However, the family is a rich source of experiential and diagnostic material that can be mined by the astute clinician. The family enters the treatment process through many channels. Sometimes the members identify the problem in the family; at other times the problem is attributed to the identified patient; still other times the therapist suggests family involvement. In any event, there is no richer way of accessing family process and multigenerational material. When members are under the naturally occurring stress of the therapeutic consultation, the therapist will see characteristic defensive styles and personality patterns emerge.

Guide to Clinical Assessment of Families

- Complete a family genogram.
- Look for features described in Chapter 3.
- Allow sufficient unstructured time to witness and experience family process.
- Carefully observe the most common defenses used by each member.
- Try to rate structural organization and defensive constellation of each member.

Assessment Procedures Although clinicians can use many assessment procedures to assess the family system, the most valuable method is to experience the relational matrix in operation dynamically and affectively. How does it feel to sit with a family? Lidz (1973) writes of his experience in the PscDps: "Indeed, sometimes after spending an hour or two with one or both of the patient's parents, I would wonder just how long my sanity or anyone's sanity would withstand living with these people, to say nothing of being raised by them" (p. 8). Does the family seem emotionally starving? Has conflict become a form of engagement that substitutes for intimacy and nurturing? Do you want the session to end so you don't become depleted? Do they engage you and *draw you in?* I believe the most accurate assessment is achieved when the therapist can emerge himself or herself in the family process a la Whitaker (Napier & Whitaker, 1978). His ability to blend with the family until he felt the unconscious life was gifted therapeutic ability.

Parent-Child Relational Assessment
Observing the parent-child or caretaker relationship is another valuable opportunity for the clinician to experience a crucial aspect of the relational matrix. The clinician can often witness the transmission of parenting, whether it is effective or not.

Guide to Clinical Assessment of Parent-Child Relationships
- Observe transactions for level of respect and nurturing.
- Notice ability to set appropriate limits.
- Notice quality of attachment.
- Monitor level of anxiety in the dyad or parental subsystem.

Assessment Procedures   "In dysfunctional families parents sometimes seek emotional ties with their children in exaggerated and inappropriate ways in response to their own ability to address these needs with other adults; other parents experience tremendous inadequacy in their parental role and retreat from setting limits or implementing consequences for fear of eliciting their children's anger" (Synder et al., 1995, p. 170). Various types of parenting styles may be more likely to result in personality disturbance although there is no known research on this issue. Parent-infant assessment can be facilitated with Sameroff and Emde's (1989) system for classifying parent-child relational disturbances. These authors categorize various factors such as intensity, duration, and rigidity of pattern. The National Center for Infant Clinical Programs (1994) has produced a system similar to *DSM* that on Axis II includes the following relationship disorders evident in infancy and early childhood: (a) overinvolved; (b) underinvolved; (c) anxious/tense; (d) angry/hostile; (e) verbally abusive; (f) physically abusive; and (g) sexually abusive.

CONCLUSIONS

Assessment of the dysfunctional personologic system is more accurate when a multiperspective diagnostic system is used. The use of the family genogram is an essential part of the evaluation that offers a visual representation of the dysfunctional personologic system and its themes, dynamics, and triangles. Classifying personality pathology accurately provides the clinician with a more focused treatment plan that enhances the process of restructuring and suggests possible fulcrum points for intervention.

CHAPTER 6

Stages of Change: Restructuring Dysfunctional Personologic Systems

E ngaging the personality-disordered individual and dysfunctional personologic system is one of the most challenging aspects of conducting clinical work. Personality disturbance, while partly offering protection against emotional pain, also causes suffering to other members of the system. It is therefore not uncommon that the first entry into the dysfunctional personologic system is through a spouse or a child who is the symptom bearer. Other channels of engagement include the legal system and medical referrals; these channels are concerned about destructive behavioral patterns but may not be aware of the predominant personality disorder or dysfunctional personologic system. Other individuals do seek treatment when an awareness of the repetitive maladaptive patterns in their lives continue to cause discomfort and negative outcome. An integrative relational approach allows clinicians the opportunity to use a tighter net to engage individuals who might slip through without being offered effective treatment.

ATTITUDES TOWARD PERSONOLOGIC THERAPY

Prior to undertaking work with personality-disordered patients, clinicians should thoroughly examine their beliefs about an individual and family's capacity for change. Some commonly held beliefs and reactions from others can undermine and cripple the treatment process before it begins. A few of these beliefs are presented in Table 6.1.

Many of the beliefs and reasons clinicians offer for not conducting personologic therapy, like many generalizations, have elements of truth to them. However, these internalized beliefs, when not addressed, may be unconsciously transmitted to the patient and are insidious to the therapeutic process.

Table 6.1   Beliefs and Reasons That Undermine Personologic Psychotherapy

Reasons Clinicians Give for Not Treating the Personality-Disordered Patient

1. Personality modification takes years of slow effort and is not worth the outcome.
2. There is no evidence to show that personality can be modified.
3. Managed care doesn't endorse personality modification.
4. I know people who have been in psychoanalysis for a decade and are still the same.
5. Working with personality-disordered patients is likely to lead to burnout.
6. Working with personality-disordered patients is not rewarding.
7. I don't want to work with difficult clients because they are too resistant to treatment.

Reasons Patients Give for Not Undertaking Personologic Therapy

1. The Popeye Syndrome—"I am who I am." My personality is fixed and is not likely to be altered.
2. Too much effort is required to alter my personality, so why bother trying.
3. If people love me they will accept me for who I am regardless of my personality flaws.
4. My defense system has worked up until now—"I'm a successful doctor, attorney, minister, scientist, etc." Why change it?
5. I know people who have been in therapy for 10 years and have not changed.
6. I think what I really need is medication.

COMMON ANXIETIES EXPRESSED ABOUT ENTERING PERSONOLOGIC THERAPY

Patients who are contemplating work aimed at addressing personologic concerns often express certain anxieties that need to be discussed and understood. These issues are valid and are realistic to face:

- If I change my family may not be able to accommodate to the new me.
- My marriage may dissolve.
- People may not like the new me.
- My family might reject me.
- My life will become more painful.
- I may have to face some unpleasant aspects of life.

PROCESS AND TYPES OF CHANGE

The process of change has only recently become the focus of scientific research but the findings and theories are not only illuminating but helpful to the clinician working with the personality-disordered individual as well as with the dysfunctional personologic system. An understanding of how we as humans change and the types of change that we have all experienced and witnessed goes a long way in restructuring our faulty beliefs about the immutable nature of personality.

DISCONTINUOUS TRANSFORMATIONAL EXPERIENCES

Transformational experiences are internally or externally induced events that result in a substantial change in the personality. This phenomenon has held much interest to religious groups and in literature, but has been largely ignored by academic and clinical science until very recently. Most clinicians have heard reports of or witnessed these episodes on occasion. One patient reported a documented change in his personality, which precipitated a major transformation, after being resuscitated from a drug overdose. Clinicians tend not to discuss these cases for fear of being discredited or not taken seriously.

Individual Quantum Change Episodes
Academic psychology has recently taken an interest in personality and the phenomenon of naturally occurring quantum change episodes (Miller &

C'deBaca, 1994). Miller and C'deBaca, in their seminal study, described individuals who on occasion experienced major, enduring transformations of their personality in brief time spans—days and weeks. Although a preliminary study, it seems to coincide with findings from clinical researchers that on occasion a massive restructuring of an individual's personality can be therapeutically induced (Davanloo, 1980; Magnavita, 1997b; Malan, 1963). Evidence of discontinuous change episodes in families has also been reported by family systems theorists and clinicians.

Family Discontinuous Change Episodes
Major change events in families that result in a major restructure do not occur as a linear process. Rather, as Hoffman (1980) observed: "One property that families share with other complex systems is that they do not change in a smooth, unbroken line but in discontinuous leaps" (p. 55). Accordingly, she reports that these rapid shifts can occur with great suddenness.

> The natural history of a leap or transformation is usually as follows. First, the patterns that have kept the system in a steady state relative to its environment begin to work badly. New conditions arise for which these patterns were not designed. Ad hoc solutions are tried and sometimes work, but usually have to be abandoned. Irritation grows over small but persisting difficulties. The accumulation of dissonance eventually forces the entire system over an edge, into a state of crisis, as the homeostatic tendency brings on ever-intensifying corrective sweeps that get out of control. The end point of what cybernetic engineers call a "runaway" is either that the system breaks down, creates a new way to monitor the same homeostasis, or else may spontaneously take a leap to an integration that will deal better with the changed field. (p. 56)

Most psychological disturbances and medical illnesses emerge during these periods of transformation and are often what brings the dysfunctional personologic system into treatment. Many clinicians have demonstrated and observed that a crisis can disrupt an individual's defense system as well as the family homeostasis, which creates an opportunity for a transformational leap.

SPIRAL PATTERN OF CHANGE

Prochaska and his associates (1992) have developed a model of change that they describe as a spiral process. They view change not as a linear, forward-moving process but as cycles among stages, like a spiral. This model has great importance to working with the personologic system. Through the use of cluster analysis, these authors have identified five stages of the change process. Although this *transtheoretical model* of change has been developed primarily from subjects with a variety of addictive behaviors, the model is also useful for understanding the process of change with the personality-disordered individual. Patients with addictive behaviors and with repetitive maladaptive patterns often have similar characteristics that are difficult to modify because of the reduced awareness of the impact of their patterns or ego-syntonicity.

Prochaska et al.'s Stages of Change Applied
to the Personality-Disordered Individual

1. *Precontemplation.* In this stage of change, the individual has no intention of making changes. Many of these individuals have little or no awareness of the impact that their personality disturbance has on their lives and those around them. For example, in this stage of the change process, an individual with a narcissistic personality might not have experienced any major setbacks or injuries and is whetted to his or her style of dominating the family and the workplace. Although spouse, children, and employees are suffering, the individual is feeling invulnerable and untouched.

2. *Contemplation.* In this stage, the individual becomes aware of the problem and may be considering changing but has not yet taken action. The pros and cons of making changes are often seriously examined. The narcissistic individual may have begun to receive feedback about his or her behavior and the impact it has on others. Maybe the spouse is threatening to divorce or the business has taken a downturn.

3. *Preparation.* In this stage of change, the individual has made some small behavioral changes and is prepared to take action. The narcissistic individual, for example, may be trying to be less demanding on those around him or her and may even discuss the possibility of couples therapy with the spouse.

4. *Action.* In this stage, the individual does something to change or modify his or her behavior in an appreciable manner. The individual may attempt to modify his or her style and may seek outside assistance from a friend, minister, or therapist. If therapy is initiated, there may be a genuine attempt at self-examination and modification of personality.

5. *Maintenance*. In this stage, the individual expends effort to protect against relapse and to consolidate the gains. The individual understands the issues and the likely results of a reemergence of self-defeating behavioral and relational patterns.

Assessing the developmental stage of each patient is crucial before the clinician makes an intervention.

NATURAL CHANGE DUE TO THE EFFECTS OF DEVELOPMENT AND PASSAGE OF TIME

"Elixir of time" often results in the modification of personality. This phenomenon has been well documented in certain personality disorders such as borderline and antisocial. Some propose a biological theory wherein the hormonal fuel that supercharges the personality starts to lessen its impact, and by middle age antisocial and borderline personality pathology loses its vigor. Although the basic personality may be recognizable, most humans make significant changes throughout the developmental process. Others make more profound changes in response to a developmental transition or challenge that seems to reorganize the entire personality, sometimes toward improvement and sometimes toward deterioration. Most people have heard of someone who seemed to be leading a successful life but then for unknown reasons dropped out of family or society, perhaps even becoming a street person. The factors involved in these events are perplexing and little understood.

FIRST AND SECOND-ORDER CHANGE

Terkelsen (1980) posits that there are two classes of systemic change. First-order change primarily focuses on adaptation and mastery of something new.

Second-order change involves transformation of the meaning and status of the system. This type of change is commonplace and is fueled by changing developmental needs in the family life cycle (Carter & McGoldrick, 1980). Second-order changes often are accommodations to normative events such as "marriage, birth of child, child entering school, child entering adolescence, child launched into adulthood, birth of grandchild, retirement and senescence" (Terkelsen, 1980, p. 41). Other events that can substantially modify the structure of the system and are less normative include "miscarriage; marital separation and divorce; illness, disability, and death; relocations of household; changes in socioeconomic status; and extrinsic catastrophe with massive dislocation of the family unit" (p. 41).

In the process of second-order change, the structure of the system is altered in a substantive way. "The index member experiences a sense of discontinuity, of being a changed person in a changed family" (Terkelsen, 1980, p. 39). This metamorphosis creates powerful affect states. "But in addition, affects such as sadness, despair, confusion, anxiety, panic, a sense of betrayal, or rage, derive from the experiences of emptiness, uncertainty, and aimlessness, all of which are in the ascendancy during second-order developments" (p. 39).

How This Knowledge and Awareness Helps in the Treatment
of Personality Disturbance
An understanding of the variety of change processes and stages of change that humans experience helps clinicians capitalize on the various change points that occur throughout the life span. Each developmental challenge and transition is an opportunity for change versus stagnation. For example, an adolescent with avoidant personality features from a DevDps may have a predictable crisis when attempting to go to college. The adolescent may feel a strong pull to stay with the family and not separate. If the family system can't help the adolescent successfully navigate this transition, a consolidation of the avoidant personality can occur. On the other hand, if the adolescent is assisted in making the transition, either from forces within the family or externally, the personality organization may loosen its hold and a period of growth may be engendered from the new social milieu of college.

Clinicians who are open to the possibility of transformational experiences may be alert to patients who are at the right place at the right time and may facilitate a rapid restructuring of the patient's personality. Hoffman (1980) describes this process systemically:

> Since family structures are under most pressure to change at natural transition points, it is no surprise that most symptoms occur at these times. The knowledgeable clinician or student of family life will know that these behaviors are expectable concomitants of family change. He or she will seek to disrupt the homeostatic sequence that forms about a symptom, so that pressure for change will be allowed to build and a transformation will hopefully take place that makes the presence of a symptom unnecessary. (p. 67)

Knowledge about the the types of change also makes it possible for clinicians to know when it is appropriate to do nothing but allow the passage of time to transpire. The field of addiction uses the phrase "hitting rock bottom" to describe a similar phenomenon. Until enough damage has been done or until a major event occurs, intervention is unlikely. In one case, a patient entered therapy and told the following story:

> I spent my teens and my twenties living on the edge. I was in jail on a number of occasions and had episodes of violent outbursts. I used every substance I could get my hands on and was addicted to heroin for many years. On one occasion I overdosed and almost died but as soon as I recovered was back out again. Then on the occasion of my second overdose I had a near death experience as I died and was resuscitated. When I regained consciousness something had changed. I began attending AA and started to take a look at my life. I began to work very hard and successfully built my own business. I work hard and expect a lot of myself and others but I am proud to pay my taxes and carry my share. I have enough money to do what I want to. I own a plane and am getting my instrument rating. I married and am faithful to my wife.

Clinicians who are open to the possibility of change see the variety of ways in which people change and personality is modified.

RESISTANCE TO CHANGE

Resistance to change is part of human nature, even though change is inevitable. However, most dysfunctional personologic systems are even more resistant to change than are those systems with a lesser degree of pathology. Hanna (1996) identified seven precursors that seem conducive to change in psychotherapy. He proposes the following questions that are relevant to clinicians' attempts at deepening an understanding of the readiness for change and the resistance encountered.

> Why do some clients change relatively quickly in therapy while others make little if any progress? Why is the change process painfully difficult for some clients and comparatively easy for others? Why do some clients welcome change while others resist and struggle against it? Why so some clients achieve core personality changes while others make minor, linear adjustments? (p. 228)

PRECURSORS OF CHANGE APPLIED TO THE DYSFUNCTIONAL
PERSONOLOGIC SYSTEM

In a review of the literature, Hanna (1996) identified the following client
variables that are associated with or are possible regulators of the change
process:

- Sense of necessity.
- Willingness to experience anxiety or difficulty.
- Awareness.
- Confrontation of the problem.
- Effort.
- Hope.
- Social support.

Dysfunctional personologic systems are especially resistant to change.
They fight the developmental process. They deny existential anxiety, especially death anxiety. They have a distorted sense of the passage of time.

A Sense of Necessity
Therapy generally deals with painful emotions, difficult decisions, and
conflicting forces. Without a sense of necessity, individuals see little reason
to undertake this endeavor (Hanna, 1996). In many dysfunctional personologic systems, the sense of necessity, or urgency to change, is kept in
abeyance by the homeostatic forces within the system. Thus, to engage the
system in the treatment process, the clinician must work at increasing the
sense of necessity for change.

What to Emphasize
- Not passing the dysfunction to another generation.
- Not waiting until things get worse.
- Increasing anxiety about the problem.

Willingness to Experience Anxiety or Difficulty
The process of change arouses anxiety, and the dysfunctional personologic
system is organized to avoid anxiety. Both the individual's and family's defensive structures are organized to resist and defend against anxiety at the
cost of rigidity and emotional constriction. Facing choices, painful aspects

of reality, and new patterns requires the patient to be willing to experience and process unpleasant emotions.

What to Emphasize

- Encourage the acceptance of anxiety as part of the growth process.
- Encourage emotional contact and expression.
- Monitor anxiety—if too high, select interventions to lower; if too low, select interventions aimed at increasing.
- Explore worse case scenarios to illuminate worse fears and address them.

Awareness

Awareness addresses the patient's perspective that there is a problem, but also what the problem is. "Awareness is the antithesis of denial" (Hanna, 1996, p. 236). This variable allows the patient to recognize the contributing factors and accept responsibility for the problem.

What to Emphasize

- Establish clarity about the nature and causes of the problems.
- Address defenses that obscure the problem at the beginning of treatment.

Confrontation of the Problem

This variable goes beyond acknowledgment to an active stance. This step requires persistence and deliberate focusing of attention in spite of the pain engendered. Patients feel a sense of determination to address the problem and find a resolution. The typical dysfunctional personologic system has been living with the problem for long periods of time, often throughout successive generations. Therefore there is a strong tendency not to confront the problem but to engage in all variety of contortions to avoid addressing the problem.

What to Emphasize

- The problem will not go away by itself.
- Sustained effort is required to address the issue.
- There are no magic cures, only hard work on the problem; the first step is acknowledgment.

Effort

Effort is the actual exertion of energy required to accomplish the change. This variable includes the effort and involvement in the therapeutic process as well as any extratherapeutic activities agreed upon. Often dysfunctional personologic systems expend tremendous effort in maintaining the status quo no matter how exhausting or destructive.

What to Emphasize

- The choice to complete or not complete extratherapeutic activities and the consequences of that choice.
- The joint nature of the therapeutic relationship.
- The fact that therapy is only a small portion of the week and that what goes on outside is most important.
- A reframing of the situation that emphasizes the good effort but challenges patients to see if the effort could be better channeled.

Hope

Hope is the belief that change is possible. It requires a realistic appraisal of the situation. Without hope, the patient capitulates to the problem and to a level of demoralization. A hopeful person feels that things can change and is empowered to take action. The degree of hope present in the dysfunctional personologic system is highly variable and needs to be carefully assessed. If hope is low, clinicians should attempt to bolster it.

What to Emphasize

- The therapist must be aware of his or her own level of hope that things can change.
- The therapist should directly inquire into the family/individual's feeling that things can change.
- The therapist can examine countertransference feelings and share them when appropriate.

Social Support

Social support is the access to various types of supportive networks and confiding relationships that are readily available. Many members of dysfunctional personologic systems have not developed the skills required to find, establish, and sustain social networks. Therefore, they often do not have the resources available that others have.

What to Emphasize
- Self-help groups when appropriate.
- The development of healthy social networks.

The Use of Persuasion

The use of methods of persuasion when dealing with unwilling and resistant clients requires a degree of spontaneity and creativeness on the part of the clinician (Hanna, 1996). The clinician must feel confident about the value of personologic psychotherapy and be willing to communicate this expectancy to the system and or individual.

RESTRUCTURING THE DYSFUNCTIONAL PERSONOLOGIC SYSTEM

Restructuring the dysfunctional personologic system can be accomplished through various approaches. Once the clinician assesses the system, he or she can make a determination as to where to intervene and in what manner. These aspects are discussed in Chapters 7 and 8. In this section, I present methods of restructuring the dysfunctional personologic system to achieve treatment gains.

Modifying the Personality of a Key Member of the System

One method of restructuring a dysfunctional personologic system is to identify and treat a key member of the system. Effective treatment of one member of the system can often result in a restructuring or reorganization of the primary system. An individual who makes a substantial improvement will experience a concomitant increased capacity for intimacy and closeness, better problem solving and enhanced emotional expression. The impact of these improvements often results in a variety of shifts in the system; like a mobile, one part moving affects the whole. Here are some shifts that can occur:

The couple can experience improved couple/marital functioning and subsequent growth of the partner. Increasing the capacity of one member of the family often results in growth in other members of the system.

The other member of a couple seeks treatment because of the perceived effective-
ness and treatment gains by partner. A partner who has a successful
treatment experience often displays great excitement. The other
member of the pair realizes that therapy can be beneficial, so he or
she seeks out a therapist for a course of treatment.

One member of the couple experiences improvement and destabilizes another
member of the family. When one member of a couple is effectively
treated, the member who was being held up can deteriorate. This
individual may or may not agree to treatment, and the partner can
then make an informed decision as to the viability of continuing or
terminating the relationship.

One member of the family experiences improvement, and couple therapy is
sought to improve the relationship. When one member of the couple
makes treatment gains, issues of dissatisfaction in the couple relationship are often exposed and a request for treatment is made.

MODIFYING THE STRUCTURE OF THE FAMILY SYSTEM

Another approach to restructuring the dysfunctional personologic system
is to directly intervene by modifying the structural relational matrix. This
approach, as well as restructuring methods, were developed and detailed
by Minuchin and Fishman (1981) and Madanes and Haley (1977). In this
manner, improvements in the relational matrix will have an impact on personality growth and development of the individuals within the system.
The therapist can use the techniques of family therapy, regardless of how
the family has arrived into treatment, to improve communications within
the system and to restructure dysfunctional relational patterns. Here are
some of the possible shifts that can occur:

Improvement in family functioning and a reduction of destructive personologic
patterns. An improvement in the family communication, level of
cohesion, and affect tolerance often leads to an improvement in
the entrenched personality patterns of the individuals within the
family. This improvement may suffice and the family may end
treatment, or individual members may seek out other growth-
promoting experiences. The change is often synergistic and spirals
upward.

Realignment of family hierarchy. Often the executive functions (problem
solving, decision making, goal orientation, and so forth) within the

dysfunctional personologic family are not adequate. In these cases another member of the family may be overfunctioning, creating a strong enabling pattern and possibly symptomatic eruptions. By strengthening the executive functions, the family hierarchy can be realigned. The parental subsystem often is unclear. For example, in one family with chronic personologic disturbance and marital conflict, the father was ejected from the bedroom and the oldest son developed sleep terrors that his mother handled by allowing him to sleep in the marital bed. This move created significant anxiety in the young boy. One restructuring intervention was to direct the mother to have her son sleep in his own bed. Shortly after, the father reasserted himself and returned to the bed.

Restructuring the Parent-Child Relational Subsystem

Another method of restructuring the dysfunctional personologic system is to directly modify the parent-child relational matrix. A change in this matrix can increase the effectiveness and emotional connection between the parental subsystem. More important enhancing parental effectiveness in the dysfunctional personologic system may be the most effective way to undermine the effects of intergenerational transmission of less than desirable parenting. The possible shifts are described:

The child is inoculated against the development of personality disturbance. An improvement in the quality of the parent-child relationship in the dysfunctional personologic system can lead to a degree of inoculation against the destructive results that these systems have on personality formation and development.

In the process of parent-child restructuring, the parent may discover pathological aspects of early relational experiences and decide to pursue treatment. Often in the process of restructuring the parent-child relational matrix, the parent makes a link between his or her parenting style and destructive child-rearing practices modeled by his or her parents. This awareness may result in an attempt to correct the process as well as motivating the parent to address his or her core issues and seek resolution.

In the process of parent-child restructuring, the parents recognize major differences in parenting styles and decide to address the ongoing relational issues underlying these differences. Sometimes in the course of restructuring the parent-child relational matrix, ongoing couples issues are exposed that lead to a change of focus to the parental subsystem. Parents who brought a child in for treatment, for example, began to examine their divergent parenting styles. One parent believed that the child should be physically corrected when all else fails; the other disagreed. A decision to address these issues led to a strengthening of the couple subsystem.

Restructuring the parent-child relational matrix leads to improved functioning of the child; this detriangulation exposes individual or couples issues. The process of restructuring the parent-child relational matrix often brings about an improvement in the child's symptom condition and a lessening of focus on the child's difficulty. This result may lead to a building of anxiety in the parental subsystem and to the emergence of unresolved relational issues that can be addressed. For example, a symptomatic child showed improvement that led to the exposure of a severe narcissistic condition in the mother and a passive-aggressive style in the father, which was creating tremendous systemic anxiety. This anxiety was being absorbed by the child while the parents were diverted from their own issue by their search for a cure and a perfect doctor to correctly diagnose their daughter's condition.

INITIAL GOALS IN THE RESTRUCTURING PROCESS

As the previous section pointed out, there are a number of ways to approach the restructuring of the dysfunctional personologic system. Each portion of the restructuring is part of an overall mosaic that invites and pushes the family and individual members toward greater levels of interconnectedness in their interpersonal functioning and of maturity in defensive organization. The clinician will encounter systems at various developmental levels and at various stages of change that exhibit the range and intensity of the precursors to change. The complexity of working with the dysfunctional personologic system is tremendous, but if the clinician keeps the basic goals in mind, treatment will be simplified. These initial goals are:

- Accept the system at the point at which the members meet you.
- Engage; develop a therapeutic alliance.

- Assess the type, degree, and level of functioning of the system as well as the individuals.
- Address safety issues—emotional, physical and sexual abuse patterns.
- Identify key individuals or subsystems that may be amenable or ready for change.
- Enlarge or limit the focus of treatment based on the stage of change and degree of readiness.
- Use psychometric instruments to gather more data and corroborate impressions.
- When the time is right, surprise the system by shifting the frame and offering a consultation to an individual or subsystem.

ADDRESSING THE PRIMARY NEEDS OF THE DYSFUNCTIONAL PERSONOLOGIC SYSTEM

Drawing on developmental family theory, Terkelsen (1980) conceived three levels of goal attainment in the developmentally disordered family that I think are useful to clinicians' work with the dysfunctional personologic system.

Restoration
The goal at this level is for the family to recapture its capacity to sufficiently promote the need attainment of the members.

Supplementation
In this case the family will not attain a level of sufficiency. Some more or less permanent attachment is required through an external helping system. Working with the family ecosystem is crucial at this level.

Replacement
When the level of deficit is so great, when the psychosocial network is so deficient, when psychobiological vulnerability is so severe, even extensive supplementation is not enough. The family is not just fragmented but severely fragmented. One or more members will require a replacement process such as a group home or halfway house.

A MULTIDIMENSIONAL PROCESS OF RESTRUCTURING

The triangles presented in Chapter 3—triangle of conflict, triangle of persons, and triangle of relationships—allow clinicians to observe and track the restructuring process. In order to restructure the dysfunctional personologic system, clinicians can either capitalize on naturally occurring developmental disruptions or discontinuous episodes or can attempt to therapeutically induce these events either by raising the anxiety level within the individual, which disrupts the defensive structure, or by raising the anxiety level within the system, which disrupts the family's homeostatic mechanism.

TRIANGLE OF CONFLICT—AFFECTIVE MATRIX

The restructuring process that takes place within the individual focuses on the use of a particular defensive style to contain anxiety aroused by emotional experience. There are three major methods of restructuring this intrapsychic matrix. Because these methods are covered in detail elsewhere (Magnavita, 1997b), I only summarize them here.

Defensive Restructuring
Defensive restructuring is the process whereby the defensive system of an individual is made explicit and the limitations and consequences of this defensive system is made known to the individual, couple, or family. McCullough Vaillant (1997) calls this procedure a cost benefit analysis. The once-adaptive nature of the defense system is explained, and the patient is asked to decide whether the system is worth keeping or should be modified. Although defensive restructuring is a very powerful method when done individually, it has increased potency when conducted in a couple session so that the partner can be used as a consultant who validates or invalidates the picture. Schneewind and Ruppert's (1998) research findings have shown that "spouses are able to rate the other partner's individual scores on personality characteristics relatively precisely. Over the course of time, wives can do this better than husbands" (p. 78).

Affective Restructuring
Affective restructuring is the process by which unacknowledged emotions are brought to the surface, are intensified, and—through contact and

experience—are fully metabolized. This method can be conducted individually or in a couple or family format. Within a couple format, affective restructuring increases the intimate bond with the partner and increases differentiation among the participants.

Cognitive Restructuring

Cognitive restructuring is a method by which the cognitive matrix—internal beliefs, assumptions about self and others—is elicited and clearly brought into awareness. This method of restructuring can also be done in various formats.

TRIANGLE OF PERSONS—INTERPERSONAL MATRIX

The restructuring that occurs in the triangle of persons relates to the current patterns of interpersonal relations and how these are linked to patterns from significant past relationships. This process is variously called early maladaptive schema (Young, 1990), repetition compulsion (Freud, 1911), and interpersonal patterns (Benjamin, 1993b). In patients with personologic disturbance these patterns are quite powerful and exert strong influence in the relational matrix. For example, a very passive, withdrawn male elicits a caretaking response from his spouse who "wants to light a fire underneath him." This strong, interpersonal current is also active in the therapeutic relationship and creates countertransference tendencies.

TRIANGLE OF RELATIONSHIPS—RELATIONAL MATRIX

Restructuring in the triangle of relationships emphasizes the dynamic processes that occur within the relational matrix. These interventions are primarily related to the strengthening or weakening of certain pathological configurations within the system. One very common configuration encountered in the dysfunctional personologic system is that of an enmeshed mother-child relationship and a distant father.

BASIC RESTRUCTURING GOALS

1. Increase capacity for emotional experience and expression.
2. Increase interconnectedness and capacity for intimacy.

3. Modify destructive personologic patterns that organize the family and constrain the developmental process.

CASE STUDY

This family was referred for treatment by a hospital clinic who tested the youngest of two sons after the parents were concerned about temper tantrums and academic difficulties. The entire nuclear family was seen for the first session. The presenting complaints were expressed and matched the information forwarded by the clinic. The mother was clearly the spokesperson. The father sat impassively while she explained the difficulties with their son. A family genogram and history was completed and showed that the father experienced the loss of his father during his early teens and had been essentially abandoned by his mother, fending for himself and becoming very isolated. When the genogram was taken, the father became sad and slightly tearful. The mother was an over-functioning, eldest sibling of a large family who was emotionally injured by her parents' narcissistic use of her. During the interview, the mother's over-functioning and enmeshment with her son became apparent.

This family displayed obvious characteristics of a DepDps. No previous contact with mental health professionals other than the referring clinic, had been made. The focus was shifted to the father. He was asked if he felt depressed, which he and his wife acknowledged, and for how long, to which he replied that it seemed like a chronic condition. He was asked if he would be willing to come in for brief treatment, to which he agreed. It also became evident that he had a long-standing personologic disturbance characterized by passivity, lack of intimacy with significant others, isolation, withdrawal, occasional explosive reactions, and a lack of ambition in his career. Following brief individual treatment that focused on his unresolved grief over the loss of his father and abandonment by his mother, he and his wife entered a course of conjoint work. It was revealed that the wife was contemplating a divorce because of her dissatisfaction over her husband's difficulties. The parental subsystem was in a severe state of homeostasis; the over-functioning spouse was becoming more frantic in her attempts to mobilize her husband and he was retreating even more. They agreed to work at improving their relationship. The focus of treatment became more effective coparenting, enhanced intimacy and closeness, detriangulation of the identified patient by strengthening the marital subsystem, reduction of the mother's over-functioning, and the passive-dependent personality organization of the husband.

Summary of this Case's Restructuring Process:

Phase one: Affective restructuring aimed at resolving pathological grief in father related to his nonmetabolized losses.

Phase two: Relational restructuring aimed at strengthening parental subsystem and moving enmeshed son out of triangle.

Phase three: Couples restructuring of current and past relationships, for example, father's neglectful mother, whom he attempted to engage by his passive style, and mother's desire to please by taking care of others.

CONCLUSIONS

When an individual or a subsystem of a dysfunctional personologic system seeks out consultation with a mental health professional, an opportunity is available for the system to be modified or restructured. This opportunity is a challenge to the clinician's ability and knowledge. The clinician who is skilled at observing family dynamics and who understands the process of change has a greater likelihood of engaging the system, which is the first step in developing a treatment alliance that can withstand the impact of the therapeutic intervention and the disruption of the homeostasis. A knowledge of what is needed to create the possibility of change also enables the clinician to know when more time is needed before an individual or subsystem is willing to embark upon the anxiety-filled and transforming journey.

CHAPTER 7

Initiating Change at System Fulcrum Points

The dysfunctional personologic system often expresses its pathology over generations in various forms and manifestations. "Awareness of the family context of the disorders also introduces a degree of 'relativism' to the criteria for personality disorders" (Perlmutter, 1996, p. 327). In one case, for example, the clinician was initially faced with a child who was symptomatic as a result of various deficits present in parenting and of the ecosystem challenge of adapting to divorce, which was exaggerated by intergenerational transmission process of personality disorder. In another case, the clinician was faced with a couple, both with personality disturbance, who had recently established their commitment and were already reenacting dysfunctional communication patterns and styles of intimacy that were creating adjustment difficulties. In this case, "the relationship itself is a basic part of the functioning of both disorders" (Nichols, 1996, p. 292). In yet another case, a woman was seeking to come to terms with an episode of abuse triggered by her narcissistic-personality-disordered husband's discovery that she engaged in an extramarital relationship. Another woman came to treatment wondering why she could not end her relationship with her ex-husband, who had a borderline personality disorder and who continued to violate her boundaries and prevent her from coming to resolution even though they divorced years ago. A man suffering from episodic and severe substance abuse with paranoid personality traits came to treatment after meeting a woman and getting engaged because he is plagued by paranoid thoughts of her unfaithfulness. These cases are all manifestations of the dysfunctional personologic system and the interaction between personality pathology and family dysfunction. An understanding of these systems will help make sense out of the complexity of variables that drive human emotions, behavior, and personality disturbance. More important for the clinician, this perspective suggests points of intervention to reduce the human suffering evident in so many people who come for consultation and treatment.

GENERATIONAL MANIFESTATION

Where do we as clinicians start? Whenever an individual comes for consultation and treatment, we start by listening to the patient's narrative and attempting to develop the context. Systems theory has taught us that the individual's presentation is more than a sum of the ingredients from the biopsychosocial model. The child seen for consultation may in fact be suffering from the effects of generations of emotional malnourishment that has culminated in the child's primary family system inadequately meeting his or her needs and expressed in the call for help elicited by child's symptom constellation. The family deficits carried forth from one generation to the next may never have been addressed and rectified. Determining the locus of treatment is probably one of the most complex issues faced by the clinician working with dysfunctional personologic systems. To find the starting point and not be diverted is a clinical art requiring discipline and theory. Gustafson (1997) borrows from Sullivan (1954) and speaks of finding the 'worthy problem'; Selvini-Palazzoli (1985) speaks of the loose end. The clinician asks: Do I intervene with the child, parents, extended family, and so on? Do I prescribe individual, family, couples, or psychopharmacologic treatment? Where do I intervene to maximize the treatment potency? These questions require a complex response based on the type, severity, and generational magnitude of the dysfunctional personologic system.

Aiming the Treatment Intervention at the System Fulcrum Point

The *Random House College Dictionary* (Stein, 1975) defines fulcrum as "the support, or point of rest, on which a lever turns in moving a body" (p. 534). If we as clinicians can determine what the system fulcrum point is and aim our intervention at it, we should be able to maximize the systemic forces and capitalize on the inherent healing forces within the system. If we miss the fulcrum point, we are likely to help but to not have the same potency of treatment impact. Although locating the fulcrum point in the system maximizes treatment potency, it must be kept in mind that these systems are very complex ones that have resisted many opportunities for naturally occurring changes as well as therapeutically induced attempts to change.

Questions to Ask to Determine the System Fulcrum Point
1. Which individual or subsystem seems to carry the most unconscious burden for the dysfunctional personologic system?
2. Which individual or subsystem seems to have the most power to affect positive systemic change?
3. Which individual or subsystem would have the most "updraft, buoyancy, or resilience" (Gustafson, 1990, p. 417)?
4. Which individual or subsystem seems to have the most chronic and enduring emotional pain?

CASE STUDY

The patient, an 11-year-old, was referred for treatment by his parents at the suggestion of the school system, who found a suicide note that he had sent to his friend. The patient appeared depressed and withdrawn and discussed his desire to end his life. When the patient was interviewed with his parents, it became clear that although this family was a high-functioning family and although both parents were professionals, there was an underlying problem with emotional neglect. The child had been regularly left home, supervised only by a teenage brother who tormented him. His parents were frequently away, working late or out of town on business. Family history showed a multigenerational history of father hunger, which the males in the family responded to by becoming hostile and abusive to younger siblings. This hostility was normalized as part of the family culture and was supported and tolerated by the parents. During family evaluation, it became evident that the father was passive and unwilling to set limits with his older adolescent son. The older son often hit the father under the guise of playfulness but the gesture represented a serious structural disturbance in the family hierarchy. When the older brother was asked to attend the session, the family resisted but conceded; he arrived for the next session petulant and openly sneering at and condemning his younger brother for the problems he had caused with his "fake suicide talk for attention." The parents did not intervene and seemed to covertly agree.

In this case the fulcrum point was not the identified, or index, patient. The fulcrum point resided within the triangular relationship among the parents and the parentified adolescent, who was furious over the expectation that he care for his younger brother, which he was ill-equipped to do. There was a history of more overt and severe abuse and neglect in previous generations. The father's passivity and the mother's complacency were evidence of chronic personality disturbance that engendered the current version of the dysfunction. Neither parent was motivated for individual or couples treatment, although such treatment would have provided the most fruitful area in which to intervene for restructuring the system. Because motivation was low, an intervention aimed at detriangulating the older brother, making the parents responsible for providing adequate supervision, and having the father set a boundary with the older son was successful as a first-line intervention.

ASSESSMENT AND INTERVENTION BASED ON THE TYPE OF DYSFUNCTIONAL PERSONOLOGIC SYSTEM

A knowledge of the type and severity of dysfunctional personologic system will enable the clinician to have a clearer view of the focal theme in which the core issues are played out and emerge in various forms from generation to generation (see Table 7.1). Once the type of dysfunctional personologic system is narrowed down, the treatment focus becomes more evident and interventions aimed at the fulcrum point more readily formulated. The sections that follow are offered as general guidelines when working with the dysfunctional personologic system. There are always many roads to Rome, and clinicians can effectively approach these disorders from different perspectives. One clinician might choose to see a patient individually whereas another might choose to see the couple or the extended family. In each case, a systemic understanding will reveal various paths along which to intervene.

THE ADDICTIVE DYSFUNCTIONAL PERSONOLOGIC SYSTEM—ADCDPS

The AdcDps has adjusted to emotional malnourishment, development deficits, and interpersonal voids by seeking out substances or addictive patterns to cope with the emotional pain. "When alcohol or drugs are abused, every member of the family suffers" (Stanton & Heath, 1995, p. 529). The dynamics of addiction are a very powerful organizing theme from generation to generation, which if not addressed will continue to produce personologic disturbances in members of successive generations.

Table 7.1   Themes, Communications, and Relational Issues
of Various Types of Dysfunctional Personologic Systems (DPS)

Type of DPS	System Themes	Communications	Relational Issues
AdcDps	Addictive processes	Reversed assumption that without substances survival is threatened	Codependence as a substitute for intimacy
NarDps	False self-protection	Public images are to be maintained at all costs	Achievement substitutes for validation of person
CNrDps	Chronic empathic misalignment	Pressure to compensate for emotional deficits in members	Affirmation provided for emotional care taking
PscDps	Adaptation to chaos	We can never feel secure	Basic attachment is achieved by assuming care functions
DevDps	Inability to tolerate individuation	Separation is dangerous to family cohesion and survival	Differentiation/ Fusion
TraDps	Accommodation to chronic abuse patterns	Family members are objects to be dominated by "powerful" members	Trauma absorption; "Use and abuse" relationships
DepDps	Attempt to adapt to insufficient emotional resources	"Make due"; there will never be enough resources to meet needs	Distortion of family developmental processes
MedDps	Overdomination of family function with medical illness and processes	Chronic medical illness predominates all aspects of family communication	Exacerbation of pre-existing personality disturbances; relations revolve around illness
ParDps	"Us vs. them" dichotomy predominates	We must protect ourselves from intrusion by outsiders	Cohesion through sharing of paranoid view
SomDps	Substitution of somatic for emotional life	The only valid form of communication is somatic	Nurturing is elicited through illness

Some clinical authors believe "chemical dependence is a disease . . . that flourishes within a social context" (Stellato-Kabat, Stellato-Kabat, & Garrett, 1995, p. 314). Regardless of whether the clinician assumes a disease model, an understanding of the biopsychosocial model is crucial. Chronic substance abuse often causes personality changes not only because of the drug action but also from the associated defenses, such as denial, that create disturbance in coping ability (Beeder & Millman, 1995). It has been established that there is a high level of comorbidity between personality disorders and substance use disorders (Tyrer et al., 1997), although the interaction between the substances and the personality changes suggest some inherent difficulties with many studies (Beeder & Millman).

The interrelationship between addictive processes and self-other deficits is clinically evident to therapists working with these systems. Murphy and Khantzian (1995) describe this relationship:

> A feeling of self-worth derives from the comforting, valuing, and valued aspects of early parenting relationships. When these relationships have been optimal, individuals can comfort and soothe themselves or reach out and depend on others for comfort and validation . . . Problems with affect defense are at the heart of substance dependence problems. We see in these patients significant developmental failures in which substances have been adopted to protect against overwhelming, confusing, or painful affect as a consequence of structural impairment. (pp. 165, 166)

"The most common relapse risk factors include negative affect, interpersonal problems and conflicts, social pressures to use alcohol or other drugs, and cravings or desires for alcohol or drugs" (Daley & Lis, 1995, p. 250). Systemic power results from this interaction among the addictive process, personality, and family functioning. As the addictive process gains ascendancy, the personality becomes more disturbed and family dysfunction increases in a constantly escalating pattern that can cycle continuously through generations; often it seems to disappear and then reappear in virulent form in the next generation. For many systems, breaking this cycle is a massive undertaking that may require successive generations of clinical intervention before the family is restructured. Additional characteristics of substance abusing families summarized by Stanton and Heath (1995, p. 530) include:

- Higher frequency of multigenerational chemical dependency, particularly alcohol, plus a propensity for other addictive behaviors such as gambling. Such practices model behavior for children and can develop into family traditions.

- Symbiotic relationships, often observed between male addicts and their mothers and often lasting well into the addict's adulthood.
- More overt alliances, for example, between the addict and an overinvolved parent.
- Parental behavior that does not mimic schizophrenia.
- More primitive and direct expression of conflict.
- Drug-oriented peer group to which the addict retreats following family conflict. This peer group gives the addict an allusion of independence.
- Preponderance of death themes and premature, unexpected, and untimely deaths in the addict's family.
- Pseudoindividuation of the addict across several levels, from the individual and pharmacological level to that of the drug subculture.
- Frequent acculturation problems and parent-child cultural disparity.

Assessment Issues

Because substance abuse problems are the most prevalent form of mental disorders (Miller & Brown, 1997), the importance of accurate assessment cannot be overemphasized. Miller and Brown report that surveys conducted since the 1960s indicate that 1 out of 10 American adults in the general population has significant alcohol-related troubles. As Stellato-Kabat et al. (1995) underscore: "Absent a multigenerational family assessment, diagnoses of chemical dependence or codependence can be missed altogether, or such diagnoses can mislead, underemphasizing the central role of family chemical-dependence dynamics" (p. 322). These authors remind us that drug and alcohol problems are not typical presenting complaints, so that routine screening for substance abuse is essential. Early identification of an addictive dysfunctional family system can save much time and needed resources. "A codependent spouse or lover may present for treatment with complaints of couple dissatisfaction, or with anxiety or depression; unless the alert clinician asks about chemical use within the family, however, the underlying and essential systemic chemical dependence may never be addressed" (p. 322).

Suggestions

- Conduct a thorough family history and genogram whenever possible so that any history of substance use can be traced.
- Screen all patients for substance use and abuse upon initial evaluation, when it is less likely to arouse resistance and dishonesty.
- Interview multiple members of the family where appropriate to achieve a more accurate assessment.

Intervention Strategies

1. Educate the system by increasing their understanding of the degree to which the addictive process is compromising family and individual functioning.
2. Illustrate the family transmission process using the genogram, and relate the multigenerational dynamics to current problems and personality disorders.
3. Increase motivation to change addictive patterns in both active and codependent members.
4. Encourage the use of community self-help groups.
5. Explain how addictive processes compromise personality and emotional development.
6. Intervene therapeutically at the fulcrum points, and attempt to modify couple, family, or individual personality patterns.
7. Address the deficits in intimacy and emotional malnourishment.

Comments

The AdcDps, although challenging, can be very rewarding for the clinician in that once the addictive process is identified, awareness is developed, and motivation is enhanced, great strides in personality development and family functioning often result. Various members of these systems often make excellent use of psychotherapeutic services, and when they make changes, the impact can be seen in succeeding generations and be multiplicative.

CASE STUDY

A woman in her 30s sought consultation for family problems. A history and genogram was revealed that the patient had married for the third time an active alcoholic. Her first husband died of alcoholism, and the second was quite impaired. Her father was a chronic alcoholic. She seemed to have limited awareness of this pattern until it was revealed graphically in the genogram. She then began to see the multigenerational transmission process and the high cost her children were paying. This knowledge provided her with sufficient motivation to begin to alter this powerful process. Her codependency and enabling were identified, and recommendations to attend AlAnon and individual treatment were made.

THE NARCISSISTIC DYSFUNCTIONAL PERSONOLOGIC SYSTEM—NARDPS

The NarDps manifests a reversal of the parent/child subsystem, with either spouse or children catering to the unmet emotional needs of one or more family members. A sense of entitlement often predominates the family system, and an air of superiority covers an essential emotional defect. Members of these systems may be prominent members of the community or society and may appear to "have it all" and elicit admiration from those who are not too close to them. Achievement is expected of all members regardless of the cost. This description fits families in American society that have been placed on a pedestal, but whose succeeding generations manifested a litany of substance abuse, inappropriate behavior, unethical conduct, and so forth that indicated a deep emotional void. Such families often are capable and powerful enough to cover up for the misdeeds of their members.

In clinical practice, a common variation of this system can be seen in children who are adopted by high-achieving, socially prominent couples. Often the match is not ideal, and as the child is seen as less and less of a narcissistic object for parental grandiosity, trouble starts. The child may reject the overemphasis on academic achievement impressed upon him or her by the parents; the parents may become more rejecting, which creates further self-esteem injuries. In successive generations, deficits in emotional nourishment may be compensated for by overindulgence combined with emotional neglect. These family constellations may become exaggerated when an only child becomes the repository of intense multigenerational conflicts that result in severe emotional injury to the child. I have encountered cases in which dying parents expected to be nursed by a "special" child, and in some cases, the child was expected to sleep with the dying parent because he or she was the only one capable of providing comfort. In other cases, children missed school to fullfill the role requirements expected of the parents.

Marital dysfunction is a common aspect of these systems, and although there are no studies to support this, clinical observation suggests a high incidence of marital infidelity. Lusterman (1995) points out that "a lengthy extramarital affair causes a remarkable degree of trauma for the discoverer, and often for the other parties involved" (p. 259). In some marriages these relationships are tolerated and enabled by the spouse; in others they are kept secret for years and often serve to stabilize the couple. Although no research documents this observation, marital infidelity appears to have a higher incidence in the Cluster B personality disorders (borderline, narcissistic, histrionic, and antisocial).

Assessment Issues

Assessing the NarDps is often straightforward. Immediately the clinician will be faced with his or her own countertransference reactions to the pressure exerted on members of the family to meet expectations and the negative reactions that result when these expectations are disappointed. The clinician will see a clear reversal of parenting functioning in that the parents' needs are penultimate and form the core structure of the family expectations. One or more clearly diagnosable narcissistic personality-disordered individuals may appear in successive generations. The family may have a high degree of public stature but the home life is often rife with neglect. In one case, while the father was out volunteering to help needy children, his own children had to face an empty refrigerator; no consistent attempt made to feed them.

Suggestions

- Conduct a thorough family history and genogram with particular attention to evidence of pathological narcissism in any of the family members.
- Note the discrepancy between the image that the family wants to present and the reality of the emotional experience for its members.
- Use psychological screening to establish and corroborate evidence of personality disturbance.
- Assess the system for marital infidelity.

Intervention Strategies

1. If possible try to engage the narcissistic individual in treatment, because shifts in the personality will have strong positive systemic repercussions.
2. Attempt to engage the couple in treatment and begin to educate the parental subsystem about the effects of the problems on the children.
3. Attempt to engage the system in treatment with various modalities to increase potency.

Comments

The NarDps is an extremely challenging system for clinicians to engage and treat. The very defensive organization often prevents this system from viewing treatment as an option. Clinicians must be very sensitive to the sense of humiliation generated by treatment contact. In an extreme crisis, the clinician who is viewed as capable and firm may often have a powerful opportunity to form a positive therapeutic alliance. The NarDps has a tendency to therapist shop, searching for the ideal therapist who will magically fix the system without intensifying the pain.

CASE STUDY

The patient, a college student, entered therapy because of academic difficulties and was in danger of flunking out of school. The only child of two prominent attorneys, the patient revealed a history of parental overindulgence, emotional neglect, and high expectations for success. Unfortunately, he was undermined at every turn by his parents' financial indulgence and enabling and by their belief that he possessed special gifts that would guarantee success. The reality was that although their son was intellectually above average, he had to work hard to excel. He experienced great difficulty taking responsibility for any of his self-defeating behavior and was often so caught up in his grandiose fantasies that he avoided activities that would genuinely build his self-esteem. He would often miss class or not turn in assignments and would then use his parent's influence or lie to avoid the consequences. In addition, he indulged in regular substance abuse and tried to live the life of a playboy. However, because of his interpersonal difficulties and low self-esteem, his only sexual experiences were with an occasional prostitute funded by his parents. The clinician brought into the open the extent of the family pattern of indulging and undermining the son as well as the crippling effect of his substance abuse and guilty acceptance of his parent's resources. It was made clear that the patient would make no personal growth unless his parents changed their pattern of overindulgence or until he decided not to accept their narcissistic crippling of him.

THE COVERTLY NARCISSISTIC DYSFUNCTIONAL PERSONOLOGIC SYSTEM—CNRDPS

The CNrDps is characterized by narcissistic dynamics but in a more hidden fashion than in the NarDps. The reversal of the parent/child subsystem has a much more subtle feel to it; it is not out in the open. The basic dynamic is that the children, but most often one child, becomes a mirror for the incomplete identity of a parent. This process is discussed in the writings of Miller (1983) and in Kohut (1977), who coined the term the "not good enough mother" to refer to a maternal/child relationship that does not sufficiently fullfill the needs of the child. There is a deficiency in the nurturing, mirroring capacity of the parental figures and an expectation that the child will inordinately satisfy the validation needs of the parental figures. Some members of these systems may appear to be highly functional and productive members of society; others, however, may function only marginally and are often described as the black sheep of the family. Emotion, if recognized, is not adequately processed or assimilated so that family members seem emotionally underdeveloped or with well-developed false selves.

Assessment Issues

Assessing the CNrDps is not as straightforward as many of the other types presented in this book because, as I have discussed, the process is much more subtle. When a child is the identified patient, the parents may show concern about complaints of depression or attention deficit. The clinician may be puzzled about the etiology of the child's symptom profile. Often it is useful to interview the parents alone and try to make an assessment of unresolved issues or history of family dysfunction. Adolescents from these systems often present with academic underachievement and sometimes behavioral disorders complicated by substance abuse.

Suggestions

- When possible, assess the marital dyad because marital disturbance is often an underlying issue.
- Especially explore parental fantasies and expectations for their children.
- Look for goodness of fit between parent and child, for example, high-achieving parents with an adopted child who is of lower intellectual ability.

Intervention Strategies

1. Address the most symptomatic individual and when that member is stabilized, expand the treatment frame and use sequential or multimodal treatment.
2. Conduct psychological testing as a way of gathering more information and as corroboration.
3. Address the reversed parent-child subsystem by providing support for the parental function.

4. Use marital therapy to assist the couple in developing greater differentiation.
5. Explore with the family the generational expectations and pressures that have been exerted from one generation to the next.

Comments
This family type is a common variant seen in clinical practice and probably accounts for a large number of individuals suffering from subsyndromal personality disturbance, although these individuals often possess more serious variants that are evident upon closer clinical inspection.

CASE STUDY

The adolescent patient was referred by a private school because of academic difficulties and suspension for drug and alcohol abuse on campus. A psychodiagnostic evaluation was performed that showed marginal learning disabilities, above average intelligence, and a narcissistic personality with antisocial traits. The first phase of intervention focused on the substance abuse and acting-out behavior, which was addressed in family therapy. The parental subsystem of two high-functioning professionals was restructured, and the hierarchy in the family established. The adolescent was referred for individual treatment, and conjoint family therapy was conducted. As the adolescent progressed, extensive marital disturbance became evident. The patient's mother became increasingly depressed and was seen for individual treatment, during which her pattern of promiscuity was revealed. Her background suggested she was from a CNrDps and, as the oldest child, served as a narcissistic object for her mother. Her parents also had a very disturbed marriage but never divorced. During the course of individual treatment, the mother was able to address many of her personologic issues. The husband who had been aware of some of the affairs, was seen for some conjoint sessions. The marriage was restructured, and the adolescent was no longer symptomatic. At follow-up the situation was remarkably improved.

THE PSYCHOTIC DYSFUNCTIONAL PERSONOLOGIC SYSTEM—PscDps

The PscDps has a range of severity based on the degree of psychopathology in the various members as well as the degree of communication disturbance present. A family in which one member has a psychotic disorder that is addressed may not qualify for this classification. Perlmutter (1996) in his chapter "Schizophrenia and Other Psychotic Disorders" writes:

> Effects vary in relation to phase and diagnosis. A family is affected differently by a first-break schizophreniform episode than by the seventh hospitalization for a chronic problem. In the first case, the family may be confused and concerned; in the second case, the family may be completely fed up with the individual's problems. (p. 73)

The psychotic process must include a level of dysfunction that impacts the entire system in a way that is detrimental to the other members and that puts individual members in a higher risk category for developing personality disturbance. In some family systems the whole family might have the same psychotic predisposition. A system may have two parents who are both functioning at a psychotic level, or one who is psychotic and the other, personality-disordered. In other systems, the level of communication has a thought-disordered quality. "Chronic psychotic thought processes severely damage the capacity for intimacy" (Perlmutter, 1996, p. 80). An even more fundamental problem is that the ability to develop trust may be severely compromised. Children in these families are in a state of extreme vulnerability, especially when they are exposed to a parent who is functioning at a psychotic level for an extended period of time. "Psychotic disorders affect every area of family life, and it is not surprising that families organize around the index person's symptom" (Perlmutter, 1996, p. 74).

Miklowitz (1995) emphasizes a history of controversy concerning the relationship between family disturbances and severe psychopathology. He identifies three alternative explanations that may not be mutually exclusive to account for this relationship: "(a) that the family causes psychopathology in individual members (primary etiological model); (b) that individual psychopathology stimulates dysfunctional reactions in the family members (the "reactivity model"); and (c) that the association is based on yet a third variable, such as genetic predisposition to psychopathology (the "shared vulnerability model")" (p. 183). A relationally based biopsychosocial model assumes that all three are interactional and multiplicative.

Assessment Issues

Assessing the PscDps is straightforward when one or more family members are actively psychotic or frequently relapsing. Assessing the system when working with adults may be more complicated. Adults often minimize or rationalize a disturbed member out of strong feelings of loyalty and protection or because of a lack of awareness. When conducting a family history, the clinician should be alert for a history of psychiatric hospitalizations. Many times, however, parents who have become psychotic have been left at home and tended to by the family doctor. This situation was more commonly seen in adults who were raised before current developments in psychiatric diagnosis and treatment were readily available to the average person.

Suggestions
- Conduct a careful family history and note previous psychiatric hospitalizations or periods in which individual members were not functional for example, long periods of unemployment.
- Take particular note of a child with severe and early developmental pathology.
- Conduct a functional assessment of the family and establish basic coping and adaptive functioning.
- Determine whether there is evidence of multigenerational psychotic disturbance.

Intervention Strategies
1. Immediately stabilize any psychotic family member and intervene with outside assistance when the welfare of the children are compromised.
2. Assist adult members in working through the developmental insults that are present in these individuals.
3. Use extratherapeutic support systems to stabilize and prevent further deterioration of the family structure.
4. Involve the extended family where possible.

Comments
These family systems can often be chronic and, as a result, they suffer from many other related problems such as unemployment, frequent disruptions of residence, poor nutrition, or abuse. Individual clinicians need to capitalize on all available resources to alter this system and to safeguard the vulnerable members of the system.

CASE STUDY

The patient, an adult female, was referred for treatment because of depression, which was treated with medication by her internist. The patient suffered from a chronic pattern of destructive relationships with males. Although a high-functioning woman, she suffered emotionally most of the time. In relating her family experiences and developmental history, it became evident that her mother suffered from a severe relapsing psychotic process, probably schizophrenia, and had been on welfare. Her father had abandoned the family. The patient, the youngest of the children, became responsible for caring for her often psychotic mother, who required frequent hospitalizations throughout the patient's early life. Every time a relationship with a male ended, the patient was thrown into a suicidal depression. Her self foundation was very weak, but she was able to come to understand this deficit was a reasonable developmental effect of never having had a parent to rely on. With intermittent therapy the patient was able to endure the pain of repeated "abandonments" and gain enough stability to establish a solid relationship. A psychoeducational understanding of the effects of the family system in which she was raised and individual psychotherapy were beneficial.

THE DEVELOPMENTALLY ARRESTED DYSFUNCTIONAL PERSONOLOGIC SYSTEM—DEVDPS

The DevDps often has a benign or inert aspect to their presentation. Although all dysfunctional personologic systems are developmentally arrested to some degree, there are distinguishing features of this particular variant. What is often apparent is a combination of enmeshment and a laissez-faire attitude. Clinicians may notice a chronic passivity and a lack of ambition, or perhaps a sense of timelessness. These systems and individual members seem to lack awareness of their "developmental dysynchrony" (Budman & Gurman, 1988). Family members who are stuck are tolerated to an amazing degree and seem to serve a primary function of protecting the parental subsystem. Loyalty issues are very strong. Family members feel overwhelming guilt when separation-individuation issues surface. Many of these cases involve multiple siblings who do not separate, and often the clinician will find more than one adult child living at home.

Assessment Issues
Assessing the DevDps that include adult children is relatively clear. A tell-tale sign in this system is their inability to launch children into adulthood.

If the children are younger, the pathological dynamics of this system are not so readily apparent. An assessment of the parents will often reveal a history of separation-individuation issues, and there may be a degree of fusion in the couple.

Suggestions
- Explore in-depth signs of separation-individuation struggles.
- Check for evidence that transition periods were particularly uneventful.
- Assess for developmental delays in the members, for example, "I was a late bloomer."
- Take note of severe career uncertainty.
- Look for signs of social or emotional immaturity, for example, children who have much younger friends or adults who seem out of phase with their contemporaries.

Intervention Strategies
1. Consider multimodal treatment packages where possible.
2. Emphasize the reality of time, goal setting, and decision making.
3. Where possible, address the parental subsystem's inability or unwillingness to appropriately push their children.
4. Emphasize the reality of not having a career and of basing a lifestyle on avoidance and dependence.

Comments
The DevDps, although often presenting as benign, are quite challenging and difficult to mobilize. Unconsciously the members feel like they are all for one and one for all in their protection of the "fusion fantasy." Their attitude is that if they ignore the anxiety inherent in their existence and life force, they do not have to suffer like other people do with problems such as aging, making poor decisions, learning from mistakes, and so forth.

CASE STUDY

The patient entered treatment in his late 30s and seemed to be living in an emotional fog. Although he was intellectually bright and had attended college part-time, he continued to work in the mail room of a large corporation. Physically he appeared more like a teenager, and he prided himself on how young people thought he was. He was also in extreme financial debt from his habit of living off his credit cards. He still harbored a fantasy from his adolescent period that he would become a rock star, although he no longer played music professionally. There was a clear sense that the patient was in a time warp. Developmentally he was always complacent, passive, and uninvolved in his unfolding life. When he graduated from high school he did not know what direction to take in his life and apparently suffered from a depression. For almost a year he stayed in his room and listened to music. His parents never said anything about his isolation, although he remembers his father, who was also very passive, eventually asking him if he was going to get a job.

THE PHYSICALLY/SEXUALLY TRAUMATIZING DYSFUNCTIONAL PERSONOLOGIC SYSTEM—TRADPS

The TraDps is, unfortunately, not uncommon in our society and is frequently encountered in clinical practice. "Domestic violence and sexual abuse are among the most distressing and controversial problems facing the professional therapeutic community and the community at large" (Geffner, Barrett, & Rossman, 1995, p. 501). This system often exhibits a multigenerational legacy of violence and unprovoked aggression toward family members. The results of long-term trauma has been well documented; it often leads to severe fragmentation of the self and severe personality disturbance (Herman, 1992; van der Kolk et al., 1996). Spousal abuse, sexual abuse, and other forms of domestic violence have reached epidemic proportions (Walker, 1996; Geffner et al.). A strong multigenerational transmission process is in effect for many of these systems; abusive patterns are evident throughout generations in various forms.

Trepper and Niedner (1996) state: "One of the most troubling of the possible relational diagnostic categories is that of intrafamily child sexual abuse" (p. 394). They note that it is common for abused children to have increased vulnerability to later abuse. Furthermore, these authors as well as others (Kirschner & Kirschner, 1996) suggest that families in which intrafamilial sexual abuse occurs are more dysfunctional than other types of dysfunctional systems. A strong relationship exists between sexual abuse and personality disturbance (Laporte & Guttman, 1996). The abusing individual often has a diagnosis of antisocial personality disorder, and the nonabusing partner often manifests a passive-dependent personality disorder.

Assessment Issues
Assessing the TraDps is not difficult because these systems are often referred by outside agencies and the history is clear. "Through a series of in-

dividual, family, and dyadic sessions—and sometimes psychometric measures—the therapist attempts to understand the interactional and intrapsychic nature of the individuals and the families" (Geffner et al., 1995, p. 504). Diagnosis may not be so straightforward in cases involving extreme denial, but multiple contacts with various family members can expose the patterns. The clinician should also assess for battered woman syndrome, which includes the following characteristics (Walker, 1996, pp. 344–345):

Anxiety and High Physiological Arousal
- Hypervigilance.
- Panic attacks.
- Physiological distress.
- Startle reaction.
- Emotional lability.
- Hysteria.

Avoidance of the Trauma and Its Effects
- Numbing of feelings.
- Depression.
- Minimization.
- Denial.
- Repression.
- Dissociation.
- Loss of interest in activities.

Cognitive and Memory Disturbance
- Confused thinking.
- Partial amnesia for some events.
- Intrusive memories of some traumatic events.
- Nightmares and sleep disorders.
- Flashbacks to fragments of memories about previous traumatic incidents.
- Perception that the abuse is reoccurring when exposed to a reminder.
- Retelling stories about abuse with or without affect, and going off on tangents.

Additionally, the clinician wants to be alert for characteristics of the batterer such as "overpossessiveness, jealousy, disrespect for women in general, insecurities often covered over by bravado, and belief in sex-role stereotypes" (Walker, 1996, p. 346).

The clinician also should assess for sexual dysfunction and dissociative identity disorders (Koedam, 1996) because adult female sexual abuse victims exhibit a high incidence of these conditions (Kirschner & Kirschner, 1996). The most common complaints given by survivors include disorders of desire, difficulties with sexual arousal, lack of ability to achieve orgasm, painful intercourse, and dissatisfaction with frequency and experience (Schorer, Friedman, Weiler, Heiman, & LoPiccolo, 1980).

Suggestions
- Interview multiple members of the family when abuse is suspected.
- Gather information from referral sources regarding the degree and severity of abuse.
- Observe for signs of battered woman syndrome.
- Observe for profiles that fit a batterer.
- Investigate the constellation of paranoid, depressed, and borderline personality-disordered males who have a high incidence of battering (Dutton & Starzomski, 1993).
- Explore a history of sexual dysfunction.

Intervention Strategies
1. Restructure the family unit extensively so that intergenerational boundaries are strengthened and maintained.
2. Encourage a more egalitarian style and reduce the commonly extreme hierarchical differences among family members.
3. Reduce intrafamily enmeshment and isolation while encouraging independence and privacy.
4. Improve communication among family members and especially reduce secrecy.
5. Emphasize marital relationship enrichment; include sex therapy if needed.
6. Help family members increase their general coping mechanisms.
7. Inculcate respect for the taboo against incest and foster awareness of the damage it causes to all involved. (Strategies 1 through 7 are from Trepper & Niedner, 1996, pp. 402–403.)
8. Establish a therapeutic context that is safe (Geffner et al., 1995).
9. File mandated reports of suspected abuse (see state and professional guidelines).

Comments
Working with the TraDps can be very taxing to the therapist emotionally. In fact, experiences of vicarious traumatization (Pearlman & Saakvitne,

1995) and secondary traumatic stress disorder (Figely, 1995) are not uncommon, and the therapist should be on alert for emotional overload.

The patient, a female physician, entered treatment for a depressive reaction that was triggered by a male coworker aggressively grabbing her neck in a hostile, threatening manner after she disagreed with him. After the depression lifted, severe marital disturbance was identified, including a lack of emotional intimacy and only a few episodes of intercourse over a ten-year period. Underneath a well-established false self, the patient had been in a chronic state of despair and suicidal preoccupation since childhood. She showed signs of battered woman syndrome and reenactment patterns of self-abuse. Long-term therapy revealed a severe pattern of early neglect and both physical and sexual abuse. Both parents showed strong indications of personality disturbance and the patient's other siblings were suffering from an assortment of personality disorders as well as post-traumatic stress syndromes. Marital problems were addressed by another therapist, and the patient divorced. Long-term individual psychotherapy allowed this patient to improve the quality of her life and to understand her victimization in the context of a dysfunctional family system.

THE DEPRESSIGENIC DYSFUNCTIONAL PERSONOLOGIC SYSTEM—DEPDPS

The DepDps is one in which affective illness or depressive personality disorders have significantly altered the family system. A severely depressed member of a family is capable of depressing the entire system (Perlmutter, 1996), especially in the case of chronic, untreated affective illness. Like other dysfunctional family systems, the DepDps begins to organize itself around the most depressed individual, and the effects on children can be devastating (Perlmutter). When a spouse or parent has been depressed for an extended period of time, certain children are likely to become parentified, and the index patient's spouse is likely to be overfunctioning or withdrawn. Because evidence indicates that many forms of affective illness are strongly heritable, such conditions are likely to be transmitted both genetically and systemically to succeeding generations unless comprehensive intervention can alter the course.

When both parents or the single parent is suffering from a mood disorder, the parental function will be greatly compromised; children will often have to fend for themselves by preparing meals, washing clothes, supervising younger siblings, and sometimes working to support the family. Developmental transitions may be greatly disrupted when a parent is relapsing or suffering from an acute exacerbation of the disorder. Depending on their developmental stage at the onset of illness, various stressors are placed on the personality integrity and development of the children. "Family communication patterns that may perpetuate a child's depression include low levels of spontaneous positive communication, ineffective conflict resolution, and high levels of hostility, criticism, and parental overinvolvement alternating with rejection" (Kaslow, Deering, & Ash, 1996, p. 179).

"Having observed a remarkably consistent association between the presence of depression and distressed intimate relationships, investigators have generated research that suggests a unique transactional process between the two conditions" (Gollan, Gortner, & Jacobson, 1996, p. 322). The spousal subsystem in these families is generally malfunctioning. Significant hostility often builds in the overfunctioning partner, which can lead to intense guilt over his or her anger toward someone so helpless. The relationship contains a high level of sexual dysfunction because depression usually robs the individual of libido and energy. Extramarital affairs may substitute for the lack of intimacy and closeness extant in the marital subsystem. Gollan et al. identify the following relational factors that are key influences in these couples: "poor communication, problem-solving difficulties, and low relationship satisfaction" (p. 329).

Assessment Issues

Assessing the DepDps requires a knowledge of affective illness and its various forms and presentations. Depression is very commonly underdiagnosed by medical professionals, which causes individuals and families to suffer needlessly when effective treatment is available.

Suggestions

- Use standard depression screening inventories as a first-line approach to assessment.
- Conduct a family history and genogram and investigate any signs of affective illness.
- Take note of the family affect and if there is a depressive element detected investigate further.
- Children with depressive symptomatology warrant a family assessment.

Intervention Strategies
1. Aggressively treat depression when severe impairment is evident.
2. Initiate marital therapy as soon as possible.
3. Have multiple members of the family treated where feasible to enhance effect.
4. Use a psychoeducational approach to increase awareness of the impact of depression on the marriage, family, and children, and educate about treatment approaches and effectiveness.
5. Restructure family system so that there is a clear parental subsystem and so that children are moved out of parentified positions.
6. Involve the extended family or ecosystem when the system is severely depleted and needs assistance.
7. Address personality disturbance in family members after depression is lifted and family is prepared to tolerate shifts.

Comments
The DepDps is often highly responsive to interventions aimed at important fulcrum points. When an individual has suffered from an undiagnosed and untreated affective disorder for an extended period of time, improvement can have major impact on the family organization. The therapist must still assist in the metabolizing of negative feeling that has built up over time, and any concomitant personality pathology should be treated. Also, the clinician must be prepared to help both the system and the individual cope with the tremendous change that can occur when a biologically depressed individual responds to pharmacological intervention. This change is often accompanied by divorce, and grief over lost time can be overwhelming.

CASE STUDY

The index patient was an adolescent female who was having academic difficulties and showing signs of emotional delay. Upon evaluation it became apparent that the patient's father was suffering from depression and had signs of a depressive personality. His wife was an overfunctioning woman who was constantly compensating for her husband's lack of ambition, energy, and family involvement. The husband's father had died when he was an adolescent; his mother began to work the evening shift and left him home alone to fend for himself. Family history indicated that the husband's mother also suffered from depression and was a very morose woman who lived an isolated existence. The husband also showed evidence of a dependent/avoidant personality constellation that inter-fered with his career development as well as family functioning. The marital situ-ation was stable, with much accommodation by the wife, but much disappointment and hostility was occasionally expressed. The husband was seen for a course of short-term treatment, and then sequential marital therapy was begun. The triangular relationship with the daughter was also addressed. The fa-ther's feeling of directionlessness, which was a source of discontent for his wife, was linked to the parents' function of spending so much time doing for their daughter. The couple began to more honestly explore their disappointment and anger.

THE CHRONICALLY MEDICALLY ILL DYSFUNCTIONAL PERSONOLOGIC SYSTEM—MEDDPS

The MedDps is overtaxed emotionally for an extended period of time, a problem that is compounded by the personality disturbance present in members of the family. An inherited illness that has grave implications, for example, Huntington's disease or cerebral palsy, will especially cause con-siderable stress and potential for disturbance of the family system.

Assessment Issues

The MedDps is readily identified by the chronic state of illness present in one or more family members and the resulting dysfunction in adaptation by the family. Chronic illness alone would not qualify a family for this ty-pology. There must also be evidence of disturbance in the basic functions of the family of sufficient degree that long-term exposure is likely to have major impact on personality development of its members.

Suggestions

- Coordinate care with a qualified health professional who under-stands the fundamental issues of the particular disease process.
- Learn as much as possible about the progression and consequences of the illness.
- Educate the family so that needs can be anticipated and addressed be-fore they become a crisis.
- Consider involving pastoral care providers as a valuable treatment component.

Treatment Strategies

1. Provide ongoing support for the most vulnerable members of the family.
2. Attempt to normalize family life and development as much as possible.
3. Encourage family members to join support groups.
4. Work with overtaxed caretakers to develop a self-care plan; try to convince them that oversacrificing themselves is not useful.
5. Provide an opportunity for members to vent feelings against the medical profession or their religious beliefs.

Comments

The MedDps is often isolated and has to deal with strong feelings of shame. The clinician, in an attempt to normalize the family process, must be careful not to invalidate the stress, and chronic burden that long-term medical illness, especially a generationally manifested illness, places on even those members with natural resilience and optimism.

CASE STUDY

The patient, a male in his 20s, was self-referred because of panic, anxiety, and depression. He also had dependent personality disorder. His history revealed that his father, to whom he was very close, died when the patient was in his teens after a lengthy illness that absorbed most of the family's emotional resources. The patient's relationship with his mother was unemotional and lacked much nurturing. The entire family was stuck in what seemed to be a pathological grief process that prevented the members from developing independent identities. The patient was seen for individual therapy, but his mother turned down repeated invitations to attend. The patient was able to contact his unresolved grief and mourn the death of his father and was able to move developmentally toward a more mature and stable personality structure.

THE PARANOID DYSFUNCTIONAL PERSONOLOGIC SYSTEM—PARDPS

The ParDps does not often engage with the mental health professional, so many of these systems are not reported. These systems function at a chronic level of paranoia and may be organized into larger systems, such as cults. According to Perlmutter (1996): "No other problem can compare with paranoia in its power to negate the trust and capacity for empathy that are required for intimate relatedness" (p. 80).

Assessment Issues

Assessing the ParDps requires an in-depth understanding of individual psychopathology as well as systemic influences that result in various types of paranoid presentations. Some of these systems are quite impervious to outside intervention, so the clinician must carefully build an alliance before proceeding too rapidly. Premature termination from treatment is always a concern, and a negative treatment experience can close off the possibility of future treatment. The clinician should proceed slowly and with caution until he or she understands the patient's problem and has developed an alliance.

Suggestions

- Use psychodiagnostic testing to corroborate impressions.
- Try to understand the paranoid position from an adaptive perspective. Take seriously persecution fantasies and attempt to understand their meaning.
- Be as nonjudgmental as possible; use a sense of humor where possible.

Intervention Strategies

1. Use a multimodal approach when possible.
2. Break up family paranoia with a reality-based approach.
3. Assess for potential for violence.

Comments

Most clinicians rarely encounter these systems because they are very suspicious of authority. The clinician who does encounter such a system has a great opportunity to impact other family members and possibly help liberate a member being held hostage.

CASE STUDY

The patient was a 15 year-old female who was hospitalized after making a suicide attempt. The patient's parents had divorced, and the mother was actively psychotic, highly unstable, and paranoid. The father remarried a highly jealous woman who resented the patient's attachment to her father; the stepmother served as caretaker for the patient. The father was a suspicious man and did much projecting onto his daughter, primarily around her sexuality. The scapegoating by both parents seemed to be an attempt on their part to keep the daughter from individuating and "abandoning" them for the outside world, which they saw as frightening and hostile. The system exuded a palpable air of hostility and suspicion. The family was seen for family treatment, and the index patient was seen for supportive therapy. That therapy provided her with a stable attachment figure to help her come to terms with the system's severe psychiatric problems.

The Somatic Dysfunctional Personologic System—SomDps

The SomDps functions at the border of the mind-body dichotomy (Mikesell et al., 1995). The SomDps are very challenging systems for the medical and mental health professional to work with (McDaniel, Hepworth, & Doherty, 1995). "The language they use to construct their problems, their solutions, and their identities, their relationships, and their lives is a language of the body" (Mikesell et al., p. 377).

> Some family cultures lack any language for emotional experience. The adults may be alexithymic and allow only language about physical experience. Children in these families receive attention for physical pain but not for emotional pain. This approach conditions children to experience any need or problem as physical, and physical symptoms become their language for a range of experiences . . . Families with severely somatizing members share patterns of interaction that seek to avoid or anesthetize emotional pain. Not suprisingly, a significant number of somatizing adults are married to other somatizing adults. These couples speak the language of body discomfort. Other somatizing adults seek out and marry caregiving partners. (p. 379)

Assessment Issues

The SomDps is often highly treatment resistant and uses the family physician in an attempt to heal its dysfunction. The communication channel of these systems emphasizes the somatic expression as a way to attain unmet needs and sometimes to control the behavior of other family members. At other times, the individual or family may receive secondary gain for maintenance of the complaints. Individuals with nonstructural chronic back pain, for example, may use their symptoms to avoid work and seek disability. The clinician must be alert for factitious disorders that are manufactured for other purposes.

Suggestions
- Investigate a chronic pattern of medical overutilization by family or individuals.
- Investigate a chronic history of headaches, gastrointestinal disorders, back pain, allergies, or asthma.
- Obtain permission to contact medical providers to gather information and make diagnoses.

Intervention Strategies
1. Attempt to increase the psychological mindedness of the family.
2. Determine the function of symptoms, for example, intimacy substitution, pathological grief, severe emotional malnourishment, or dependency bonds.
3. Avoid in-depth emotional exploration until there is a readiness (McDaniel et al., 1995).
4. Work with medical professionals to create an alliance. Consider team consultations with the family at the physician's office.
5. Encourage activities outside the family to stimulate growth.

Comments
The SomDps is very difficult to treat effectively, especially when there is evidence of widespread personality disturbance in the family members.

CASE STUDY

The patient, a 30-year-old married male with children, was referred by his family internist after years of somatic complaints with no evidence of physical disease. He had an avoidant personality disorder. His family history showed a high level of neglect in his background, and the development of somatic symptomatology was a way of extracting nurturance and affection from depleted and somatizing adults. The family seemed to communicate all emotional states via physical descriptions such as tiredness, headaches, body aches, and gastrointestinal illness. The patient suffered from severe gastrointestinal problems, but he could only discuss his affective state through terms of physical symptoms. It was recommended that his wife join him for a marital consult, which he resisted. Unfortunately, like many of these patients, he terminated prematurely and did not return. His somatic process seemed to function as a means to control his current family and unconsciously punish them for what he had not gotten from his nuclear family.

CONCLUSIONS

A relational model of dysfunctional personologic systems enables clinicians to formulate a focused intervention plan. Subtypes encourage specific treatment application that is best suited for a particular system. Clinicians have many possible ways to intervene and, often, multiple fulcrum points to consider. An understanding of the dynamics of the dysfunctional personologic system encourages a more coherent and focal intervention that may initiate the process of change and facilitate interpersonal and intrapersonal growth patterns heretofore dormant.

CHAPTER 8

Treatment Matching and Selection Factors

THE RELATIONSHIP AMONG SYMPTOMS, PERSONALITY, AND FAMILY DYNAMICS

Because the concept of dysfunctional personologic systems is a new one there is no research that provides empirical data concerning the types of clinical conditions that coexist within these systems. This area requires future research. However, substantial evidence from clinical observation and other lines of research suggests a high rate of prevalence of various clinical conditions and personality pathology in the dysfunctional personologic system. These conditions often appear as a complex array of interrelated disorders and personality pathology akin to a ball of yarn that is tangled and knotted and that has no visible loose end. For example, avoidant and dependent personalities as well as anxiety disorders (social phobia, agoraphobia, panic disorders) are often encountered in the Dev-Dps. Members of these systems will often show evidence of interpersonal difficulties. They might have trouble establishing peer relations or sexual and intimate relations or committing to a partner. They also often have job-related disturbances and have not found productive careers that would enable them to become autonomous. The dysfunctional personologic system is often the wellspring from which many of these associated conditions and relational disturbances emerge. Clinicians' understanding of the interrelatedness of these relational disturbances, dysfunctional personologic systems, and clinical conditions alert them to the presence of deeply ingrained, multigenerational disturbances and pathology that are being transmitted.

EXPANDING THE CONCEPT OF DIFFERENTIAL THERAPEUTICS FOR THE DYSFUNCTIONAL PERSONOLOGIC SYSTEM

Selecting the appropriate treatment for the personality-disordered individual and knowing where to focus intervention in the dysfunctional personologic system is currently more an art than a science. *Differential therapeutics* was the term coined by Frances et al. (1984) in their book on the art and science of treatment selection, which was one of the first devoted to this important topic. Offering the right treatment at the wrong time will often result in poor outcome. The appropriate treatment applied at the correct time will have maximal effect, and a synergistic reaction or positive feedback loop in the system can result. This treatment-matching paradigm may not be useful when dealing with complex systems and multidetermined syndromes. Instead, what is more meaningful is to understand what Pinsof (1995) describes as the *problem-maintenance structures*, or underlying features that form the biopsychosocial matrix.

COST/BENEFIT ANALYSIS

The cost/benefit ratio of any treatment intervention or program (combination or sequence of modalities) will improve with careful treatment selection and application. For example, offering an expensive modality such as long-term individual psychotherapy or even short-term individual psychotherapy to a poorly motivated individual who is likely to miss sessions and terminate prematurely may be an inefficient allocation of expensive treatment. A series of family consultations in this case might be more effective to mobilize the systemic forces toward change. For example, the SomDps case study in the previous chapter described a man who prematurely terminated; it would probably have been more effective when the initial contact was made to suggest a family consultation instead of an individual one. Motivational forces can wane very quickly after the recommendation is made to contact a mental health provider. Clinicians may find that inviting the family in for consultation will help determine the loose end to pursue. A spouse may be an ally who can enhance motivation of an index patient or subsystem.

Considerable research needs to be conducted in this area before we as clinicians can confidently know the most efficacious methods of intervention, and it may be that, because of the complexity of variables, intervention will always be more an art than a science. Until more research is done, we must use clinical judgment and experience to guide our treatment selection and matching decisions. We often learn more from our treatment failures than from our successes. We should examine the failures as carefully as the successes to see if another focus or different modality might have given us an edge. The previous chapter illustrated that once the system dynamics are clarified through assessment and the fulcrum point has been identified, intervention strategies can be developed with greater precision. This chapter discusses the various types and modalities of treatment and how they can be combined to intervene at the system fulcrum point.

COMPONENTS OF THE TREATMENT PROGRAM

Personality disturbance can be treated through various well-established treatment modalities and types of intervention. Clinicians who effectively treat the dysfunctional personologic system should have familiarity with a variety of treatment modalities and should creatively interweave these modalities to create an individualized treatment mosaic. This decision should be based on the type of dysfunctional personologic system, stage of change, motivation, and resources available. The basic building blocks of a treatment program are specific treatment modalities, which can be applied alone, sequentially, or concurrently.

TREATMENT MODALITIES FOR THE CLINICAL TOOLBOX

Previously discussed methods of treatment have been depicted schematically by three triangles (triangle of conflict, triangle of persons, and triangle of relations); these methods are used for restructuring intrapersonal, interpersonal, and systemic phenomenon. Clinicians also can add to their clinical toolbox various modalities of treatment that can be delivered by the clinician, if trained in them, or by a treatment team. Familiarity with each of these modalities is required for the clinician to develop comprehensive treatment programs.

Individual psychotherapy is considered a basic modality of treatment for the personality-disordered individual. Individual therapy can have a high level of potency for someone who is at the contemplative or action phase of change or for someone at an optimal period of gestation. Individual psychotherapy is an essential element of the overall treatment of patients interested in an in-depth and comprehensive restructuring of the personality (Magnavita, 1993b, 1993c, 1994b). A recommendation of individual treatment can exert a powerful systemic influence; in the case of someone who is fused and needs to differentiate, for example, individual treatment can disrupt the homeostasis. One woman who sought treatment for concerns about her depressed, controlling, and hostile husband wanted to bring him to treatment even though he had walked out of the previous therapist's office. Instead, she was instructed to tell him that she would be working on her own problems; thus a step was made to detach her from his problems. This induced a positive structural shift.

Group psychotherapy is another modality that is often used in the treatment of the personality-disordered individual (Linehan, 1993). Group psychotherapy is an intensive stand-alone treatment, especially when offered in a partial hospital or inpatient setting. Group therapy for the personality-disordered patient has many advantages. It provides a rich relational matrix for patients to experiment with social skills and interpersonal relationships in a safe environment. Group therapy may reduce the anxiety that is aroused in patients more threatened by the intimacy of individual therapy (Piper & Rosie, 1998). The pressure of the peer group is essential for some types of personality pathology, such as antisocial. Piper and Rosie also emphasize the efficacy of treating greater numbers of patients simultaneously. Group therapy may be useful for patients whose motivation is low and who need the pressure of a group to break through defensive reactions.

Couple therapy is another modality of treatment for the personality-disordered individual, although much less has been written about the use of this modality. Schnarch (1991, 1995) has developed a potent couples therapy model for conducting sexual therapy that seems to address the long-standing personality issues often driving the sexual dysfunction. The action-oriented interventions available in couple work often has much impact. Bergantino (1994) offers the following insight after observing a renowned couples therapist encourage the wife of a very destructive physician to take action: " 'Oh, so that is what EFFECTIVE ACTION is with character disordered people.' With such people, words or more normal therapies I have found to be nearly a total waste of time" (p. 65). Because the major subsystem in most dysfunctional personologic systems is the couple in the triangular variations that were presented in Chapter 2, couple therapy is a viable method of intervention. It is covered in greater depth and specificity in Chapter 10. Couple work is highly beneficial in situations in which individuation needs to be promoted.

Pharmacotherapy is the administration of psychotropic medication, usually aimed at specific biologically based symptoms such as mood stabilization, anxiety reduction, and thinking and perceptual disorders (Koenigsberg, 1997). This treatment modality for personality disorder is gaining attention in the clinical literature, especially when integrated with psychotherapy (Feldman & Feldman, 1997). Joseph (1997) actively treats the symptomatic profile with various medications and believes that this method is an efficacious one for many personality disorders. Medication can reduce symptomatic disturbance that interferes with the ability to make use of psychotherapy. Medication is essential in controlling psychiatric illness in some patients that is biologically based, such as bipolar disorder, major clinical depression, and schizophrenia, and that, if left untreated, creates increased family dysfunction. Other conditions such as ADHD may warrant biological treatment.

Family therapy has not been a traditional approach to the treatment of personality disorders but holds much promise as a potent treatment modality. Family therapists have tended to downplay the concept of personality pathology and instead focus on the dysfunctional system, so that in effect the "medical model" view of personality disorders has been avoided. However, the clinician who uses strategic family interventions can mobilize the powerful systemic factors that reinforce and maintain personality disturbance. Family therapy can be especially useful in families with narcissistic and borderline pathology in which splitting and projective identification complicate adolescent members striving for autonomy (Berkowitz, et al., 1974; Shapiro, Zinner, Shapiro, & Berkowitz, 1975).

Psychoeducational intervention for personality-disordered patients and their families is not a widely used treatment modality but can be used to increase awareness and educate family members to enhance coping. One of the outcomes of current diagnostic conceptualizations of personality disorders and the dysfunctional personologic system is that this knowledge can be used to increase both public and professional awareness. Greater awareness may encourage more individuals and families to seek treatment. A psychoeducational model can be used to help family members understand and cope more effectively with personality disturbance. Psychoeducation can be employed to address other biologically based disorders (Pinsof, 1995) present in the dysfunctional personologic system, such as schizophrenia, affective disorders (bipolar and depression), and ADHD.

Support groups can be a useful adjunctive treatment and, for some individuals, can trigger major changes. Support groups are not only economical, but they also offer ongoing support during the maintenance stage of recovery and thus prevent relapse. Support programs often do not emphasize personality as the direct focus, but programs such as Alcoholics Anonymous do recognize the importance of character change in their step program. Increased public awareness and destigmatization may lead to the development of personality support groups similar to the specialized groups now formed for people with, for example, bipolar disorders or eating disorders.

Ecotherapy focuses on changes in the broader context or system that generates, reinforces, and maintains personality disorders. Ecotherapy is especially important for prevention, which is discussed in Chapter 12.

A recommendation for no treatment, although obviously not a modality of treatment, has its place in the armamentarium of the clinician. A recommendation for no treatment can deliver a powerful systemic message that, for example, an individual is not ready or willing to undergo the pain required to change. It can also serve as a powerful paradoxical intervention to induce motivation.

FLEXIBLE TREATMENT FORMATS—LENGTH OF SESSIONS, SCHEDULING OF SESSIONS, AND LENGTH OF TREATMENT

The use of flexible treatment formats with regard to length of session, scheduling of sessions, and length of treatment (short-term vs. long-term) are important variables to be considered in the development of effective and efficient protocols for the dysfunctional personologic system. Experimenting with various configurations, although anxiety provoking at first, will enable the clinician to organize the treatment around the patient's strengths, limitations, financial resources, proximity to therapist's office, and motivational factors. For some systems and individuals, longer sessions on a monthly basis are an excellent format, and for others in times of crisis, multiple extended sessions in the same week can stabilize a system and prevent costly hospitalization. Of course, when working with flexible formats in the era of managed care, the clinician needs to communicate with the various insurance companies and to offer an explanation for why the treatment is being delivered in a particular format. Usually when the reasons are explained, third party payers are more than eager to authorize these sessions as a way to avoid the cost of more expensive inpatient or partial hospitalizations. Hospitalization or residential treatment are needed at times, of course, but many systems can benefit in multiple ways from a more intensive outpatient experience.

Length of Sessions
Although most therapists ascribe to the standard treatment format of 45- to 50-minute sessions on a weekly basis, no research indicates that this format is the most efficacious (Budman & Gurman, 1988; Magnavita, 1997b). The use of extended sessions of two hours or more has tremendous advantage when the clinician is working with dysfunctional personologic systems. Extended sessions afford the clinician the opportunity to engage in the system with enough time to make a high-impact intervention by maintaining focus and deepening the experience for the individuals present. The reports from families and individuals who have experienced these extended sessions corroborates the clinical observation that these sessions are a powerful and welcome alternative to the limitations of the standard session.

Scheduling of Sessions
The flexible scheduling of sessions when used therapeutically can have a powerful effect on the system. In many instances, the scheduling of sessions every two or even three weeks is a metacommunication to the family that they have the necessary resources to resolve their situation without extensive dependency on the clinician (Budman & Gurman, 1988). Some systems and individuals may do well with sessions scheduled monthly; others may respond better if they are told to schedule the next session when they feel the need to address or work through another aspect of their problem. The point is that each system and individual should, in a collaborative relationship with the therapist, formulate what is most efficacious. In some cases, an entire day or even two days in a row spent with an individual or family can provide a highly impactful experience that can shift the system or individual in a brief period of time. Although some systems require the security of a trusting, more dependent relationship built over a period of years, most systems and individuals can benefit from longer sessions spread further apart.

Length of Treatment
The next section of this chapter discusses various treatment protocols, but it is important to underscore the topic of how long treatment should last.

Generally speaking, treatment is initiated now with the expectation that, in most situations, a short-term format is appropriate. The format can be modified later as other information becomes available and as the response to treatment is assessed. However, the length of treatment can never be predicted until the clinician is engaged in the treatment process, and even then the length is sometimes difficult to determine. Some systems immediately become mobilized; others quickly regress and let the pathology surface in the most virulent form. Clinicians' attitudes about the capacity for human transformation and about the therapeutic process should be examined (Budman & Gurman, 1988). Short-term and long-term therapists usually hold very different views about the process of change and the methods used. Clinicians must examine their own expectations as well as those of the family or individual member at the beginning of the treatment process.

DELIVERY OF TREATMENT—THE BENEFIT OF A TREATMENT TEAM APPROACH

The delivery of treatment to the dysfunctional personologic system is best done in a collaborative treatment team in which each treatment team member's individual growth and clinical development is supported. Treatment teams are usually multidisciplinary in composition; various members offer specialized knowledge in assessment and treatment modalities. In situations in which it is not possible to have a close collaborative treatment team, clinicians can develop relationships with other providers in their community who can offer quality treatment and, most important who are willing to collaborate and coordinate treatment so that the work being done is coordinated and focused. A collaborative treatment approach is essential for severely disordered systems in which splitting and projection occur.

DEVELOPING COMPREHENSIVE TREATMENT PROTOCOLS

Comprehensive treatment programs can be developed and administered in several settings (in-patient, out-patient, partial programs, or some combination of these) and can combine various modalities of treatment individually, sequentially, or concurrently.

SEQUENTIAL TREATMENT

A *sequential treatment approach* refers to the application of various treatment modalities in a specified order. The goal is to offer treatment in a series in which each modality capitalizes on the previous one. For example, in a NarDPS, treatment may begin with family therapy that focuses on parent/child problems and is followed by individual therapy, group therapy, or a support group. In a DepDps, the initial course of treatment might be to actively focus on one member who is severely depressed.

CONCURRENT TREATMENT

A *concurrent treatment approach* refers to the application of multiple treatments simultaneously. Concurrent application of treatment theoretically offers more potency because of its greater breadth. For example, in a PscDps, medication management, family therapy, and psychoeducation might be combined to stabilize the individual and the system. Then, on an ongoing basis, medication management and individual treatment with intermittent family sessions can be used.

FORMULATING TARGETED INTERVENTION STRATEGIES

Formulating a targeted intervention strategy is no easy task that can be reduced to simple algorithms or cookbook recipes. However, I can offer some basic clinical guidelines and considerations. Clinicians may find so many interacting variables that they become overwhelmed by the task at hand. The selection of one or more interventions is based on an understanding of the biopsychosocial model as it is embedded in the relational context and on knowledge about the precursors and stages of change covered in this text.

Pinsof (1995) offers a well-articulated framework that he terms "problem-centered therapy." This approach formulates intervention around the *"problem-maintenance structure, which embodies the constraints that prevent resolution of the presenting problem"* (p. 7). The constraints are factors from the biopsychosocial model that inhibit the system from solving the problem. Pinsof explains that "problem-maintenance structures vary at least along three dimensions—depth, width, and darkness" (p. 23). When numerous constraints are present in the system, the structure is *deep*. *Width* refers to the number of constraints present within a particular level of the biopsychosocial matrix, such as when various biological disturbances are evident. The *darker* the structure is, the more potent the constraints are from a domain. Pinsof uses this helpful conceptualization to guide the intervention program.

> The narrower, simpler, lighter, and more superficial the problem-maintenance structure, the quicker the problem is likely to respond to intervention. In contrast, the wider, darker, and deeper the structure, the more time and effort will be required to resolve the problem. (p. 25)

Dysfunctional personologic systems are likely to be the deeper, darker, and wider structure. Nevertheless, Pinsof's conceptual framework has much clinical utility and assists in organizing the treatment as efficaciously as possible.

INTERVENTION SELECTION FACTORS

How does the clinician organize and select the type of intervention to apply to a particular case? This question cannot be answered simply, but the method used to answer it will dictate how treatment is provided. When a patient or family seeks out a clinician for an initial consultation, the clinician is the demanding position of having to, in a fairly rapid period of time, come up with an initial strategy. With experience, the clinician may quickly be alerted to the presence of personality pathology or discern evidence of a dysfunctional personologic system. With this knowledge, the clinician must quickly assess the stage of change, examine the various precursors of change, and observe the stage of the family life cycle (Gerson, 1995) to determine the initial intervention strategy. Each strategy has an inherent risk (premature termination; flooding the family with affect too quickly and causing regression) and a potential gain.

Motivation

Fluctuations in motivation are apparent in all humans and in the systems in which we function. When motivation is ebbing, one modality of treatment or type of intervention may be called for; when motivation is at a high point, another one may produce better results. For example, a low motivation may require an approach that emphasizes engagement, such as family or couple therapy. Engagement is a crucial phase of developing a therapeutic alliance. It is covered in detail in Chapter 11.

Degree of Homeostasis
When the level of homeostasis is powerfully maintained and the system is heavily invested in not changing, the clinician may want to consider a potent approach, such as a paradoxical intervention, to create a state of disequilibrium. Intervention with this approach is risky because the family may flee, but without such intervention the clinician may face a greater risk in being rendered ineffective because the family pathology is reinforced.

Family Life Cycle Transitions
It is common in general psychotherapy and family psychology practice to encounter personality pathology that is exacerbated by family life cycle transitions. For example, couples often enter treatment with severe marital disruption as the result of an affair following the birth of children. The dynamics in most cases take a similar course and are recognizable. Usually the husband enters into an affair after the birth of the first or subsequent children; this affair is discovered by the wife, which creates a severe marital crisis and a demand for therapy. Sometimes the couple will agree to come together for consultation, but more often the husband wants to be seen alone and is not ready to terminate the affair. Suprisingly, many of these couples report good sexual relationships even with the demands of children and are unclear about what has led to the disruption. In many cases, long-standing personality pathology emerges under the stress of the transition and presents in the form of relational disturbance. Many patients refer to these events as midlife crises or existential dilemmas: "Do I really still want to be married?" The wife is often an enabler who has always worked to please and care for her husband and is shocked when the rug is pulled out from under the family just when she is feeling dependent and emotionally involved with the demands of young children. Often, one spouse suffers from a personality disorder or both suffer from complementary disorders that were not evident until professional demands and family responsibility increased and called for an added degree of maturity and restraint that was not there.

Locating the Individual in the Family Life Cycle   Whether the clinician is working with the family or with an individual, it is worth the effort to locate the family in the life cycle and understand the developmental implications. A family with an adolescent who is stuck while trying to leave home suggests a situation far different than one in which an adult is living in the basement and functioning only marginally with retired parents. Clinicians should consider the implications of a generational pattern of difficult life transitions, for example, a delay in marrying, running away from home, or not marrying.

OTHER FACTORS TO DEVELOPING A TREATMENT PROGRAM

The array of treatment approaches can be staggering, but selection of an approach, be it individual, couple, or so forth, can be simplified with an understanding of systems dynamics. Chapter 7 discusses the importance of finding the fulcrum point in the system. Once the fulcrum point is established, the clinician can offer a treatment approach that is consistent with the level of motivation and readiness demonstrated by the system and that is at the proper depth of intervention.

CAPITALIZING ON LIFE EVENTS

Various experiences in life are potentially transforming and are often overlooked as domains of intervention for the psychotherapist (Magnavita, 1996). For example, in modern culture, the opportunity to experience a college education is a highly transforming experience; it exposes the student to aspects of the world, self, and others that are powerful and immediate. Other experiences—such as travel, spiritual quests, accepting new challenges, or extending in new ways—can lead to personality change and emotional growth.

COMORBIDITY

The concept of comorbidity is a relatively new but important one in the mental health lexicon (Lyons et al., 1998; Magnavita, 1998c). Comorbid refers to the co-occurrence of two or more separate syndromes or disorders. This concept is relevant to the clinician's purposes because so many personality-disordered systems and individuals typically present with syndromes and family pathology related to or coexisting with personality pathology. The presence of a history of an Axis I anxiety disorder, for example, can alert the clinician to the possibility of borderline personality (Zanarini et al., 1998); major depression may be traced to a history of childhood physical or sexual abuse (Levitan et al., 1998). Clinicians will find it useful to be aware of coexisting syndromes as well as individual personality pathology that are

2

suggestive of dysfunctional personologic systems. As I have discussed previously, knowing where to intervene is one of the greatest challenges to the therapist. Does the clinician start with symptom constellations, such as depression and anxiety, or with personality disturbance as manifested by repetitive maladaptive patterns, or with relational disturbances? An understanding of psychopathology and its manifestation in both the individual and the system is central to effective therapy. Therapists can often be sidetracked by focusing on a symptom that is a red herring and that prevents more comprehensive work in more important areas.

Personality Disorders and Comorbid Clinical Syndromes
In a review of the literature, Tyrer et al. (1997) found a number of comorbid syndromes that occur with personality disorders:

- Borderline personality disorder and depression.
- Depressive personality disorder and depression, especially dysthymia.
- Schizotypal personality disorder and schizophrenia.
- Avoidant personality disorder and generalized social phobia.
- Cluster B personality disorder and substance use disorder.
- Cluster B and C personality disorder and eating disorder.
- Cluster C personality disorder and anxiety disorder.
- Cluster A personality disorder and schizophrenia.
- Somatization disorder and cluster C and B personality disorder.
- Cluster C personality disorder and hypochondriasis.

Other comorbid conditions that have not yet been researched are often evident to the clinical practitioner:

- Stuttering and avoidant, passive-aggressive personality disorder.
- Dysthymic and obsessive-compulsive personality disorder.
- Sexual dysfunction and cluster C personality disorder.

ASSOCIATED RELATIONAL DISTURBANCES

Johnson et al's (1997, p. 388) summary of the research indicates "that dysfunctional family relationships and parental behavior are associated with Axis I and personality disorder symptomatology, and that personality disorders predict subsequent Axis I symptomatology." Further, their "findings suggest that future research may be likely to confirm that adolescent personality disorder symptoms tend to mediate the association between parental behavior and Axis I symptomatology." One premise of this book is that dysfunctional personologic systems have long-standing patterns of relational disturbances. These relational disturbances are very commonly the reason that individuals, families, and couples seek consultation with mental health professionals. As I have already reviewed, the most common relational disturbances occur in two crucial arenas: marriage and family. Although it is true that not every couple that presents with marital and family issues is a member of a dysfunctional personologic system, it is true that most dysfunctional personologic systems exhibit relational disturbances. These disturbances include:

- Marital/couple disturbance.
- Parent-child problems.
- Separation-individuation difficulties.

INDIVIDUAL TREATMENT PROTOCOLS

An understanding of the various treatment modalities and categories of intervention provides for a more reasoned and informed treatment plan formulation. Benjamin (1997) writes:

> Principles of intervention in psychotherapy need to be operationalized in such a way that the clinician can create an individualized approach while still adhering to protocol. Not every patient, even in a group with the same "diagnosis," will need the same interventions, especially not in the same sequence. It is an oversimplification to imagine that a given therapy intervention (e.g., encourage assertion; interpret; support; point out; enhance self esteem) is categorically constructive. (p. 316)

We as clinicians therefore must construct an individualized treatment program for each patient and family system that we encounter. Contextualizing the treatment with regard to the time frame is a critical first step. In another words, we must decide if treatment is going to be long-term, brief, intermittent, or consultative. We must also decide what depth of treatment we are attempting to achieve. To do so we must take into consideration both practical issues—such as reason for referral, individual or family resources, proximity, and additional therapeutic resources—and extenuating circumstances, such as a family or individual who is about to relocate to another area. Once we determine these issues, we further sharpen our treatment formulation by assessing the precursors of change. We can then select one of the following intervention frameworks: (1) short-term intervention; (2) long-term intervention; (3) intermittent intervention; and (4) maintenance intervention.

SHORT-TERM INTERVENTION

A short-term intervention is one in which the clinician believes that (1) the patient or family will experience a substantial treatment impact for an intensive, focused, in-depth personality therapy; (2) the patient's motivational factors are low, and the patient or family would benefit from a focused partial modification of personality; or (3) because of other factors, the patient or family is only available or amenable to a brief course of therapy.

Treatment Goals
- Comprehensive or partial restructuring of personality.
- Systemic restructing of family or couple.

LONG-TERM INTERVENTION

A long-term intervention is still considered by many clinicians to be the only potent form of treatment for personality disorders. Benjamin (1997) comments: "It takes a long time to address core issues" (p. 316). She goes on to say that "personality disorder, and/or personality traits, are too complex, and have too many determinants, to be amenable to short-term interventions" (p. 316). I agree that for many patients, a long-term intervention is the treatment of choice and may actually be cost-effective when compared to repeated hospitalizations or to long-term medication treatment. However, I disagree with the generalization that modification of all personality traits or disorders is necessarily a long-term endeavor.

Treatment Goals
- Restructuring of the personality or trait modification.
- Major modification of family system.

INTERMITTENT INTERVENTIONS

The use of intermittent interventions is probably the most common form of intervention. Intermittent interventions are ones whereby the patient or family returns at various points in time for a course of treatment, either to a single therapist or to multiple therapists who are not connected in any collaborative fashion. This type of intervention is based on a family psychology model of care and, I believe, offers much promise for the treatment and prevention of personality disorders.

Treatment Goals
- Step-wise personality transformation.
- Primary prevention.
- Modification of family system.

MAINTENANCE INTERVENTION

This type of intervention differs from long-term intervention in that the patient is not able to function without the support of some type of therapeutic regime. Maintenance therapy may only be required in severe refractory cases in which other intervention strategies have proved ineffective.

Treatment Goals
- Maintain highest level of functioning.
- Prevent suicide, homicide, or major catastrophic occurrence.

SUGGESTED TREATMENT PROTOCOLS

Specific treatment protocols need to be developed for each family system on an individual basis. However, certain treatment modalities are used when working with certain dysfunctional personologic systems. In this section, I emphasize the treatment modalities that are most important in a treatment protocol. A systemically based treatment protocol takes into consideration the factors that have been previously reviewed. In addition, treatment modalities and sequencing vary depending on whether the index patient is a child brought in by parents, an adolescent referred by the school system, or an adult.

THE ADDICTIVE DYSFUNCTIONAL PERSONOLOGIC SYSTEM

Determining the treatment protocol for the AdcDps will vary from case to case, but certain features of these systems require standard intervention. The first step in the treatment is to address the addictive cycle, focusing on the members of the family most motivated for change. These systems are often highly refractory because the addictive process and personality commingle to form an entrenched pattern. Issues of abuse and neglect, where they exist, also need to be addressed early. Once the family is stabilized, the system triangles and intrapsychic pathology can be addressed.

Recommended Treatment Modalities

Psychoeducational Intervention   The system must be educated about the addictive process and its effects on individual and family functioning.

Substance Abuse Treatment   Treatment must at some point address the primary addictive disorder with outpatient, inpatient, or partial hospital therapy or with a 12-step program.

Family Therapy   Family therapy is useful in keeping the family focused on their goals to lead a nonaddictive lifestyle and to break the pattern of addiction.

Individual Therapy   Individual therapy is often a necessary treatment to deal with the long-term effects of addiction on the individual's emotional functioning.

Couples Therapy   Couples therapy addresses issues of personality that are maintaining the pattern. A focus on codependent issues can often be best addressed together.

Psychopharmacological Intervention   Treatment with medication can be aimed at the comorbid disorders that are amenable to this approach, such as psychotic disorders, depression, and severe anxiety.

The most effective treatment approach for the AdcDps is often a combination of substance abuse treatment and other modalities.

THE NARCISSISTIC DYSFUNCTIONAL PERSONOLOGIC SYSTEM

The NarDps often activates strong countertransference feelings in the therapist. There may be a powerful sense of entitlement and exaggerated demands on the therapist or team. These systems may devaluate previous therapists and look for someone who is well known. Often the therapist is idealized and then quickly devaluated. The therapist who works with these families must have a solid footing and a realistic understanding of the process of change.

Recommended Treatment Modalities

Individual Therapy   Often it is necessary to conduct some individual work with key members of these systems because shame is usually a prominent affect that needs to be metabolized. The therapist may feel that individual therapy for a child is necessary to address developmental disturbances.

Couples Therapy   Focusing on the spousal subsystem where possible is a useful way to address some of the disturbed communication patterns that occur in these systems.

Family Therapy   Dethroning an individual in a narcissistic system can be very powerful if done in an empathic way. Individuals often find that giving up the throne is a relief, and the dethroning allows other members of the family to take responsibility for the family functions.

Psychoeducation   Focusing on parenting and relational skills will enhance the family environment and is often a nonthreatening way to engage the system.

THE COVERTLY NARCISSISTIC DYSFUNCTIONAL PERSONOLOGIC SYSTEM

The CNrDps has a tendency to reverse the parent-child emotional relationship by unconsciously eliciting and reinforcing the development of a false self that gratifies parental needs for affirmation and reinforcement. Over generations these families, although appearing healthy to the untrained observer, systematically rob their members of ambition, autonomy, and capacity for healthy affection. The family members are not aware that the CNrDps system serves to protect the fragile subsystems.

Recommended Treatment Modalities

Family Therapy   Modeling appropriate interpersonal and affective communications can be accomplished with family therapy. It is also helpful to identify the missing links in the family development and to provide a corrective emotional experience.

Individual Therapy   The individual focus can provide a useful forum to address some of the issues related to carrying a false self.

Couples Therapy   This modality is quite beneficial to the system at large. Strengthening the couple dyad enhances overall functioning.

A sequential treatment approach is the best way to organize this treatment. Family therapy with a child or adolescent as the index patient is often a starting point, which can be followed by individual or couple therapy.

THE PSYCHOTIC DYSFUNCTIONAL PERSONOLOGIC SYSTEM

The PscDps varies depending on the type and lineage of psychotic disorders in the system. When multiple family members are functioning at a psychotic level, a treatment team should be utilized to handle the system and individual treatment needs.

Recommended Treatment Modalities

Family Therapy   Family therapy is a recommended treatment of choice in these systems. Emphasis on emotional patterns of communication is crucial to prevent relapse.

Pharmacotherapy   When an active psychotic process is occurring, the clinician must consider appropriate medication management.

Individual Therapy   Various members of these systems can benefit from individual treatment.

The PsyDps requires a combined treatment; various treatment modalities need to be presented in a multimodal format.

THE DEVELOPMENTALLY ARRESTED DYSFUNCTIONAL PERSONOLOGIC SYSTEM

The DevDps often have tight boundaries around them that protect them from outside influence. The family contains powerful triangular configurations that keep individuals locked into rigid roles. These triangular relationships need to be identified and disentangled.

Recommended Treatment Modalities

Family Therapy The treatment of choice for DevDps is often family therapy that focuses on concrete issues such as leaving home (Haley, 1997), attaining and holding a job, dating, and establishing peer relationships.

Couple Therapy The couple is often a necessary focus of treatment, or it at least should be seen for consultation. Parenting differences should be addressed. Roles are often polarized; for example, the father is too harsh and the mother is too lenient. Both usually support dependency.

Individual Therapy Seeing a family member for individual treatment can assist in the process of emotional differentiation. The therapist needs to be aware of the system's tendency to undermine progress and maintain the homeostasis.

THE PHYSICALLY/SEXUALLY TRAUMATIZING DYSFUNCTIONAL PERSONOLOGIC SYSTEM

The TraDps needs immediate intervention to interrupt the cycle of abuse and protect the members who are being subjected to mistreatment. Intervention is a difficult task because the fragile therapeutic alliance can be disrupted before it forms, and families may retreat. Chronic patterns of abuse are highly toxic to all family members, and all members should be assessed for post-traumatic stress disorder.

Recommended Treatment Modalities

Group Therapy The batterer often requires the power of a group that exterts significant pressure on the individual to change.

Family Therapy The family often needs the support and boundaries provided in family therapy. Patterns of communication and emotional responding can be modified and restructured.

Ecosystem Intervention Addressing the greater social system through social services, job training, and so forth is often a necessary treatment component.

This treatment is best organized through a combined approach. Various treatment modalities often need to be delivered to the TraDps to enhance the potency.

THE DEPRESSIGENIC DYSFUNCTIONAL PERSONOLOGIC SYSTEM

The DepDps, although often functioning at a depressed level, may have one or several members who are acting-out as part of the family dynamics. In fact, the system often enters treatment as a result of acting-out behavior on the part of a child or adolescent. The first line of treatment is to address the crisis if one is presented. Careful assessment is required to determine the level of chronicity and previous attempts at amelioration. It is not uncommon for individuals to be unaware of the legacy of depression and to not realize that effective treatments are available.

Recommended Treatment Modalities

Family Therapy   Initially, the family in crisis should be seen so the clinician can intervene and stabilize the situation and then conduct a thorough history and genogram.

Pharmacotherapy   Those members suffering from clinical depression require appropriate medication evaluation and treatment.

Individual Therapy   The clinician may initiate individual courses of therapy with depressed individuals who require more intrapersonal work to restructure their inner schema.

THE CHRONICALLY MEDICALLY ILL DYSFUNCTIONAL PERSONOLOGIC SYSTEM

The MedDps is typically in a constant state of overtaxation, and the clinician needs to be ready to differentiate that chronic stress from frequently occurring crisis states. For example, a family with a severely asthmatic member might have to be prepared at any moment to take the person to the emergency room. This constant edge makes a normalized family function difficult. Other situations may be dealing with a generational manifestation of medical illness, which is accepted as part of the family culture, that leads to neurological decline, blindness, or deafness. A medical illness that exists throughout generations, as opposed to an illness that is an act of fate, leads to different implications for how the system organizes itself.

Recommended Treatment Modalities

Group Therapy   Group therapy should be used to provide support to affected members.

Family Therapy   Family therapy is the cornerstone of the treatment protocol. Dealing with the chronic challenge that must be managed is best handled through family therapy.

Individual Therapy   Working with individuals within the system is often useful in strengthening and inoculating the member against personality disorder.

Consultation   Collaboration with medical providers is necessary to reinforce and coordinate treatment.

THE PARANOID DYSFUNCTIONAL PERSONOLOGIC SYSTEM

The ParDps, like the other systems, exists on a continuum of severity. When severe, these systems often lead an isolated existence and may go unnoticed. The family may share a paranoid view of the world. These individuals may be overly concerned about self-protection and must be assessed for the potential for violence.

Recommended Treatment Modalities

Family Therapy   To fully understand and assess the degree of family and intergenerational pathology, family therapy is important. Often, these systems because of their disturbance eschew this modality of treatment.

Individual Therapy   More commonly, the clinician is in the position of treating a less disturbed member of the system or someone from the extended family. In some cases, a vicarious traumatization occurs when, for example, children cut off contact with their parents or do not allow the grandparents to have contact with their grandchildren.

Pharmacotherapy   Severe paranoid conditions necessitate medication consultation and management to bring the condition under control.

THE SOMATIC DYSFUNCTIONAL PERSONOLOGIC SYSTEM

The SomDps is often a refractory system, especially when generations of individuals have substituted somatic communication as their preferred mode. Emotional tolerance and capacity for intimacy are quite low. The emotional communication revolves around symptomatic conditions. The clinician must be prepared to learn the family communication style and find the most likely fulcrum point.

Recommended Treatment Modalities

Family Therapy   The best way for the clinician to experience and map the family structure of these systems is to have the family together and to observe the nuances of their communication. The clinician will also be able to observe the biases toward various personality disorders and how they are maintained.

Individual Therapy   Although individual therapy can be potent, patients often experience disappointment when they realize that they are expected to give up the communication style that they have relied on.

Group Therapy   Enhanced coping can be emphasized in group therapy sessions.

THE THERAPEUTIC FIELD

The therapeutic field is the domain of possibilities in which the therapist can intervene. The therapist can choose to move from a microscopic level to a macroscopic one, for example, from a level of intervention at the ecosystem by contacting community agencies and broader networks to a detailed focus on the intrapsychic or biological process of an individual. Various strategic moves are called for at certain times and under certain clinical conditions.

DEEPENING THE THERAPEUTIC FIELD

Many therapeutic approaches and modalities attempt to deepen the therapeutic experience so as to stimulate as much structural change as possible both individually and systemically. Various modalities of treatment and approaches or combinations of approaches can serve to deepen the therapeutic experience.

Suggested Modalities
- Individual therapy.
- Couples therapy.

Broadening the Therapeutic Field

At times the therapist may elect to broaden the scope of the therapeutic field.

Suggested Modalities
- Family therapy.
- Support groups.
- Ecosystem intervention.
- Group therapy.

Narrowing the Therapeutic Field

On occasion the therapist may decide that the therapeutic field needs to be narrowed to effect change in a subsystem or individual.

Suggested Modalities
- Individual therapy.
- Pharmacotherapy.

Shifting the Treatment Frame

The therapeutic frame is the manner in which the patient and therapist define the treatment goals and parameters. For example, a SomDps might initially enter treatment at the suggestion of a pediatrician who determines that a somatization process is occurring. The initial treatment frame is that the parents are concerned about the health of their child and want it improved; the parents believe that something is "wrong" with their child. The therapist initially accepts this treatment frame and then, in the course of the assessment, realizes that dysfunctional personologic system is driving much of the symptom pathology and that the frame of treatment needs to be expanded. Following are various possibilities that clinicians can consider.

Accept the presenting problem, engage the system or individual, and then when the time is right broaden the intervention. Family psychologists who treat children often find that a behaviorally disordered child is delivered by a dysfunctional personologic system in which one or both parents could benefit from treatment. The motivational factors present in the parental subsystem, however, are often low; they want the child fixed. In this case, the clinician may consider an intermittent intervention to be the best possible outcome. Intermittent intervention may build an alliance that will keep the door open for more comprehensive intervention.

Reframe the presenting problem or complaint and intervene at a different level of the system. Sometimes the presenting problem is so obviously a diversion from the central issue that a shift can be made and accepted by the family. One family, for example, presented an adolescent who was treatment refractory and out of control. During the initial consultation it became evident that this adolescent was deflecting conflict from the marital dyad. The adolescent in fact gave a good portrayal of the family disturbance and was relieved when the parents were asked to come in for the next session to focus on their concerns. The father's long-standing personality pathology made it difficult for him to provide the basic level of nurturing for his family, and all members were reacting with anger and opposition. One of the children even mentioned that the father had threatened to kill himself.

Offer short-term treatment and attempt to enhance motivational factors. During a brief treatment, a patient with poor motivation for change can experience enhanced motivation. Once an initial awareness is built and the presenting problem is viewed in the light of personality factors, the patient may consider a more comprehensive treatment package aimed at the personality disturbance.

Act as a consultant, identify the disturbance, and refer the system to another clinician for a course of treatment. Acting as a consultant to the system or individual and then referring for treatment has certain advantages that can accelerate the treatment process. The consultant can rapidly make a recommendation to another therapist for, say, couples work to address parenting. This recommendation is a preliminary way to engage parents in some couple-focused work with a competent therapist who can begin to identify the deeper, personality-related aspects of the problem matrix.

CASE STUDY: A TRADPS—THE FAMILY THAT WAS HELD HOSTAGE

The patient, a 15-year-old adolescent male, was referred by his parents. The entire family, which included the index patient and his mother and father and younger sister, was seen for the initial consultation. Immediately it became clear that this adolescent was hostile and resistant to the idea of treatment. The parents had in fact consulted various mental health and medical professionals, but the patient's behavior continued to be out of control. Immediately the patient started harassing his father and provoking him by calling him names, mimicking him in the most unflattering manner, and blaming all his troubles on his parents. The patient revealed that his father was angry because he believed his mother had an affair with someone she worked with and that his father threatened suicide when he was upset. The younger sister sat and watched the antics and laughed and encouraged her brother. The father responded to the provocation by complaining and engaging his son in argumentative interactions. The mother sat and watched, sighing with contempt at the interaction and adding that it is worse at home and goes on nightly. The patient had a history of oppositional defiant behavior, depression, and hyperactivity.

Sitting with this family was unpleasant. The index patient seemed on the verge of completely losing his temper; he escalated with the merest hint of criticism. At one point he jumped out of his chair, sarcastically hugged his father, and rubbed the man's head, saying in a sneering tone, "I really love you Dad." He complained that his parents were old, and he made fun of his father's job. The level of communication within the family was clearly disturbed. The parents seemed ineffective and helpless, like they were being held hostage by this adolescent. The structure of the family was out of alignment. The index patient held far too much power; he was intimidating and ruled the family with his demands and behavior. The parents also reported that the son was violent at home toward the younger sister and that he attacked the father. The department of child service had been called in after a number of these incidents.

The family history shed some light on the multigenerational transmission process in effect. The patient's mother reported being raised by two alcoholic parents and being exposed to violence and emotional abuse. There were seven children, and she desperately wanted to get away from this traumatizing system. The father was also from what he described as a dysfunctional family; he had been exposed to harsh treatment and occasional physical abuse by his father who was large and whom he feared.

THE FIRST SESSION WITH THE FAMILY

During the first consultation session, the family quickly enacted the dysfunctional family interactions. The index patient was clearly offering himself up as a target for the family rage. Although defiant and oppositional, he clearly communicated his sense that there was a severe lack of emotional nourishment in the family. He was articulate and dramatic about the problems. Once the therapist acknowledged these issues and set some limits to his behavior, the patient calmed down. He talked about the family's previous therapeutic encounters in the most disparaging manner. When the children were out of the consultation room, the therapist directed questions toward the parental subsystem that corroborated initial suspicions. The marital relationship was in severe distress; it suffered from a tremendous amount of hostility and a lack of sexual or positive emotional involvement. Both parents had a desire to walk away and never return. They agreed to schedule a session for the two of them to discuss some of the marital issues. The patient, upon hearing this result, shook the therapist's hand and commented that his parents were the ones with the problems.

THE COUPLE ASSESSMENT

The couple arrived to the session with a thick file documenting the accumulated educational, neurological, and psychological evaluations that had been conducted. They also talked about the desperate state of affairs and their feelings of helplessness. They both felt impotent and discussed in greater detail their son's volatility and the verbal abuse he showered on them. Indeed their marriage was on the rocks, and their entire family existence focused on coping with the ever-increasing demands their son made on them for clothes, material goods, and entertainment. The parents also disclosed that an older son had similar problems and was extremely violent and abusive. This son had previously been in a residential placement and was leading a marginal existence.

The couple's relationship was tenuous at best. They had disconnected from one another years ago. The husband was feeling abandoned by his wife and angry about her emotional withdrawal; the wife believed she could cope with almost anything by putting up a wall and not letting things get to her. They were unable to communicate together about what to do. The wife said she wanted to run away from the whole mess, and the husband declared that he would not blame her.

INTERVENTION STRATEGIES

• *Stopping the cycle of violence.* The first step was to deal with the issue of violence and emotional abuse. Ongoing violence is a threat not only to the psychological well-being of the individual who is the target of the abuse but also to those who witness violence. Children who are exposed to violence are at risk for developing a wide range of emotional and behavioral disturbances (Holden, Geffner & Jouriles, 1998) that, if not addressed, may develop into chronic personality disturbances. During the couples session, the parents were informed of the options available: intensive outpatient treatment, inpatient hospitalization, or residential treatment.

• *Empowering the parents.* The parents were encouraged to set a clear limit with their son: All physical and emotional abuse must be stopped; otherwise he would be removed from the house. The parents were told to contact the department of child service and have a case worker assigned to prepare for possible emergency placement if the abuse continued. The father cried at the thought of "putting my son away." The therapist reframed this attitude in terms of getting appropriate treatment for the son before it is too late, before someone is severely hurt and his son is lost. This intervention was aimed at restructuring the family system by strengthening the parental subsystem and taking the index patient out of the seat of family power.

• *Treatment modalities and settings.* Following is a chronological list of the treatment modalities, including settings, that were utilized in this case: Family therapy; ecosystem intervention (hospitalization) and family therapy; group therapy (partial program) and family therapy; group therapy (outpatient basis); family therapy; couples therapy; individual therapy.

Using Pinsof's (1995) models, this case would be described as having a deep, wide, and dark structure. Many factors commingled to produce this multigenerational level of disturbance, and multiple and sequential interventions were required to sufficiently restructure the system.

CONCLUSIONS

The art of treatment selection can be a staggering challenge for a clinician facing a dysfunctional personologic system. However, careful evaluation and an understanding of the developmental disturbances and dynamics in the dysfunctional personologic system clarifies the necessary setting, type, and modality of intervention. Shifting treatment modalities and combining them sequentially and concurrently can enhance the treatment potency of the protocol and can have more and deeper impact on the dysfunctional personologic system.

CHAPTER 9

Language of the Therapeutic Alliance

L anguage is the medium we use to conduct psychotherapy and heal the injured and wounded who come for our care. Bandler and Grinder (1975) remind us in *The Structure of Magic* that "all the accomplishments of the human race, both positive and negative, have involved the use of language" (p. 21). Dysfunctional personologic systems are masterful in their use of confusing, contradictory, and double bind communications. The direct expression of feeling and needs that occurs in intimate relations is avoided. Mixed communication is substituted, such as by the SomDps, who uses a language of somatic communication, or by the PscDps, who commonly uses double bind or contradictory messages. Affirming words might be stated with hostile, nonverbal expression or tonality in a confusing communication matrix. What we as therapists attend to and what we dismiss has a powerful influence on the direction of the therapeutic process. The impact that our language has can be seen in the responses of the systems and individuals we work with. Some words increase anxiety; some serve to soothe and reassure.

Understanding the language and metaphors of personality and systemic modification enhances therapeutic potency. This chapter presents the elements of language and metacommunication, such as metaphor and paradox, that can be used to deepen the therapeutic process and add to the momentum of transformation. Anderson (1996) writes about the power of language:

Language and words are like searching hands. One might say that language is a sense organ. But words are more. Like a hand, they grasp on to meanings. So, the words we select influence the meanings we come to reach. (p. 122)

Andrew Weil (1995), in his book on spontaneous healing, discusses the often overlooked power of expectancy that is expressed by the medical profession, often unwittingly, through negative predictions and attribution. Expectancy is no more evident than in the field of transforming personality. Many mental health professionals openly discuss their skepticism about the possibility that personality can be transformed. This view is often reinforced by other systems, such as managed care companies, who pronounce that personality disorders are not treatable conditions.

These attitudes are communicated to patients and often reinforce a popularly held belief that personality cannot be changed. This attitude is detrimental to the delivery of effective psychotherapy. Paradox may, at times, be an effective intervention, but therapists must realize that their attitudes about change are consciously and unconsciously communicated to families. In my clinical experience, I have observed that even small changes in behavior patterns, attitudes, or emotional reactions can have an enormous influence on personality. I have witnessed a seemingly hopeless individual on the fringe of society experience a quantum change, triggered by a near death experience that primed the pump of the change process and resulted in major personality transformation. I have watched the evolution of families, in which some branches have managed to extricate themselves from generations of pathology and establish better lives for themselves and their progeny.

I began this book with an example of the often dismal and condemning attitude expressed by some mental health professionals. A six-year-old boy was labeled a "natural born killer." Such labels and language used in a moralistic or condemning fashion may influence the treatment of this child; the system may have a difficult time remaining optimistic and continuing to treat this boy as a product of the complex biopsychosocial model that exists in the relational system. Ninety percent of abusive parents were themselves abused as children; one of the five leading causes of death for children under age twelve is homicide (Emory & Laumann-Billings, 1998).

CONTROVERSY OVER THE LANGUAGE OF LABELING

Before proceeding, I want to identify a current controversy in the field of health. There has been a reaction to the pathology and deficit model of human behavior that is the foundation of modern psychology and psychiatry. In its place, many clinicians have recommended a health model that is not based on the concept of pathology. When pathology is described and labeled, as I have been doing in this volume, there is the possibility that labeling will be used to confine and limit rather than expand and promote growth. Anderson (1996) expresses concern about "the strong effect labeling might have on the forming of the labeled" (p. 123). Social constructionism goes even further, with its point of view that questions whether the development of relational diagnosis is a worthwhile pursuit (Gergen et al., 1996). Gergen et al. raise many valid questions that must be struggled with:

> What is the intent of a diagnosis? What questions are believed to be answered by diagnosis? What information is thought to be gained? What do we want a diagnosis to communicate and to whom? If there are many ways to think about, to describe what may be thought of as the same thing (i.e., behaviors, feelings), how can we respect and work within all realities? Should we consider the possibility of multiple diagnoses? How can we bring the client into the process? How can, and is it possible for, a diagnosis to be meaningful for all involved? How can it be collaborative, tailored to the individual, useful? What other words can we use? If we reject diagnostic terms, should we try to persuade the helping system to change its nosology? How do we develop a way in which multi-verses can coexist? (p. 105)

I have already addressed many of these questions, and the rest will be discussed throughout the remainder of this book. The social constructionistic perspective is an important part of a dialectic process that serves to alert therapists that we have gone too far in the direction of misusing language, that we have narrowed the range of options and reduced expectancies. Much of this divisive language seems to be a reaction to the hopelessness that many practitioners have experienced while working with difficult populations; this hopelessness may have led to complacency among mental health practitioners. Our attitudes, beliefs, and labels are aspects of our metalanguage that may occur outside our awareness.

ASPECTS OF METACOMMUNICATION

All behavior represents a communication; this communication may be expressed actively or passively, as by an individual in a catatonic state. In their classic book, *Pragmatics of Human Communication*, Watzlawick, Beavin, and Jackson (1967) introduced seminal axioms of metacommunication. The most cited axiom is "the impossibility of not communicating," which they elaborate on as follows:

> First of all, there is a property of behavior that could hardly be more basic and is, therefore, often overlooked: behavior has no opposite. In other words, there is no such thing as nonbehavior or, to put it even more simply: one cannot *not* behave. (p. 48)

To accept this assumption is to believe that all behavior is interactional and communicative. All behavior and inactivity communicates and influences others. This axiom is one of the basic tenets of systems theory. As therapists we enter the system and become part of the metacommunication about change; therefore, we need to understand our own assumptions as well as the system we are engaging.

ACKNOWLEDGING AND CHALLENGING ASSUMPTIONS ABOUT CHANGE

What we as therapists say to our patients and families emerges from our deeply held assumptions about human nature, the human condition, and the capacity for change. When we don't really believe that people can make major changes in their personality and systems, we become limited by these expectations. We as therapists must challenge these assumptions. We will not be able to take our patients and families to places that we can't imagine. I encourage therapists to think in the language of possibility.

THE LANGUAGE OF POSSIBILITY

Patients and their families are often stuck in a defeated position and feel hopeless about change. The system may also exhibit strong motivation to defeat the therapeutic process and thereby hang on to the familiar and predictable. Negative language is such an intrinsic part of personality disturbance that therapists can become immune to its powerful effect. The therapist must expand the field of operation and challenge the defeated language; otherwise, the therapy will be sunk in a morass of hopelessness and helplessness. The therapist should ask questions that go to the core of the defeated position: "Why don't you think you could change this pattern or behavior?" The therapist at other times may have to go with the resistance and ask, "Why should you change?" The language of possibilities encourages people to fantasize about what they want to change or how they would like their lives to be different.

The language of possibility expands rather than limits the framework. Language that expands the framework approaches the idea of change with questions like, "Why can't you change your attitude?" or "What stops you from changing this behavior if you desire?" Inevitably the clinician will engage the patient's negativistic thinking and resistance to change that blocks options. A typical response is, "We have tried this or that, and it didn't work." This response can then be challenged, and cognitive restructuring or systemic interventions can proceed.

The language of possibility views incremental change as a synergistic process. Language that reinforces and affirms incremental change is valuable to the process. Incremental steps often activate important systemic changes that further enlarge the scope of change.

The language of possibility believes that an individual's will can be stimulated. The concept of will is central to psychotherapy and change. Often, patients and families enter treatment without much evidence of the will to change. Usually a series of demoralizing life experiences have crushed the will. Therapists can pick a focus that is likely to be successful and then allow the patient to own the gain; this method gradually strengthens and builds motivation. Patients find that changing one aspect of their life can inspire hope.

The language of possibility recognizes that human beings are capable of great feats and have much untapped potential. A belief in the potential for change is not necessarily an element of most therapists' belief systems. Throughout history, however, many average individuals have achieved great feats or overcome tremendous obstacles that challenge assumptions about the human capacity for change.

PARADOX, COUNTERPARADOX, AND CHANGING THE FRAME

Watzlawick, Weakland, and Fisch (1974) comment on the language of paradox:

> On the one hand, although logic and common sense offer excellent solutions when they work, who has not had the frustrating experience of doing his very

best in these terms, only to see things going from bad to worse? On the other hand, every once in a while we experience some "illogical" and surprising but welcome change in a troublesome stalemate. Indeed, the theme of the puzzling, uncommonsensical solution is an archetypal one, reflected in folklore, fairy tales, humor, and many dreams—just as there are both popular and more erudite conceptions of the perversity of other people, the world, or the devil to explain the converse situation. (p. xiii)

CONFUSION

Milton Erickson taught that confusion was often a precursor to reframing: Thus, confusion is an important step in the process of reframing and effecting second order change (see Watzlawick et al., 1994). Many therapists cannot tolerate confusion in themselves or their patients and may rush in prematurely to reduce the confusion.

REFRAMING

The technique of *reframing* (Minuchin & Fishman, 1981; Watzlawick et al., 1974) is to view the problem in a more positive intention or denote a positive connotation (Seaburn et al., 1995). "To reframe, then, means to change the conceptual and/or emotional setting or viewpoint in relation to which a situation is experienced and to place it in another frame which fits the 'facts' of the same concrete situation equally well or even better, and thereby changes the entire meaning" (Watzlawick et al., p. 95). This technique has also been variously called *noble ascription* (Stanton & Todd, 1979) and *positive connotation* (Selvini-Palazzoli, Boscolo, Cecchin, & Prata, 1978). Reframing is a method of utilizing language to open up the possibility for change. Reframing is used in individual, couple, and family therapy. In individual therapy, for example, a patient who is manifesting characteristic defensive responding can benefit from an explanation about these adaptive responses to certain dysfunctional family patterns and dynamics. A man who is severely emotionally numb can be reminded that his emotional reaction was a method for handling the affective storms of a disturbed mother, but behavior that may have been adaptive in that context may now be limiting his enjoyment of life and capacity for closeness and intimacy. In couples therapy, reframing may be used to help the family see the benefit of a triangular configuration. The therapist can point out to the couple that while the affair was going on, neither had to face the emotional and sexual issues. Not until the affair was in the open did the couple decide to work at their marriage.

THE COUNTERFORCE—THE LANGUAGE OF RESISTANCE

Counteracting the language of possibility is the language of resistance, which is the counterforce to will, hope, and transformation. Resistance is a natural phenomenon that protects people from the anxiety of change and the unknown. Therapists have all heard variations of the cliche, "The devil we know is better than the one we don't know." Therapists must have many methods for working with resistance, or therapy will be swamped. Many approaches and models of therapy deal with resistance in a direct or indirect manner. Watzlawick et al. (1974) discuss the common dilemma encountered by the therapist:

> Uncommonsensical as it may seem to the layman, quite a few people seem to enter therapy not for the purpose of resolving a problem and being themselves changed in the process, but behave as if they wanted to defeat the expert and presumably "prove" thereby that the problem cannot be solved, while at the same time they clamor for immediate help. Eric Berne has called a very similar pattern the "Why don't you—yes but" game. Within the context of reason and common sense, this attitude establishes a typical impasse in which somebody's demand for help leads to common-sense advice from others, to which he responds with more of the same (i.e., with more reasons why this advice cannot be used, and with more demands for "better" help), to which others react with giving more common-sense help, and so on. In terms of the pragmatics of human communication, they respond to him predominantly on the *content* level and ignore his communications on the *relationship* level—until sooner or later, usually later, the relationship becomes so painful or frustrating that one party or the other gives up in desperation or anger. (pp. 133–134)

Watzlawick et al. suggest a number of powerful interventions for handling resistance and addressing the metacommunications of systems. These interventions are discussed in the following sections.

Why Should You Change?
Therapists are often in the position of recommending change or suggesting how to go about it. When resistance is high and there is an investment in

the pattern, albeit a destructive one, the therapist may be better off challenging the rules of the game or the metacommunication. No matter how competent, dedicated, or hardworking the therapist is, the family has the power to sabotage the process. The system often wants to change but is looking for a painless way to do so. By taking the position, *"Why should you change?"* and by challenging the need for change, the therapist can assist the system or subsystem in finding their motivation and will to change. Couples, for example, who come to treatment after years of circular conflict that has never been addressed are highly invested in their stalemate. They are aware at an unconscious level that changing the pattern will require an increase in existential anxiety and pain in choices and personal responsibility.

One couple who had spent 20 years in a marriage that looked perfect to the outside world was asked, "Why should you change this pattern?" The couple was financially successful and appeared to have it all. The wife had sacrificed her personality in the name of the marriage; the husband was a controller who could not allow his wife to express any thought of her own. Change for this couple would require substantial pain and anxiety. Either they would have to rework their entire marriage or get a divorce. They had no way around the pain. Instead of encouraging them to face their pain squarely, the therapist asked why, at this point in their lives, they would want to tackle such an enormous task that would clearly result in substantial pain and suffering.

The Judo Technique
The judo technique requires the therapist to accept the forces of resistance and turn them around on the family so that the resistance is confirmed as having important value. "In more than one sense this form of problem resolution is similar to the philosophy and technique of judo, where the opponent's thrust is not opposed by a counterthrust of at least the same force, but rather accepted and amplified by yielding and going with it" (Watzlawick et al., 1974, p. 104). This position requires that the therapist abandon the notion of change by counterforce. When the system expects a counterforce from the therapist, the therapist instead moves with the resistance. One young woman in a PscDps had a family who was exerting a great deal of pressure on her to find employment after she had been dismissed from a previous job for irrational behavior. She responded to the pressure with increasing stubbornness and avoidance, retreating to her bed. This behavior escalated the family's controlling attempts to get her on the right track, or at least get her in the train. The therapist went along with her lack of desire to work and supported her right to live on welfare or be-

come a street person if she wished. Once the woman's attempt to assert her ability to destroy herself if she wished was validated, she then began talking about her interest in finding a job.

Relapse Prediction
Relapse is part and parcel of working with dysfunctional personologic systems. Relapse is inevitable and should be accepted as a valuable learning experience. The therapist can use relapse prediction as a method to deal with the inevitable resistance to change. The spiral model of change shows that, after a period of growth, patients often have a tendency to backslide or relapse. This relapse can be predicted to occur by the therapist and accepted as a normal part of growth and recovery.

Prescribing the Symptom
Systemically oriented theorists view the symptomatic presentation as a communication. The DevDps, for example, often communicates that they can't tolerate the pain of their children growing up or their death anxiety or their concerns about being alone. Therefore, the symptom presentation is a metacommunication by the system. Prescribing the symptom is a method of creating a paradoxical injunction: "You really ought to hang on to your children as long as possible because childhood is so short-lived!" Once the symptom is prescribed, it can no longer be viewed as a spontaneously occurring phenomenon. A symptom that is thus performed allows the patient to express volition (Watzlawick et al., 1967). In the case of a young man whose presenting symptom is agoraphobia in the setting of a DevDps, for example, the therapist might encourage the father to drive the son to job interviews because his son has such a crippling condition. The son should be refrained from leaving the house for any other occasion. Thus, the dependency is encouraged and will be resisted.

CASE STUDY: THE ENTITLED MAN WHO HELD HIS PARENTS HOSTAGE

The parents of a man in his 30s came for consultation. The family system fit the profile of a NarDps. In this very wealthy family, one of the children, the son, was tied by a financial leash to his parents. There was a clear pattern of enabling and rescuing this son from his many falls in business and in life. He worked for his father and demanded special financial considerations. When those favors were not met, he informed his parents that they would not see their grandchildren, whom they were quite fond of and interested in. This extortion had tremendous impact on the parents. They blamed one another for their son's difficulties, blame that escalated into severe marital conflict. In one session, it was suggested that they deliver the following message to their son by telegram.

> Please don't contact us until you are ready to stand on your own two feet. We are off to Europe.
> Love, Mom and Dad.

This paradoxical communication served to remove the parents as victims of their son's entitlement. It also took the wind out of the son's sails in terms of the power of his emotional rejection of them. The parents were planning a vacation together for the first time in many years and were encouraged to go and enjoy themselves and allow their son to learn how to stand on his own two feet. The marital subsystem was strengthened, and the son detriangulated from his parents' marriage.

DETERMINING THE DEEP STRUCTURE

The deep structure of the individual or the system must be recovered so that it can be modified. "The importance of clear sensory channels, the uncovering of patterns of coping with stress learned in the family system, the childhood traumas, the imposition of therapeutic double binds—are all examples of the emphases which the various forms of psychotherapy have selected as their way of challenging the client's impoverished model" (Bandler & Grinder, 1975, p. 45). This deep structure can be observed in various intrapsychic, interpersonal, and systemic triangular configurations. The deep structure is communicated both verbally and nonverbally by the system.

The Language of Emotions — Facilitating Emotional Development

The emotional language of most dysfunctional personologic systems is quite limited, as is the access to emotion. This affective/cognitive matrix is compromised by developmental vicissitudes and trauma that occur within the relational context and by associated communication disturbance of the dysfunctional personologic system. The ability to use language to mediate and control emotional overreactions is often lacking, like it is in small children. This capacity for emotional language, or emotional intelligence (Goleman, 1994), is also underdeveloped in the various types of dysfunctional personologic systems that have been presented in this book. The language of feelings and emotions needs to be demonstrated and taught to the family and individual. Many patients do not possess an emotional vocabulary; the therapist needs to address this lack of words and formulate a remedial plan of affective education. Other patients have the words but are not connected to the emotions. Still other families seem allergic to any emotional expression and quickly become somatic when an emotional breakthrough is imminent.

Affective science has underscored the adaptive value of the often trivialized statement, "getting in touch with your emotions." Ekman and Davidson (1994), in their groundbreaking work *The Nature of Emotion*, bring together a number of scientists of affective science who support the contention that "quick onset is central to the adaptive value of emotions, mobilizing us quickly to respond to important events" (p. 16). Also, humans' ability to label emotions with appropriate words is a crucial element of our intimate capacities (Pankseep, 1994). If we cannot differentiate and label our affective state, we must rely on others to interpret and reflect. In the same book, Pankseep writes: "Few individuals need any formal training to know what it means to feel happy, sad, frustrated and angry, scared, full of lust or other innumerable desires, or to identify the environmental events that trigger these feelings" (p. 20). However, clinicians who work in the world of dysfunctional personologic systems and personologic disorders are well aware that this quotation presents a precise description of what hasn't occurred but needs to be remedied.

One of the major goals of therapists who work with dysfunctional personologic systems is to advance emotional development of the members within the system and of the system as a whole. Izard (1994) delineates this concept of emotional development:

> Conceived as an integral part of individual or personality development, emotional development might be viewed primarily as a matter of achieving intersystem connections and communication lines. Indeed, much of the current body of research on emotional development concerns the development of relations between the cognitive and emotional systems. I think of this aspect of emotional development as the development of affective-cognitive structures and view these phenomena as the most common building blocks of mind, memory, and the traits of personality. (p. 356)

Emotional development is facilitated in the context of the system in which individuals live and is shaped by the quality of their interpersonal relationships. This process begins at birth, and some theorists even believe that the interpersonal milieu occurs in vitro as the developing fetus experiences the maternal hormonal bath that communicates her affective state.

Current research is providing insight into early observations about the "unfocused, unclear, and contradictory" family transactions that characterize schizophrenic families (Miklowitz, 1995). The concept of communication deviance (CD) was introduced by Wynne and Singer (1963) and refers to a familywide communication disturbance. This line of research was further developed by Brown, Birley, and Wing (1972) and by Vaughn and Leff (1976) in their categorization of risk among families using the concept of expressed emotion (EE). High EE is seen in families with a high level of criticism, hostility, or emotional overinvolvement (characterized by too much concern and overprotection). When EE is high, the risk of relapse for psychiatric disorders such as mood disorder and schizophrenia is higher. A stress-diathesis model predicts that if the genetic predisposition is high and EE is high, the co-occurrence of personality pathology will exist in the context of a dysfunctional personologic system. Therefore, therapists might also be alert for personality pathology that could benefit from treatment.

NONVERBAL COMMUNICATION

Nonverbal communication provides the therapist with a great deal of information about the change process and unconscious communication patterns. Grinder and Bandler (1976) suggest that the therapist attend to the following visual and auditory communications:

Visual Paramessages
1. The person's hands;
2. The person's breathing;
3. The person's legs and feet;
4. The eye fixation patterns;
5. The head/neck/shoulder relationship;
6. The facial expression, especially the eyebrows, the mouth, and the cheek muscles. (p. 60)

Auditory Paramessages
1. The tonality of the person's voice;
2. The tempo of the person's speech;
3. The words, phrases, and sentences used by the person;

4. The volume of the person's voice;
5. The intonation patterns of the person's speech. (p. 61)

Once the therapist becomes aware of and observant of the paramessages communicated by the individual and within the family, he or she can often begin to address the incongruities by assisting the individual and family to come to terms with the communication pattern. In a CNrDps, for example, the index patient refused to speak to his parents about what was upsetting him. Instead he began to play charades with the therapist and to richly communicate his feelings nonverbally. Both parents were embarrassed and attempted to make him act appropriately. The therapist engaged in the nonverbal communication and interpreted these actions to the parents. They were surprised by how accurately the son was dramatizing the family conflict.

METACOMMUNICATION

Metacommunication can be used to amplify the voltage and shock the system into a state of activation. Whitaker (Whitaker & Keith, 1980), the master family therapist who worked from his unconsious process, wrote: "The power to change anything in the family, whether schizophrenia, divorce or internecine fighting, requires a voltage amplification in the suprasystem." Bergantino (1993), who trained with Whitaker and studied his technique, comments: "This is quite different from a great deal of therapy that attempts to minimize anxiety. On the one hand it is important to reduce stress anxiety that accrues from self-torture, but on the other it is important to increase patients' tolerance for existential anxiety as a movement toward a fuller, more engaged way of living" (p. 275).

In one case, a couple entered treatment with an assortment of marital complaints including sexual dysfunction, poor communication, parenting disagreements, and frequent distancing and blowup patterns. Both came from dysfunctional personologic systems. The wife was severely obese, suffered from diabetes, and had a very stressful job. She complained of not having enough of her husband's attention. The issue of her obesity was never mentioned. When the therapist asked the wife how long she had felt suicidal, she and her husband were both startled. Neither one had viewed her overweight in such a stark aspect, even though she had recently been told by her physician to lose weight because of her diabetes. She did nothing about her weight, but the anxiety between the couple escalated. The weight served as another corner of the triangle in their marriage. He would frequently nag her to lose weight; she would claim that she had tried everything but nothing ever worked. She continued to overeat, would frequently binge, and did not exercise. As long as the weight was there, the wife was saved from her husband's demands for a sexual relationship, and he was able to justify his workaholic escape valve. Because they could not openly discuss the seriousness of the situation, they worked at pretending the situation wasn't so bad. When the therapist raised the issue of the wife's premature death, grief was elicited and the couple were able to more fully come to terms with their destructive relational patterns.

SCRIPTS

Transactional analysis focuses attention on the scripts that guide people's lives and that are developed at an early age. There are individual scripts and family scripts, and these two types are intertwined.

CASE STUDY: THE WOMAN WHOSE PARENTS WERE GOING TO THROW HER OFF A BRIDGE

A woman entered treatment later in life for depression following the death of her husband. A family genogram and history indicated a TraDps. The patient reported a lifelong history of abuse, abandonment, placement in foster homes, and violence. She always saw herself as "no good." She had been an illegitimate child, and her parents had contemplated throwing her off a bridge when she was an infant. Her biological father disappeared, and her mother was ashamed. Her mother never talked of the father; instead she projected her hatred and shame onto the patient. The family story of wanting to throw her off the bridge was part of the family legacy that was retold and kept alive. This basic belief that she was "no good" plagued her all her life, and only as a woman in her 60s did she begin to understand the roots of her suffering. She also began to see the generational transmission process that led to estrangement with her own children as a result of abuse by her deceased husband, who she felt had rescued her from hell. Part of her therapy was to rewrite and work through her feelings about her lifelong principle that she was "no damned good."

METAPHOR AND PERSONALITY

The use of metaphor in psychotherapy is another pioneering accomplishment in the field of systemic and family therapy. Metaphors are a way in which the individual and family unconscious process can be spoken to without the activation of defense systems that might surface with more direct forms of communication. Effective use of metaphorical communication is difficult to re-create because it is most effective when it emerges from the unconscious of the therapist, primed by his or her experience with the family or individual. Some therapists are highly gifted in their ability to use metaphorical language that mimics the deep structure of the system or individual. Metaphors provide a useful way of anchoring the metacommunication that often stays with the system or individual long after other aspects of the therapeutic process have receded into the background. Therapists should listen for certain key phrases or words that can be turned into a metaphor that will crystallize the deep structure.

CASE STUDY: THE MAN WHO WAS ALLERGIC TO SUCCESS

The depressive personality-disordered individual often exhibits strong masochistic elements. In this case, the patient had grown up in a NarDps and was continually destroying everything he worked so hard to achieve. The therapist used metaphor to frame his dilemma as an "allergy to success." Each time the patient met with success, he would respond with depression and temper tantrums, which were destroying his relationships with those who supported him. Through this allergic behavior, he was able to maintain his relationship with his father, albeit at a high cost to his development.

A most useful metaphor is to compare personality transformation to what the hermit crab experiences when it needs to shed its shell. When the crab outgrows its shell, it must find a larger one to accommodate its growth. Once it finds a suitable shell, it must leave the old and enter the new. At the moment it leaves the old, it is most vulnerable to any hungry and alert predator. A family who alters their patterns and becomes more adaptive and less rigid is shedding the shell that they protectively lived in. Finding a larger, roomier shell is exciting!

CONCLUSIONS

The manner in which we as therapists experience and understand the family systems that we are engaging relies on our ability to interpret the nonverbal and verbal communication patterns that we are witnessing. The power of language to capitalize on the positive forces of change is enhanced with the use of techniques such as paradox, metaphor, prescribing the symptoms, and reframing. An understanding of the positive and negative currents and their identification within each system will enable the system to view transformation as a viable option in its development.

CHAPTER 10

Treating the Couple Through the Integrative Relational Approach

The most common, essential dyad in dysfunctional personologic systems is the couple. Couples with personality disturbance in one or both members are not an uncommon phenomenon in our society (Masterson, 1988) and probably account for the majority of relational disorders seen in treatment, especially the refractory cases. In their landmark longitudinal study on personality and family development, Schneewind and Ruppert (1998) describe their study as "based on an approach that views personality and family development in context. This assigns a major role to the relationships between parents and children, between (marriage) partners, and among members of the entire family" (p. 32). The couple dyad is the most common intergenerational transmission vehicle for the dysfunctional personologic system. It is therefore paramount that work with the dysfunctional personologic system include therapeutic interventions aimed at restructuring the dyad either directly or indirectly.

Various authors have begun to address characteristics and features as well as treatment implications for couples with personality disorders. Solomon (1996) describes the dynamics and therapeutic goals of the borderline couple. McCormack (1989) identifies the borderline-schizoid constellation and its treatment with long-term intensive couples therapy. Glickauf-Hughes (1996) delineates some of the criteria and treatment approaches to sadomasochistic interactions, and Nichols (1996) focuses his attention on relationships between antisocial and histrionic personality-disordered individuals. Slavik,

Carlson, and Sperry (1992) recommend conjoint therapy when one member displays passive-aggressive pathology. These dyadic relationships all require an understanding of the complementary communication process and systemic dynamics that occur in the couple. The therapy of these dysfunctional personologic dyads is not formulaic; "each couple is unique in what they need for negotiating each stage of development" (McCormack, p. 307). However, certain themes and similarities can be observed. There are fundamental problems in couples in which one or both members suffer from personality disturbance. The greater degree of disturbance in the individuals, the more likely it is that the relationship will be disturbed, will lack differentiation, and will compromise the other subsystems. Nichols (1988) states his assumption "that most family therapy eventually becomes marital therapy, either in an informal, implicit sense or in a formal, explicit manner"(p. 5).

THE DISTURBED PERSONOLOGIC COUPLE—A DYAD PRONE TO TRIANGULAR CONFIGURATIONS

When two individuals couple, they are entering into both a real and an imagined contract to meet one another's real and unrealistic needs. "The emotional challenge of long-term coupling is for each partner to adjust his or her needs and wants to the demands of the relationship" (Gerson, 1995, p. 97). Generally speaking, individuals establish relationships with another person who is developmentally at the same level. McCormack (1989) comments on the findings noted by many clinicians:

> Marriage is not a random event, and the choice of marital partners is understandable, even if not understood. The spouses are on approximate levels of personality organization and share developmental needs, even if these are not apparent. The pace at which both spouses come to accept shared responsibility for the marriage is determined by their level of defensive needs. (p. 303)

The unstable dyad, as has been mentioned in previous chapters, is prone to various triangular configurations. Guerin et al. (1996) describe the various triangular forms that the unstable dyad may assume, including extramarital relationships, in-law triangles (wedding gift triangle, loyalty triangle, and dominant father-in-law triangle), social network triangles, and occupational triangles. When a couple cannot maintain the intimacy or resolve their relational struggles, they very naturally develop multiple triangular configurations to stabilize their relationship and reduce their anxiety to a manageable level. Unfortunately, this tendency results in a stagnation of the natural maturation that would occur in less compromised couples. Understanding the dynamics and systemic issues necessitates knowledge of the various stages in the family life cycle.

THE FAMILY LIFE CYCLE

Carter and McGoldrick (1980), in their seminal work on the family life cycle, identified six distinct stages traversed by most couples. Each couple will navigate these stages in a unique manner depending on the type and severity of personality pathology and dysfunctional relationship. The six stages are:

1. The launching of the single young adult.
2. The joining of families through marriage.
3. Families with young children.
4. Families with adolescents.
5. Launching children and moving on.
6. Families in later life. (p. 17)

The point in the family life cycle at which any subsystem or individual of the dysfunctional personologic system accesses treatment is crucial to understand. As I have presented in previous chapters, the goal should always be to have maximal input at crucial fulcrum points. An understanding of how normal life cycle transitions are exaggerated for the dysfunctional personologic system allows the clinician to utilize these stressful transitions in order to engage the system and often broaden the range of treatment intervention.

Personality pathology in its various forms and levels of severity compromises smooth transitions through the family life cycle and are often points at which the dysfunctional system seeks treatment. "When a family has difficulty meeting the challenges of a particular life cycle or moving on to the next stage, there may be a crisis" (Gerson, 1995, p. 99).

1. *The launching of the single young adult.* Leaving home is often a difficult task that may become problematic for many (Haley, 1977). The manner in which the adolescent moves into adulthood and becomes autonomous sets the stage for later developmental challenges and how these challenges are resolved. The type of dysfunctional personologic system might predict some of the issues that will arise; the therapist can then move to intervene and smooth out the developmental process. In some types of dysfunctional personologic systems,

the adolescent is prematurely launched into pseudoautonomy after a blowup with a parent and a decision to move out or run away. This action may interfere with pursuing a trade or higher education, which obviously can have dire consequences for the adolescent. Some of these adolescents or children are motivated by a desire to get away from the abuse that occurs in their family system. In other cases, the family is unwilling to encourage the separation and individuation because of the anxiety that is aroused in the couple.

2. *The joining of families through marriage.* When individuals come together in a committed relationship they are required to shift their primary attachments from their nuclear family to their new relationship. For many individuals from dysfunctional personologic systems, this transition is very difficult to achieve and may in fact continue to be a struggle after many years of marriage. Often the original loyalty ties are so strong that they interfere with the development of a solid and stable marital dyad. One configuration that may develop is what Guerin et al. (1996) term the wedding gift triangle, in which the husband turns his relationship to his mother over to his wife. This configuration may exacerbate symptoms in the husband and blur his attachment.

3. *Families with young children.* The arrival of children is often another major stressor for the dysfunctional personologic system. Depending on the type of system, the arrival of children will have a differential effect. For instance, in the NarDps the arrival of a child might severely activate the narcissistic issues in the male, who feels that he has moved from center stage and that he cannot sustain the wife in her nurturing of the child. It is not uncommon to see this reaction become a precipitant for marital infidelity, which leads the couple to therapy.

4. *Families with adolescents.* Many families find that adolescence is the most difficult period of the family life cycle. Adolescents can create increased tension because of their unique developmental struggles, rapid sexual changes, and mood swings. The resolve of the couple or single parent is often stressed. Parenting disagreements surface with tremendous force. Disagreements over boundaries, limits, and age appropriate behavior are common. For many dysfunctional personologic systems, this period is the "straw that breaks the camel's back." Various comorbid or primary psychological problems—such as eating disorders, conduct disorders, substance use disorders, or suicidal behavior—that have been fueled for years by dysfunctional patterns often emerge in virulent form during this time.

5. *Launching children and moving on.* The cycle continues back to the start, back to the step of launching children into adulthood. As the

next generation of children launch into adulthood, marry, reproduce, and establish their own families, the primary couple may continue to exert power and influence in a variety of positive or negative ways. Some financially well-off NarDps may exert control over their progeny with financial rewards, which can further cripple adult children and rob them of their self-worth.

6. *Family in later life.* As parents mature and age, there is often a reversal in caretaking roles. Children become more responsible for their parents, and parents become more dependent on their children. Adult children from dysfunctional families are often thrust into the position of having to care for or supervise aging, chronically ill, or dying parents with whom they are still highly conflicted. This situation can exacerbate preexisting conflicts and lead to increased personality dysfunction and symptomatic behavior in individuals and in the family system. Already difficult transitions associated with the aging process and increased medical illness can thrust the family system into a state of crisis. Often, aging parents demonstrate personality changes and expect that extended family members will offer forgiveness for past misdeeds without any apology or genuine effort to achieve some resolution.

SHIFTING OF ATTACHMENT

In order to establish an effective couple relationship, each individual must be able to shift his or her primary attachment from the nuclear family to the new dyadic relationship. "The more successful the shift in primary attachment from parents to mate, the greater the influence each person has over the other" (Guerin et al., 1996, p. 170). Gerson (1995) describes this process, first identified by Bowen (1976): "The relational challenge is the shifting of allegiances of each partner from their families of origin to the new family unit while at the same time maintaining the earlier emotional ties" (p. 97).

DIFFERENTIATION

Individuals couple and marry at various levels of differentiation of the self, which directly molds the capacity of the relationship to further development or stifles it. Many undifferentiated individuals move immediately from their primary family to a marriage without having experienced a sufficient level of maturation and differentiation to sustain a vital, healthy marriage. When this abrupt movement occurs, idealization at the beginning of the relationship may quickly turn to disillusionment and negative affect states. Guerin et al. (1996) identify three primary functions of triangles in the couple:

1. *Displacement of conflict.* When the couple has many issues that are not within their means or ego capacities to resolve, conflict is often displaced in the form of the many triangular relationships delineated in this volume. The displacement of conflict is therefore a systemic defense against anxiety over fear of intimacy or abandonment in the couple.

2. *Defense against intimacy.* As I have detailed and described in my previous book (Magnavita, 1997b), intimacy is an approach-avoidance paradox for the personality-disordered individual. The craving for intimacy and closeness is deeply rooted in the primary drive system and is necessary for survival. When a couple is formed, the promise of intimacy is attractive until anxiety over unresolved relational issues unconsciously surfaces. These issues of unresolved loyalty or enmeshment are defended against with individual defenses. This anxiety mobilizes one or both members of the couple toward triangular configurations.

3. *Containment of tension.* When tension in the couple is too high to be metabolized, a third party is often used to stabilize the situation. One couple's anxiety over the partner who was obese and diabetic, for example, led to a triangular configuration with their son, who on one level enjoyed feeling needed by his parents and their desire to have him around but on another level was angry with them over the position they put him in.

CHARACTERISTIC CRISIS POINTS OF COUPLES FROM DYSFUNCTIONAL PERSONOLOGIC SYSTEMS

Some commonly observed crisis points of couples from dysfunctional personologic systems are characteristic of the relational disturbances that each member of the couple brings to the union. Frequently seen are couples with marital infidelity, sexual dysfunction, parenting conflicts, divorce issues, and remarriage complications. Other dysfunctional systems at times have similar issues, but what often differentiates the dysfunctional personologic system is the severity, chronicity (multigenerational manifestation), and interrelatedness that makes these issues complex.

MARITAL INFIDELITY

Many couples and individuals from dysfunctional personologic systems enter therapy to address the disruption created by an extramarital affair. Sometimes the individual is caught in the triangle between his or her lover and spouse and is suffering from severe ambivalence characterized by the question, "I'm not sure which one I want to be with." With other patients, a long-term affair has stabilized a dysfunctional marriage. Yet others come to treatment with serial, seemingly meaningless, dangerous sexual liaisons that virtually destroy their careers and marital relationships. Because the triangular configuration of marital infidelity is often a precipitating event that results in consultation and treatment, the clinician who wishes to comprehensively treat dysfunctional personologic systems should also be adept at navigating the often complex dynamics of extramarital affairs. The discovery of these affairs is often highly traumatic, as Lusterman (1995) describes: "A lengthy extramarital affair causes a remarkable degree of trauma for the discoverer, and often for the other involved parties" (p. 259). Lusterman recommends the model of post-traumatic stress disorder as a tool to understand the often volatile reaction that results in the revelation and reaction to the affair.

Recently there has been increased clinical interest and focus on understanding and treating marital infidelity (Humphrey, 1987; Lusterman, 1995; Moultrup, 1990; Guerin et al., 1996). Lusterman, summarizing the literature, identifies the following types of extramarital sex (EMS): "(1) brief sexual encounters, (2) lengthy relationships that may be emotionally intense and erotically charged, but not necessarily sexual and (3) lengthy affairs that are emotionally and sexually charged" (p. 260). The deception necessary to continue an extramarital affair has severe negative consequences for the marital relationship. The constant deception not only destroys the intimacy and trust but often further consolidates intrapsychic personality pathology.

Peck (1983) in his book *People of the Lie* writes about the gradual erosion of the character that takes place in the individual who lies and deceives. From a personologic standpoint, therefore, an individual who has maintained a long-term affair is utilizing powerful defenses to contain the anxiety over the betrayal and deception. There may be antisocial elements to the individual—histrionic, borderline, and so on—so that it is important for the clinician to have some sense of the individual personality. I have treated a few men who have established separate families while maintaining the illusion of their primary family. The system then functions under the weight of "unknowable" secrets. These relationships, unfortunately, are not as uncommon as we might like to believe. In some cases, there are children with the same names.

Restructuring Extramarital Triangles

Lusterman (1995, p. 267) delineates three phases of treatment of infidelity: (1) restoration of trust, (2) examination of predisposing factors, and (3) rapprochement. One of the first issues in the restructuring of the marital dyad is to assist the unfaithful spouse in making a decision to terminate the affair, which many are unwilling to do. Until the affair is terminated, it is unreasonable to expect that the marital relationship can be improved. The therapist who encounters resistance to the termination of the extramarital affair must allow the individual a period of time to make a decision and explore the consequences and ramifications of the choices.

SEXUAL DYSFUNCTION

Personality disturbance is often associated with forms of sexual dysfunction that may contribute to and intensify marital dissatisfaction. Some personality-disordered individuals suffer from severe forms of sexual dysfunction "varying from premature ejaculation to impotence in men and inability to experience orgasm in women" (Masterson, 1988, p. 123). Other dysfunctions include vaginismus, hypoactive sexual desire, and avoidance of sex. Therapists may see a higher prevalence of certain types of sexual dysfunction in specific personality disorders, such as impotence or ejaculatory dysfunction in narcissistic men, inhibited sexual desire in obsessive-compulsives, and promiscuity in borderline and histrionic personalities. Sexual dissatisfaction is therefore a reason that many couples enter treatment.

Schnarch (1995) also points out that "in family or couples therapy, a couple's sexual and intimacy problems often become evident, either at the outset or later in treatment" (p. 239). He recommends, and I agree, that the therapist must take the initiative to raise the issue of sex and that the therapist must become comfortable with frank discussions.

When couples have a sexual dysfunction or are dissatisfied with their sexual relationship, emotional intimacy is often not being achieved at a satisfactory level. Schnarch (1991) describes his approach in his book *Constructing the Sexual Crucible: An Integration of Sexual and Marital Therapy:* Providing a holding relationship that enables each member of the couple to achieve greater levels of differentiation balances the need for autonomy and togetherness. Guerin et al. (1996) describe the interrelationship among sexual dysfunction, degree of maturity, and infidelity and depict how an affair can stabilize this type of configuration:

> A triangle can, and very often does, allow the relationship system to continue without change and without resolving issues that need to be resolved. For example, an extramarital affair makes it "unnecessary" to address the sexual immaturity of a couple in which one spouse is sexually demanding and the other sexually constricted. The lover is meeting the demands of the spouse having the affair, and that takes the pressure off the constricted spouse, who therefore feels less pressured. If the therapist persuades the spouse having the affair to end it, the sexual issues are likely to become explicit and can be dealt with in treatment. (p. 33)

Individual personality pathology is often reflected in the couple's sexual functioning. For example, the borderline-narcissistic combination may contain a good deal of sexual acting-out, and infidelity may be an ongoing issue. On the other hand, in couples with passive-aggressive, obsessive-compulsive, dependent, and avoidant personalities, sexual functioning may be inhibited or nonexistent. The window that is opened by discussing sexuality and sexual functioning reveals much about the relational system as well as the intrapersonal functions of the individual. Further exploration may also expose a history of sexual abuse and evidence of a dysfunctional personologic system that need assessment and the proper treatment regime. Power and control dynamics may also be revealed. In some cases, it becomes clear that one member of a couple may be suffering from an addictive sexual disorder that has been enabled by a docile or pleasing mate.

In cases in which sexual dysfunction is secondary to the personality pathology and in which disturbance in the relational system enhances differentiation, the therapist should address the tolerance for intimacy and emotional closeness. In cases in which sexual dysfunction is severe and refractory, referral to an appropriate clinician and medical specialist should be made. For some sexual dysfunctions, such as impotence, therapists should seek to rule out organic pathology and contributing medical conditions such as high blood pressure, diabetes, or vascular problems. Most of the time, sexual dysfunction has a personologic and developmental foundation that requires psychotherapeutic intervention. Vaginismus and erectile problems, for example, can often be the result of repressed anger and a defense against intimacy. Erectile problems are often noted in individuals with passive and dependent personalities. The complexity of these issues is a good reason why a team approach, in which various professionals can collaborate and contribute their unique expertise, is highly beneficial for couples with personologic issues.

MALADAPTIVE PARENTING AND CONFLICTING PARENTING STYLES

Maladaptive parenting, including abuse, neglect, and foster care placements, is often associated with various disruptive behavior disorders (Alexander & Pugh, 1996) and is another common reason why a dysfunctional personologic system may initiate treatment. "Child centered problems need to be seen as part of a whole or a larger system. The child never owns the problems solely. The cooperation of the family's intrapsychic and intersystemic patterns and issues provide a setting for the growth and the maintenance of health or dysfunction" (Pitta, 1998, p. 24). Parent-child relational disturbances may also contribute to learning disabilities and attention deficit disorders. According to Beren (1998), learning disabilities and attention deficit may be partially a function of familial and cultural narcissism. In fact, what therapists may be observing in some of these disturbances is an artifact of a certain type and severity of dysfunctional personologic system. Morrel (1998) points out, and I have witnessed in some NarDps and CNrDps, that some parents attempt to find the right medication that will provide them with a perfect child, one that reflects their narcissistic needs. These parents want the child to be fixed without the parents' engaging in any self-reflection.

Parenting assessments are useful tools to help the therapist to determine one aspect of the degree of dysfunction and type of dysfunctional personologic system.

SEPARATION AND DIVORCE

Although no statistics confirm this observation, clinical experience suggests that dysfunctional personologic systems have a higher rate of divorce than do less dysfunctional families. Couples and individuals enter therapy in various stages of the divorce process. Some are contemplating separation or divorce as a way to extricate themselves from the unresolved and seemingly unresolvable pain of the relationship. "The intense anxiety raised by a possible breakup may motivate the couple to enter therapy" (Kaslow, 1995, p. 271). The therapist needs to know where in the process the couple and each member is. Couples often come to treatment with unrealistic expectations; each member usually expects that the partner will change. Many sessions start out with a litany of the faults of the other member. In conducting treatment with couples considering or entering into a divorce process, the therapist needs to get a reading from the couple as to how they view the relationship and if they hope to improve it. By the time many couples enter treatment, it is too late; the couple is looking for the therapist to pronounce the relationship moribund and assist with the grief process.

The Three Painful Choices

Because patients are often in a state of confusion and are involved in complex and repetitive relational interactions, I find it useful to assist them in attaining some clarity. I usually inform them that they have three choices: "One, you can continue to go the way you are. Two, you can separate or file for divorce. Or three, you may elect to work on the marriage to improve the situation. Obviously, whichever choice you select to pursue, the process will be painful. Working on a long-neglected marriage is very painful, but so is divorce and so is staying together and continuing to live the same problems for the next ten or fifteen or however many years." Most couples recognize that there is no easy way out of the dilemma. An extramarital affair may have stabilized the situation, but the cost was high for both parties. Partners may have escaped into work or into drugs, alcohol, or other forms of anesthesia.

Many of these marital relationships may seem hopeless, but the fact that one or both of the couple have entered treatment presents an opportunity to achieve some treatment gain. If the couple decides to stay together and work on the marriage, the other members in the system can benefit from the enhanced capacities of the couple. If they decide to divorce, the therapy can provide for a smoother termination and, especially when children are involved, a far better outcome. Working with a couple through their divorce often affords the therapist the opportunity to help both parties resolve their issues so that the same mistakes are not made in their next relationship.

STAGES AND DYNAMICS OF DIVORCE

A couple must navigate various stages before their "legal divorce marks the culmination of a painful process that began earlier in the marriage and has numerous sequelae in the postdivorce period" (Kaslow, 1995, p. 271). These stages include (1) predivorce, or the emotional divorce; (2) legal aspects;

(3) economic divorce; (4) coparenting and custody issues; (5) community, social, and extended family aspects; (6) religious aspects; and (7) psychic divorce.

As Kaslow (1995) points out, and which is true of couples from dysfunctional personologic systems, the greater degree of dysfunction that existed prior to the breakdown of the marriage, the greater is the degree of acrimony and bitterness. Many individuals remain stuck in a pathological grief reaction and are not able to resume their life in a meaningful way. Kaslow reminds us that "[a] family systems perspective should be maintained because changes in one family member will affect other family members" (p. 281).

Divorce mediation offers the couple an alternative to the adversarial process that often occurs in these systems. "The purpose of divorce mediation is to help couples resolve conflicts and to make their own decisions concerning child custody and visitation, division of property, child support, and spousal support" (Sauber, Beiner, & Meddoff, 1995, p. 285). In my experience, mediation is not often seen as an option for the couple from a dysfunctional personologic system. However, some couples have been able to make themselves amenable to this less adversarial divorce process. Sauber et al. outline various types of divorce mediation—integrative, structured, therapeutic, and negotiatory—that all contend with potential imbalances in power, especially if one party is submissive or financially weaker. An understanding of each partner's personality configuration and an understanding of the relational dynamics can help the clinician make a better determination. For example, mediation for two high-achieving, narcissistic professionals has a better chance of being equitable than does mediation in a couple in which one party is a passive-submissive homemaker and the other is a narcissistic attorney who commands much authority and power.

One positive outcome of divorce mediation is that the therapist may be able to engage one or both parties in follow-up treatment. The therapist can then shift the frame of treatment to the personologic work that needs to be achieved in order to prepare the individual for future relationships and postdivorce family demands. Children who have suffered the consequences of long-standing marital dispute can often be engaged in treatment for preventive work, to address any developing personality pathology before it becomes consolidated.

REMARRIAGE AND BLENDING SYSTEMS

Dysfunctional personologic systems often enter treatment to deal with the stress of blending families following divorce. Sometimes these systems are very complex, so it is imperative that a careful and thorough history and genogram be attained. Approximately 33 percent of children in the United States will live in a stepfamily before age 18 (Glick, 1989). Probably a disproportionate percentage of these families are dysfunctional personologic systems. When treating a blended dysfunctional personologic system, the clinician needs to carefully consider the stage of the family life cycle to better understand the issues that the family is struggling with. Various factors need to be considered, such as age of parents and children and their relationships with biological relatives. "Thus, the multiple developmental trajectories of family members and the stepfamily life cycle are important to consider in understanding the functioning of stepfamilies" (Bray, 1995, p. 126). Bray's comparison of clinical and nonclinical stepfamilies showed that "clinical stepfamilies reported less-effective problem solving, less spousal individuation, poorer marital adjustment, and more negative and less positive child-parent interactions than nonclinical stepfamilies" (pp. 134–135).

TREATMENT CONSIDERATIONS

The basic couples treatment strategy is for the therapist to provide a holding environment, a container for the work of increased differentiation, restructured defenses, emotional development, and capacity for intimacy and closeness. The degree of difficulty will increase as the level of personality disturbance moves to the more severe types and pathology. Treating two borderlines in a couples format will be highly taxing without the support of individual or other treatment modalities.

Establish Basic Personality Structure of Couple
The basic personality type and structure of each member of the couple should be assessed. The therapist needs to determine, for example, if one member is structurally at the neurotic level and the other at a psychotic level.

Determine Basic Emotional Transaction That Limits Couple's Development
The therapist should determine the basic emotional transaction between the couple and begin to develop the couple's awareness about how this transaction limits emotional growth and satisfaction.

Develop Awareness for What Intimacy Is and Enhance Level of Intimacy
Masterson (1988) points out the dilemma that I have previously termed the *approach/avoidance paradox:*

A close emotional involvement with another person activates and reawakens his fear of being engulfed or abandoned. If he gets too close the feelings of being pulled back into the symbiotic whirlpool become too intense. If he gets too far away, the possibility of being abandoned looms before him. (p. 113)

The capacity to build an intimate relationship is necessary for the healthy functioning of the couple. Each type of personality pathology has a different, distorted version of what intimacy is (Masterson). The borderline seeks a mate who will support him or her through regressive episodes; the narcissistic looks for perfect mirroring and admiration; the dependent looks to be taken care of; the avoidant looks to be excused for not facing responsibility; the passive-aggressive looks to remain self-centered; and so forth. The relational field between the couple is set by their personality style and is endlessly reinforced in their patterns of interaction. The therapist should encourage nondefensive communication and expression of feeling. Defensive responses that block intimacy should be pointed out, and awareness of how such responses stifle intimacy should be underscored.

Develop an Awareness of and Address Codependency
Couples with personality pathology are likely to have issues with codependency. Codependency is another way to describe the lack of differentiation that is evident in the self-structure of the two individuals and to describe the poor differentiation that extends to the relational field of the couple.

THE RESISTANT COUPLE

Couples may be resistant to treatment. Resistance takes many forms. One common form is when one spouse refuses to participate in couples therapy. In other forms of resistance, one spouse may try to control the treatment by canceling sessions after a fight, by not rescheduling, or by not showing up for a scheduled session.

Encourage Treatment-Engaged Spouse to Continue to Attend Treatment
Generally speaking, therapists will find it useful to encourage the treatment-engaged spouse to continue to attend sessions and to not pressure the spouse to attend. If the therapist feels uncomfortable shifting to an individual format, he or she can make a referral. In my experience, however, it is better to continue with a spouse in individual treatment because transferring the person to another therapist may be interpreted as a rejection.

Use Spouse as Therapist Extender

When one member of a couple seeks out therapy but the other is resistant and initially unwilling to participate, the therapist can often use the participating partner to function as an extender for the therapeutic process. Systems theorists assume that changes made in one member of the system will affect the rest of the system. Using the involved spouse as a therapy extender capitalizes on this principle. The therapist can coach and direct the patient in various methods of direct communication, limit setting, and constructive feedback. Eventually the resistant spouse will agree to participate. Sometimes the therapeutically engaged member of the couple has an unconscious motivation to keep spouse out of treatment. This motivation usually involves the triangular relationship that has developed among the therapist, patient, and noninvolved spouse. Including the spouse will trigger intimacy anxiety in the engaged spouse, because the triangular configuration will be brought under therapeutic control and the anxiety will no longer be displaced onto the third party, the therapist.

COUPLE COMBINATIONS

Various combinations of couples exhibit different and similar forms of personality pathology. This very interesting area requires future clinical research. At the beginning of this chapter I mentioned some of the research reported by various investigators, but obviously these reports only scratch the surface of possible combinations. It would be impossible to cover the multitude of combinations and their dynamics in one chapter or even in one volume, so what I have included here are some commonly seen combinations that deserve attention and that can be used as models for less frequently occurring combinations.

The Borderline and Narcissistic Couple

The borderline and narcissistic couple is the classic example of being caught between a rock and a hard place. This combination represents one of the more primitive combinations seen in clinical practice. The borderline requires a tremendous amount of emotional caretaking and is often moving from one crisis to another. The narcissistic individual may at first enjoy the special feeling of being idealized by the mate, but when the climate shifts and devaluation occurs, a highly conflictual situation may quickly escalate to self-destructive gestures or physical violence. The therapist can best handle this combination by placing both members of this couple in individual treatment and in conjoint couples therapy. The narcissistic member of the couple will generally tend to view the therapy as less important, which may require the therapist to help the engaged spouse individuate and start to address issues in a constructive fashion.

The Narcissistic and Cluster C (Dependent, Avoidant, Obsessive-Compulsive) Couple

Narcissists are controlling by nature and often attract those who are seemingly not so in control. These combinations are often described as codependent. As long as the non-narcissistic spouse is paying homage, the ego of the narcissistic spouse will remain intact; but when ego supplies aren't forthcoming, a crisis may result. The repressed personality disorders are often attracted to the narcissist's assertive style and confident manner.

The Histrionic and Passive-Aggressive Couple

This couple struggles on all fronts with activation. The passive-aggressive individual often has difficulty with activation, so the histrionic spouse is constantly attempting to get his or her attention. This struggle creates more negative feelings, which are expressed with greater degrees of passive nonresponding.

The Borderline and Obsessive-Compulsive Couple

This configuration is drawn to one another primarily for affective reasons. The borderline seeks the calm, organized, intellect-driven style of the obsessive but becomes disappointed about the lack of affective intensity. The obsessive looks to the spouse for his or her unacknowledged and feared emotionality.

The Schizoid and Cluster C (Avoidant, Dependent, Obsessive) or Histrionic Couple

The schizoid is looking for attachment and emotion but is often enticed and overwhelmed by the affective responding of the histrionic. This combination actually works to a certain degree for some higher functioning schizoid personality-disordered individuals in that the schizoid can become more comfortable, although at times he or she may be overwhelmed by the emotion.

CASE STUDY: THE WOMAN WHO BELIEVED SHE WAS INCOMPETENT

This client came for consultation with a presenting complaint of depression. In the following session, she revealed that she was involved in an ongoing affair. The patient was very concerned and could not understand why she continued to deceive her husband, whom she described as a "nice guy." Her father had behaved in a similar way, and it was apparent that through this affair she was maintaining her attachment to him. After a course of individual work, the patient, who manifested dependent and avoidant personality features, agreed to invite her husband in for consultation. Their relationship was structured in an unusual manner in the care-taking of their three children: The husband was the primary force and the wife's role was peripheral. He was responsible for most of the parenting; whenever she expressed any anxiety about parenting, he would step in and relieve her so that she never had the opportunity to master her anxiety. The couple evaluation revealed, however, that he was highly emotionally detached, unresponsive, and parental with his wife, who was a well-functioning teacher in a private school. Family history on the wife's side revealed evidence of a dysfunctional personologic system and paternal abandonment. Severe family dysfunction was reported, with many underfunctioning or disturbed siblings. The husband was a man with an obsessive-compulsive personality who modulated intimacy by controlling the family. He was encouraged to back off on the parenting and let his wife grow through her anxiety. Couples and individual work was recommended to detriangulate the couple, restructure the marriage, and enhance intimacy.

TECHNICAL ISSUES

Working with couples with personality pathology, especially when the pathology is severe, is a challenge to the therapist. The therapist becomes a third member of the subsystem and will experience a strong force to become triangulated in order to reduce the couple's anxiety over intimacy or to displace anxiety over unresolved issues. The more primitive the organization of the couple and their defensive system is, the more likely that the therapist will have to deal with their tendency to externalize or blame one another for the relational disturbance and disappointment. Oftentimes, as the couples therapy proceeds, a previously triangulated member of the family may quickly become detriangulated, but the force will be shifted dynamically to the therapist. Guerin et al. (1996) write that "triangles stabilize such patterns by allowing them to be repeated over and over without ending the relationships (and without forcing them to change). Having a third person (or thing) to focus arguments and resentments on sustains the illusion that the real problem between them is that third party" (p. 27). Couples who have committed to treatment are faced with the dilemma to change themselves or leave the relationship. Failure by a member to accept the inevitable choice requires the continuation of a repetitive process that is often tumultuous and disruptive to other members of the system.

The therapist who works with these couples must be willing to become part of the triangle but not stay too long in one position. The therapist will find it useful at times to side with one member of the couple, but then must be able to shift to the other member or an imbalance will occur. These patients are often highly sensitized to bias the therapist may have.

Abuse, Control, and Domination

Probably the most difficult situation encountered by therapists working with dysfunctional personologic couples is when one member of the couple begins to intimidate, degrade, or dominate his or her spouse during the session. Often, these dynamics have never been displayed in front of outsiders, especially if the couple is a high-functioning couple. When this intimidation occurs in the session, the abusive spouse, usually the male, will express shock and denial that his behavior is considered "abusive treatment." In one case, a highly prominent individual began degrading his spouse during the first consultation and was asked to stop. He continued his behavior, and when he was told again that he was being abusive, he stood up and in a denigrating fashion called the therapist a quack, left the session, and did not return. The situation of an abusive partner, although rare, does present a difficult conundrum for the therapist. Should we as therapists attempt to develop a therapeutic alliance before addressing the abuse patterns? Even when we take this strategy, if there is no outside pressure and if the spouse tends to be submissive, the therapy will usually break down. Without court referral, these individuals are not motivated to undergo the self-scrutiny that treatment would entail. Walker (1996), in her seminal work in spousal abuse, reminds us that battering is cyclical in nature and that it consists of three main phases: "(1) a period of tension-building; (2) the acute battering incident or explosion; and (3) a period of living contrition" (p. 342). Batterers do show some consistently described behaviors, "such as overpossessiveness, jealousy, disrespect for women in general, insecurities often covered by bravado, and belief in sex-role stereotypes" (p. 346). Batterers are often diagnosed with personality disorders such as borderline and paranoid (Dutton & Starzomski, 1993).

CONCLUSIONS

The couple is an essential subsystem of the dysfunctional personologic system. Restructuring the couple and increasing emotional maturity has great benefit for the rest of the system. The severity and type of individual personality pathology and the dynamic interplay between the couple and triangulated other(s) need to be addressed in systematic treatment that often includes couples therapy.

CHAPTER 11

Maximizing the Therapeutic Alliance in the Relational Matrix

U p until now, this book has addressed the theories and techniques of working in the relational matrix to treat the dysfunctional personologic system as well as its subsystems and individual members. Although the therapeutic alliance is the cornerstone of all therapy, there are advantages to presenting it last, after a thorough review of the necessary theory, constructs, and techniques. Readers can now approach this topic with an appreciation for the complexity of the clinical work and plethora of variables that therapists contend with. The therapist who works in an integrative relational model must be adept enough to conduct concurrent therapy and be flexible at shifting modalities and treatment foci. A shift from the couple or family modality to the individual requires structural considerations. Pinsof (1995) calls this "the most demanding and complex relational structure to manage" (p. 82).

Although the concept of the therapeutic alliance has not been widely considered in the family therapy field (Rait, 1995), it is becoming a focus of attention. Fifteen years of empirical investigation demonstrates that the concept of the therapeutic alliance is a robust predictor of eventual therapeutic outcome and is constant across diagnostic categories and theoretical orientations (Horvath, 1995; Horvath & Symonds, 1991).

Without a solid therapeutic alliance, therapy does not proceed. Hovarth (1995) emphasizes that "building an alliance is one of the most urgent tasks in the beginning of treatment: If a good alliance is not developed by the fifth session, then the likelihood of successful treatment outcome is significantly diminished" (p. 16). When a positive therapeutic alliance is nurtured, the system can withstand the anxiety and pain of transformation. Identifying and working through the inevitable ruptures that occur is a powerful corrective emotional experience.

WHAT IS THE THERAPEUTIC ALLIANCE?

The therapeutic alliance is the quality of the relationship or strength of bond that develops between the therapist system (team members, consultants, supervisors) and the patient system, subsystems, and individual members (Pinsof, 1995). A therapeutic alliance encompasses therapeutic conditions such as empathy, warmth, unconditional positive regard, and collaboration that enable the tasks of therapy to be achieved. More than this, however, therapeutic alliance is collaboration on the tasks and goals of therapy, collaboration that takes into account the features and characteristics of both the system and the therapist.

THREE ASPECTS OF THE THERAPEUTIC ALLIANCE AND SYSTEMIC EXPANSION

Bordin (1979) has developed a well-accepted concept of the therapeutic alliance that entails three interconnected components: (1) making the bond, (2) collaborating on the tasks of what is to be done, and (3) setting mutually defined goals. The first step in building an alliance is to show an interest in exploring the individual or the subsystem's view and perspective of the problem. One of the most cogent presentations of the therapeutic alliance from an integrative systems perspective is by Pinsof (1995). Pinsof expands our concept of the patient-therapist alliance to include the *patient system* and *therapist system* and underscores the fact that "the therapeutic alliance exists simultaneously on multiple levels between and within the patient and therapist system" (p. 66). The patient system includes the *direct system* that is involved in the treatment process and the *indirect systems* that often influence the process. The therapist must strive to attain an alliance with all systems, direct and indirect, and where possible and appropriate, must engage the indirect systems.

THERAPEUTIC CONDITIONS NECESSARY

ENGAGEMENT

Probably the most challenging aspect of working with dysfunctional personologic systems is the ability to effectively engage the family and appropriate subsystems in the treatment process. Engagement requires the therapist to put aside his or her agenda and view each case anew. Engagement is an important task of the early phase of any therapy (Watson & Greenberg, 1995). The *Random House College Dictionary* definition (Stein, 1975) of *engage* is "having chosen to involve oneself in or commit oneself to something, as opposed to remaining aloof or indifferent" (p. 438). Therapists must demonstrate engagement to the individuals they are working with or the therapeutic alliance will not be activated. Engagement requires emotional presence; therapists must be willing and able to evaluate their personal reactions on an ongoing basis and use this evaluation to deepen their understanding of the process and unique style of each individual, subsystem, and system.

ACTIVATION

To activate the therapeutic alliance, therapists must start with a careful assessment so that they know what needs to be emphasized at the onset of treatment. Assessment then becomes an ongoing process by which the therapist continually refines his or her hypothesis about the interrelated factors in the biopsychosocial system. A therapist cannot address issues of intimacy and closeness in a system in which the capacity to establish basic trust is tenuous. In a case such as this, the family would be overwhelming with anxiety and unable to make use of the therapeutic situation. Therefore, the therapeutic alliance must encompass the expectations and capacity of the system as well as therapeutic ingredients such as structure, acceptance, authority, and education. Of major importance is the therapist's ability to accept the presenting problem and engage the appropriate subsystem with the goal of deepening the involvement and moving to the focal issues.

System's Capacity for Attachment

Underlying the capacity for an individual or system to engage in the treatment process and develop a therapeutic alliance is the ability to form attachments. Attachment entails the sense that an individual can trust someone else. If a patient's capacity to develop basic trust with the therapist is underdeveloped, then the patient will have difficulty forming a therapeutic alliance. Major issues with trust may be particularly evident in some types of dysfunctional personologic systems, such as paranoid, traumatic, and psychotic. The clinician will need to make a major effort to address these issues and to give the system an opportunity to attach. These systems often believe that their trust has been been betrayed in the past, and they are going to protect themselves from being burned again.

System's Fear of Intimacy and Closeness

The therapeutic situation activates fears of intimacy and closeness that can be terrifying to many individuals. Many types of dysfunctional personologic systems have substituted less acceptable interpersonal variations for true intimacy. The SomDps, for example, engages in somatic communication as a vehicle for attempting intimacy and closeness, using the language of the physical rather than the emotional self. The NarDps uses the false self to establish a safe haven for intimacy that is less vulnerable to injury or wounding. Intimacy is less of an issue in the more disturbed dysfunctional personologic systems, in which basic attachment is more primitively guarded by psychosis or projection. If trust is a major issue, the therapist may do well to narrow and deepen the treatment frame by providing individual treatment that aims toward the establishment of a trusting holding relationship (Pinsof, 1995).

CLASSIFICATION

Alliance building is facilitated if the therapist classifies the dysfunctional personologic system. Classification alerts the therapist to the therapeutic stance that should be assumed early on in the treatment process and to the steps necessary to build an alliance. The therapeutic stance toward the more severe forms of dysfunctional personologic systems, for example, must often be less formal and more engaging, so that trust can be invited and not forced. A clinician who is attempting to engage with a system in which attachment is a major block might spend more time in social chit chat, playing with the children or offering the family coffee or drinks, to establish a basic level of comfort before proceeding. More psychoeducational intervention is suggested and useful in the initial stages of the treatment process. When I think of working effectively with the more severe forms of dysfunctional personologic systems, I think about Carl Whitaker's style, which was down to earth and genuine but had a toughness that even the most disturbed systems responded to.

THERAPEUTIC STANCE

The therapeutic stance sets the tenor of the therapy at the onset. Is the therapist authoritarian and prescriptive, as is seen in a medical model, or collaborative and nondirective? Is the therapist revealing or neutral? Does he or she engage in small talk or get down to business immediately? Clearly no one stance is best; what is important is that the stance meet the needs of the system while allowing the therapist to be true to his or her beliefs and personal preferences.

Flexible Stance

For maximal effectiveness in treating the dysfunctional personologic system, the therapist must have flexibility, which includes the capacity to enter into the conflict and to energize and influence the relational matrix (Ackerman, 1966). Flexibility should not, however, be misconstrued with sloppiness or poor boundaries. Flexibility refers to the therapist's capacity to take an experimental stance and to become a participant-observer (Sullivan, 1953) with each system. This flexibility must be tempered with firmness when required. Many dysfunctional personologic systems have learned to function by being manipulative in a variety of ways. Their behavior ranges from intimidating to seductive as they maneuver to outwit the therapist and avoid disrupting their equilibrium. Flexibility does not mean that a therapist should be a pushover or allow his or her values to be compromised.

RELATEDNESS

The effective therapist has a capacity for relatedness and an enjoyment of the intimacy of the therapeutic process. The therapist's capacity for relatedness includes a genuine fascination with the human experience as well as an ability to establish a developmentally appropriate level of contact. Therapists who are out of contact with their own feelings are going to be at a tremendous disadvantage in understanding the system and in responding to helpful countertransference themes that emerge from their unconscious and conscious processing.

CHARACTERISTICS OF A GOOD THERAPEUTIC ALLIANCE

At the most fundamental level, a good therapeutic alliance maintains clear, firm boundaries between the patient and therapist. This essential building block of trust, when violated, threatens the therapeutic alliance in the most basic manner. The specifics of a good therapeutic alliance are beyond the scope of this book, but the essence of a good alliance is a safe therapeutic environment maintained by the therapist. Therapists must avoid any behavior that interferes with this safety, such as sexual relationships or aggression. Much controversy exists about dual roles. Dual roles often present a conflict of interest and should be carefully considered. Some prominent therapists have encouraged socializing for therapeutic benefit, advocating such activities as playing tennis and having lunches. I think such dual roles can be potentially destructive and countertherapeutic.

WHAT THE THERAPIST BRINGS

Enjoyment of the Process
Therapists who don't enjoy their work are unlikely, in my estimation, to be effective. Although therapy is hard work, it offers joy in the process of seeing systems transform and individuals grow. It is important that therapists take their work seriously but that they also maintain a sense of humor and an ability to laugh at themselves.

Nurturance
An effective therapist has a capacity to nurture others by providing them with affirmation, support, and genuine interest in their development. Therapy for dysfunctional personologic systems especially requires a nurturing capacity because these systems have experienced generations of emotional malnourishment.

Movement in and out of the Frame
An effective therapist must be able to move in and out of the various perspectives and subsystems that are offered. The ability to immerse himself or herself in the emotional process in order to experience the tenor of the system or to identify with an individual is as crucial to the therapist as the ability to pull back and process the experience. The therapist must be capable of multiple identifications and must use empathy to achieve a sense of

what each person experiences. I concur with Pinsof (1995), who believes that the therapist working at this level must have developed advanced interpersonal and psychodynamic skill and, I would add, a knowledge of systems. Pinsof writes: "It requires considerable skill on the part of the therapist to conduct individual therapies with members of the same patient system, interspersing them as needed with conjoint sessions" (p. 82).

A Belief in the Capacity for Change
Positive expectancies are important to the process. If the therapist is demoralized and does not believe in the power of change, those negative expectancies will be communicated and can create a demoralizing effect.

THE ISSUE OF SELF-DISCLOSURE—HOW MUCH? HOW LITTLE? IF ANY?

Self-disclosure is a controversial issue in the field of psychotherapy. Whether it should or should not be done is too simplistic a question. Rather, therapists must examine their feelings and beliefs about self-disclosure and determine what form of disclosure is appropriate with whom. A self-disclosure to one family or individual may be helpful; to another family, the same self-disclosure may have the opposite effect. Self-disclosure with the more severe forms of dysfunctional personologic systems can be helpful in establishing a trusting alliance. Whitaker, for example, would often disclose his feelings about the challenge of being a parent or of raising a family; those disclosures had the result of humanizing him, (Whitaker & Keith, 1980). Deep personal disclosures, however, with rare exception are not indicated and may in fact have a distracting or detrimental impact.

THE COMPLEXITY FOR THE SYSTEMICALLY ORIENTED THERAPIST

Rait (1995) notes that the systemically oriented therapist must contend with the challenge of developing and monitoring the therapeutic alliance with more than one individual. He writes: "Because there are multiple participants in couples or family treatment, the task of 'conducting the session' can be arduous, especially for the beginning therapist" (p. 60). Contending with family members and subsystems who are at different levels of motivation and willingness to engage in collaborative treatment is a crucial aspect of successful alliance building and maintenance. The therapist needs to remember that the system seeks out certain reactions in interactions. The therapist must be able to develop an alliance with various members of the system and subsystems as well as maintain his or her flexibility to shift within the system and to put pressure on an individual or a subsystem without fracturing the multiple alliances.

Understanding the System Dynamics

To address the alliance, therapists must think beyond dyadic and complementary interactions to triangular configurations that include the therapist as well as other members of the family (Rait, 1995). Therapists who understand the power of triangular configurations are likely to see that an intervention that prematurely threatens the homeostasis will be rebuffed. The therapeutic alliance is developed and strengthened when the therapist becomes part of the triangular configuration but does not become emotionally stuck in the triangle. The therapist needs to be able to disengage so affects that cannot be processed can be experienced by members of the system. A therapy-resistant husband for example, is victimizing his family in one or more ways; the therapist finds it easy to identify with the plight of the victimized spouse. Siding too closely with the victim, however, creates a triangle that can siphon off the anxiety that the victim may have about making necessary life changes. In maintaining the system equilibrium, this victim may never address the questions, Should I stay? Should I make the ultimatum that he get treatment? Or should I leave?

ALLIANCE BUILDING AND STRENGTHENING

Building a therapeutic alliance has many elements that must be understood and attended to. Developing an alliance with an individual has different demand characteristics than does developing an alliance with a couple or a family. Regardless of the system or subsystem that is being targeted, the therapist must begin with an understanding of the stage of change that the individual or subsystem is at. Once an alliance is developed, the therapist can shift the treatment frame and increase motivation as the alliance grows. The tasks that need to occur differ depending upon the stage of the change process. The accompanying case study illustrates this concept.

CASE STUDY: A NARDPS IN THE PRECONTEMPLATIVE STAGE OF CHANGE

The index patient was referred to treatment by a child psychiatrist who was prescribing medication for ADHD. The parents were seen with the child for the initial consultation and were tremendously concerned about their daughter. Psychological testing was completed and showed that the daughter was functioning in the low, near-borderline, range of intelligence and did suffer from a moderate case of ADHD. The couple reacted with disbelief and anger when confronted with the findings of the intellectual assessment and attempted to question the validity or the results. As the consultation continued, it became clear that the family was functioning as a NarDps and that the findings were a deep threat to the narcissistic equilibrium of the parents. They were in the precontemplative stage of change because they could see no problems other than those with their daughter. The first phase of treatment focused on individual work with the daughter, and conjoint sessions focused on parental expectations and psychoeducation. As the alliance with the parents developed, the therapist began to address the deeper and more troubling issues within the marriage that were being deflected by their daughter's problems. The focus was slowly shifted to the couple and then to some individual work in which both parents addressed their narcissistic vulnerability.

USING THE LANGUAGE OF THE SYSTEM TO SPEAK TO THE FAMILY

As I discussed in Chapter 9, language is the medium of the therapeutic process. Discovering the language and metaphors that crystallize and captivate the family is helpful in establishing and maintaining a therapeutic alliance. The therapist must also be aware of differences in the language of various socioeconomic systems and ethnic groups. I am not saying that a therapist should take on the language of the system with which he or she is working, but that the therapist should speak in a manner that is understandable and is aimed at the system's level of education and sophistication.

CREATING AN ATMOSPHERE OF FREE EXPRESSION

A positive therapeutic alliance is one in which there is a free expression of thoughts, feelings, and emotions in a considerate and respectful manner. What is being expressed is often painful, uncomfortable, or shameful, but the atmosphere that is encouraged and modeled by the therapist must be one of tolerance, respect, and understanding.

MAINTAINING SAFETY

Above all else, safety must be ensured for the system and for the therapist. When fear of aggression is an issue, the therapeutic process will suffer and the alliance will weaken. The therapist must do whatever is necessary to ensure safety. An inpatient setting may require the presence of aides, for example. In an outpatient situation, the therapist may discontinue family work until an individual can maintain greater impulse control, either through medication or an anger management program.

THERAPEUTIC HOLDING

An adequate bond between the therapist and the patient system creates a holding environment that allows the work of therapy to be conducted. The therapist is in a sense providing a container to hold the nonmetabolized affects and conflicts that are being exposed until these conflicts be integrated and resolved. Therapists must also be willing to allow their patients the freedom to terminate therapy, to seek outside consultation, or to take a vacation when appropriate. One patient reported that after he had been in nondirective long-term therapy, he decided to terminate because his therapist did not seem engaged with him. When the patient announced that he was terminating, the therapist jumped out of his chair and declared, "But you're too sick to leave treatment!" Holding is good, but the relationship also needs an adequate level of engagement; sometimes "fleeing" treatment is adaptive.

BEING AN AUTHORITY WITHOUT BEING AUTHORITARIAN

Mental health professionals are authorities on human development, systems, psychodynamics, psychopathology, and various other topics that concern change and problem resolution strategies. Requested information should be freely provided. However, assuming an overly authoritarian stance is counterproductive to the developmental process. Patients often have a way of engaging in complementary power struggles with authoritarian therapists that are destructive and a waste of time.

SETTING APPROPRIATE LIMITS

The willingness to set and maintain appropriate limits is necessary for strengthening the alliance. The therapist must be comfortable intervening if the situation is out of control. Some therapists avoid the necessary limit setting; they do not, for example, file a child abuse report that would provide intervention in an out-of-control system. This situation is probably one of the most difficult interventions to make, but it should not be avoided; otherwise we as the rapists add to the conspiracy of silence around the issue of abuse.

DEEPENING THE ALLIANCE

There are various methods or procedures for deepening the alliance when more intensive or in-depth restructuring is needed. Pinsof (1995) describes four of these methods: (1) relational focus—processing the transference reactions or how the system experiences the therapist; (2) increasing the frequency of sessions; (3) shifting the context of the therapy, that is, decreasing the number of people in direct treatment; and (4) the passage of time. I would add two more to Pinsof's list; (5) increasing the duration of the sessions by using extended sessions; and (6) increasing the affective intensity. (Magnavita, 1997b).

CASE STUDY: THE MAN WITHOUT A PROBLEM

The patient, a man in his middle 40s, was referred by his employee assistance program after testing positive for cannabis on a random drug screen required to maintain his position as an air traffic controller. He was unable to return to work until he was evaluated. Tony reported an 18-year history of marijuana abuse on the weekends. He denied ever having smoked pot while on duty. He did not see a problem with his substance "use" pattern but did realize that his job would be endangered if he did not discontinue, which he agreed to do. This patient was definitely in the precontemplative stage of the change cycle. He also displayed a strong tendency to externalize his problems and to view himself in an excessively positive light. Clearly he had personality issues that were long-standing; however, his resistance to change was high. Instead of recommending a course of treatment that the patient would resist, the therapist gave the patient the opportunity to return for follow-up in a month and asked if he would be willing to bring his wife. The patient had mentioned that she did not approve of his marijuana use and was concerned that their two children might discover him using it and follow in his steps. The therapeutic alliance was tenuous because this patient did not see himself as the kind of guy who needed a shrink. However, the therapist's strategy in inviting his wife in for the next consultation was to broaden the treatment frame and to obtain more information that might be useful in having this patient look at the impact of his personality and behavior on those he said he loved.

Resisting Change—The Counterforce to the Therapeutic Alliance

Resistance, or the counterforce to change, is a move away from the therapeutic alliance. Therapists must identify the resistances in operation in the system in order to counteract or neutralize them. This topic has been covered comprehensively in numerous volumes. For a contemporary review, I refer readers to the special edition of *In Session: Psychotherapy in Practice* titled "Resistance to Change in Psychotherapy" (Arkowitz, 1996). Resistance is a vital process occurring from the beginning to the termination of treatment that seeks to maintain the homeostasis and contain anxiety. Resistance is demonstrated in the calls that clinicians inevitably receive from patients who make an appointment and cancel it, only to reschedule and cancel again. Resistance can be aimed against the treatment process, as in those phone calls, or against the development of the therapeutic alliance itself and the attachment, intimacy, closeness, and collaboration that the alliance entails. Resistance has both behavioral and affective sequences (impulse/feeling and fantasy). Resistance is not to be thought of as the enemy of the therapist (Messer, 1996) but rather as an expression of the very disturbances that the system is attempting to master. Resistance can be considered psychodynamically as a form of transference, or what the system brings to the therapist to prevent the anxiety of change from becoming too great. The displayed resistance is a direct manifestation of the personality functioning of the individual or the system, known as trait or character resistance when repetitive in nature. The resistance manifested in individual defenses gives the therapist a clear picture of the type of defensive system and level of adaptive capacity. For example, resistance manifested at a behavioral level, such as missing or forgetting appointments or acting-out, indicates a more primitive level of functioning than does resistance manifested by a patient who avoids expressing feelings for fear of humiliation.

ENCOUNTERING MULTIPLE TRANSFERENCES, COUNTERTRANSFERENCE, AND THE CONUNDRUM OF OPPOSING SYSTEMS

The field of object relations has taught therapists that the transference and countertransference dance is the most crucial intrasubjective experience of the therapeutic process. In other words, reactions that are activated within the therapist can serve to guide or deepen the therapeutic process. The various dysfunctional personologic systems will often pull for certain reactions in the therapist. The TraDps can activate fear or anger over abuse scenarios and can incite rescue fantasies. The PscDps may engender confusion or a state of feeling overwhelmed. The MedDps often activates grief in the therapist.

Individuals within the system can also create various reactions in the therapist. The victim elicits a desire to direct, the victimizer, to punish, the neglected child, to rescue. Regardless of his or her reactions, the therapist should attempt to monitor countertransference at the system, subsystem, and individual levels. These subjective, often preconscious reactions are a way of deep channeling into the family process and unconscious dynamics. Sometimes therapists find it useful to share these reactions as a way of developing awareness in the system, for example, "I feel like King Solomon, like I want to tell you to cut your child down the middle and each take half."

The Split Alliance

Pinsof (1995) offers useful guidelines for dealing with *split alliances*—a positive alliance with one subsystem and a negative one with another—which are ubiquitous in this approach to dysfunctional personologic systems. He suggests that the major alliance needs to be developed with the more powerful subsystem, because therapy is often not viable when the main alliance is with the weaker subsystem. "Subsystem power is usually a function of age, economic resources and control, and psychological influence" (p. 68). Ultimately, the therapist must vigilantly monitor alliances with all the relevant subsystems and individuals, often walking a tightrope that balances therapeutic thrusts against alliance monitoring and repair. Moving the focus from the index patient to another subsystem such as a marital dyad has to be done while taking a careful pulse of the alliance.

THERAPEUTIC RUPTURES

Therapeutic ruptures entail a negative shift in the quality of the therapeutic relationship; they vary in duration, intensity, and degree (Safran, 1993). Ruptures can be subtle or severe and can result in premature termination or iatrogenic disturbance. Hovarth (1995) writes: "one can think of these alliance disruption–repair cycles as opportunities for the client to practice, in vivo, new, more productive interpersonal behaviors with the assistance of the therapist, who is able to respond emphatically, honestly, and knowledgably to both the surface and the underlying issues" (p. 14). After the initial therapeutic alliance is established, mending these disruptions provides an opportunity for the patient to experience emotional problem solving and for the therapist to adjust the pace and focus of treatment.

Therapeutic Misalliance

Therapeutic misalliances are a common feature of working with the dysfunctional personologic system. Therapists who are going to conduct treatment of the dysfunctional personologic system should be prepared to encounter therapeutic misalliances, because they are inevitable. "Recent research suggests that the course of the alliance over time is not linear, that is, it does not improve or deepen with successive session, even in treatments that have very successful outcome" (Horvath, 1995, p. 13). The crucial aspect is how the therapeutic misalliance is handled. The therapist should always attempt to understand the nature of the misalliance and should respond with empathy to the hurt feelings. Therapy then needs to be adjusted to the right pace and focus. In one case, the behavioral problems of a preadolescent were clearly linked to his father's chronic back pain, unemployment, and explosive treatment of the youth. When the therapist gently brought these issues up in a couple consultation, however, the patient's father responded with indignation that he was only interested in his son doing well in school. Although the wife agreed with the therapist, she was in a less powerful position, and therapy was thwarted.

Power Struggles

Both novice and experienced therapists working with dysfunctional personologic systems can get entangled in power struggles that are counterproductive. Power struggles, which can develop for a number of reasons, are detrimental to the therapeutic alliance. Once they develop, power struggles can spiral downward and severely disrupt therapy. Therapists can avert power struggles by being aware of the following tendencies:

- Feeling inadequate and wanting to effect change when the family isn't ready.
- Unconsciously reenacting abuse patterns with patients, for example, control attempts, punitive reactions, and so forth.
- Turning patient relapse into a personal failure.
- Attempting to force patients into a position they are resisting or are not ready for.

How to Mend Therapeutic Misalliances

Minor Miscommunications

Minor communication problems can be handled in a straightforward manner once they are identified. Often the therapist is aware of an underlying anger that is not addressed; this anger should be pointed out. The therapist who has some awareness of what the problem might be can offer that information. If, for example, the patient misinterpreted or misunderstood something that was said, the therapist can clarify the statement and validate the feelings of the patient.

Major Misalliance

When a major misalliance occurs, therapy may be in jeopardy and the misalliance must be addressed to prevent acting-out or premature termination. If, as a result of frustration or countertransference, the therapist says or does something that is countertherapeutic, the therapist should identify the problem, ask the patient how he or she feels, and offer an apology. These actions often will suffice and allow therapy to get back on track. If the misalliance is the result of a systemic shift or confrontation, the therapist can carefully explore the reaction and try to understand what it indicates in terms of system and individual deficits that may require another approach or another therapist. If, for example, active substance use needs to be addressed in an AdcDps, the therapist might attempt motivational counseling techniques to explore the alternatives.

CASE STUDY: AN EARLY MISALLIANCE

The couple, married about five years, came for a conjoint session because they were considering divorce. The husband was an entrepreneur who had started a new company six months ago and was working 80 hours a week. He wanted to devote all his time to his enterprise and felt it was his due, because he had "never complained" when his wife, in her previous job, had worked as much. The couple had very little emotional engagement; they had sex about once a month. The wife wanted to support her husband but also encouraged him to find some balance. The husband seemed to be passive-aggressive in his personality style, and the wife seemed more dependent with a need to please. During the initial session, the husband passively refused to talk but did say that he didn't think the job was the issue. This partner was, in essence, having an affair with his career. When the therapist pointed out to the husband that he seemed willing to sacrifice his marriage to become a millionaire, the husband felt belittled. The husband had much invested in maintaining his career. Although his workaholism was destroying his marriage, he was not ready to consider altering his position. Because the husband was in the precontemplative stage, the therapist should have spent more time building an alliance with him to ensure his return. Instead the premature focus on the husband's career created an early misalliance, and the couple did not return.

In retrospect, the therapist would have been better off to emphasis engagement. Engaging the husband might have entailed spending more time valuing his ambition and work ethic and asking him details about his company. The initial impression was that the husband had a passive-aggressive personality; he reported that he never got angry but seemed to retaliate by distancing and withdrawing from his wife. However, his response suggested a deeper narcissistic disorder that the therapist needed time to get to. That the therapist was examining the triangular relationship that was in operation was frightening to the husband. The wife, on the other hand, continually felt rebuffed and tried to be more pleasing; she was alternately demanding and enabling. For the wife, altering the triangle might have meant that she would have to assume a more direct and demanding approach that would either strengthen or terminate the marriage.

Therapeutic misalliances, especially early in the treatment process, often result in premature termination (Magnavita, 1994a). At times, the misalliance is the result of a therapeutic blunder; at other times, a misalliance represents patient characteristics that were not discernible until an intervention was made. An emphasis on shorter treatment increases the likelihood of early misalliance. Some patients are just not ready for treatment; they have been forced into it and have no intention of making the best of it. Therapists should routinely examine the dynamics of misalliance, especially the ones that lead to premature termination. Much can be learned from therapeutic failures that will prepare therapists for the next challenging system.

CONCLUSIONS

This chapter explored and presented some of the crucial aspects of maintaining a positive therapeutic alliance and mending inevitable therapeutic ruptures in the dysfunctional personologic system. No therapy will be successful for these systems unless the therapist has a deep appreciation for how multiple alliances are managed and how misalliances are navigated. Traditional forms of individual therapy in which the therapist maintains clear boundaries around the therapeutic relationship are not as problematic as are therapies that simultaneously treat various systems and subsystems. Although individually oriented therapists may disagree, systems therapy clearly benefits from a more flexible, adaptive stance. Interested readers should refer to Pinsof's (1995) excellent book for a cogent discussion of these issues.

CHAPTER 12

Prevention and Early Intervention: Using the Relational Matrix

T he identification of those at risk for personality disturbance can be enhanced with the use of a relational diagnosis and treatment model. The best hope for breaking the multigenerational transmission process is to *intervene as early and comprehensively as possible.* Tackling this problem requires early identification of the dysfunctional personologic system and intervention at the appropriate level. For example, a second grader who is showing signs of being overly aggressive toward peers should be considered for a family consultation to determine whether there is a more pervasive pattern of disturbance that would suggest a dysfunctional personologic system. Perhaps the father is modeling aggressive behavior as a method of controlling his wife and children. Is this pattern entrenched? Is immediate intervention and follow-up treatment required to restructure the family system?

In one case, a patient reported that he suffered from severe anxiety when he was going off to school and was given a placebo by the pediatrician. His "school phobia" was only the tip of the iceberg. The family system was characterized by severe alcohol abuse and emotional abuse. In fact, a number of members died from chronic alcohol abuse and others were headed in the same direction. An understanding of the dynamics and generational transmission process by the pediatrician may have alerted her to the need for early intervention. Social policy and planning must strengthen existing

239

programs and develop new ones to aid in early intervention of the dysfunctional personologic system.

HEALTH PROFESSIONALS
AND THE COMFORT OF DENIAL

Medical and mental health professionals often use the defense of denial when working with the dysfunctional personologic system. The pervasive nature of the dysfunctional personologic system is evident in so many areas in current society. Daily newspaper reports and news broadcasts indicate the various manifestations these systems often take. The sports pages contain articles about sports parents who are verbally and physically abusive to coaches and to their children. I wonder about the presence of a NarDps in many of these cases. Some parents seem to use the athletic event to reflect back a level of glory to the parent; when the glory isn't forthcoming, the parents may be severely narcissistically wounded and may retaliate.

Medical and educational professionals are often on the front lines in being confronted with manifestations of dysfunctional personologic systems. A patient who medically overutilizes and never gets better may reflect a SomDps that needs systemic intervention. An educator observes siblings coming to school poorly groomed and lethargic but does not realize that a DepDps may be in operation here. The widespread dysfunction evident in these systems often makes it easier for us as professionals to engage in denial rather than open Pandora's box and face the overwhelming needs of the dysfunctional personologic system. In addition, the personality pathology of individual members is often highly off putting. That unpleasantness tends to cause us to proceed through our contact with these systems without truly recognizing the problems. Denial may reduce our anxiety but it allows the problems in the dysfunctional personologic system to continue from one generation to the next without improvement.

POLITICIZATION OF SOCIETAL FACTORS

Beyond the level of heath professionals and educators is a world that politicizes the problems of the dysfunctional personologic system. Prevalent are attacks on social welfare programs and perpetuation of the belief that individuals should be able to rise out of generations of reliance on social welfare to embrace the values of the dominant culture.

SOCIETAL FACTORS AND ISSUES AFFECTING THE DYSFUNCTIONAL PERSONOLOGIC SYSTEM

Societal factors account for a large amount of variance in the relational biopsychosocial model. In summing up the research, Matsen and Coatsworth (1998) write:

> Over the past 25 years, signs of trouble emerged for child development in the United States, spurring considerable attentions to the status of children in terms of school success, behavior, and physical and mental health, and growing interest in the origins of competence in development. High risks for children have been apparent in rates of divorce, births to single parents, teenage pregnancy, child abuse, homelessness and poverty among young families with children, and surges in problems like suicide, substance abuse, and violence. (p. 205)

However, an entire issue of *American Psychologist* (Hetherington, 1998) devoted to developmental science made little mention of the dysfunctional personologic system and minimal discussion of the impact that these systems have on developmental processes. Matsen and Coatsworth (1998), in an article in that same issue, do emphasize the "attachment system" and state: "This system is so basic and universal that lack of behavior associated with attachment usually occurs when there is something fundamentally wrong with the organism or the environment, with high risk for adaptive failure" (p. 208). Cicchetti and Toth (1998) describe what they term "depressotypic developmental organization" and write that "the organization of biological, psychological, and social systems as they have been structured over development must be fully examined" (p. 221). These authors advise professionals to "consider a depressotypic developmental organization to be a potential precursor to depressive illness" and to seek "to understand how those components have evolved developmentally, and to understand how they are integrated within and across biological and psychological systems of the individual embedded within a multilevel social ecology" (p. 221). In fact, children with depressed parents may experience a sense of loss akin to an actual loss of a parent.

ADOLESCENT PREGNANCY

For many dysfunctional personologic systems, the generational transmission is furthered by adolescent pregnancy. This situation tends to require an individual to take on a parental role before he or she has developed a solid sense of self or the maturity required to fulfill a parental function. Adolescent pregnancy often leads to generations of individuals who are emotionally incomplete and lack the ego development necessary to be productive members of society and to provide a solid familial base. The consequences of teenage pregnancy are widespread. Coley and Chase-Lansdale (1998) sum up much of the evidence: Delays in cognitive development are noted in the preschool development of the offspring of teenage mothers, and these delays proceed throughout schooling. These children "also tend to show behavioral problems, including higher levels of aggression and lower impulse control than peers born to older mothers" (p. 158). As teenagers these offspring have a higher incidence of academic failure, incarceration, grade failure, delinquency, sexual activity, and pregnancy. Adolescent mothers are often depressed and are likely to drop out of school, so their ability to provide a financially stable family is compromised.

ABUSIVE FAMILY RELATIONSHIPS

According to Emory and Laumann-Billings (1998), "violence within the family is disturbingly common" (p. 122). These authors argue that there should be "a basic differentiation between *family maltreatment*, characterized by minimal physical or sexual harm or endangerment, and *family violence*, characterized by serious physical injury, profound psychological trauma, or sexual violation" (p. 121). Summing up the findings of Pianta, Egeland, and Erickson (1989) Emory and Laumann-Billings state that "personality factors such as low self-esteem, poor impulse control, external locus of control, negative affectivity, and heightened response to stress all increase the likelihood that an individual will perpetrate family violence" (p. 126). These authors also highlight the intergenerational transmission process in the violent family and suggest that children are at increased risk of becoming violent as adults.

SOCIOECONOMIC DISADVANTAGE

"Poor individuals living in high-poverty communities, as compared with their counterparts residing in communities with lower rates of poverty, are disadvantaged by reduced accessibility to jobs, high-quality public and private services (e.g., child care, schools, parks, community centers), and informal social supports" (McLoyd, 1998, p. 185). McLoyd points out that the family system can provide a protective function that can be used by those working in the relational matrix. "Parenting that is strict and highly directive (i.e., well-defined house rules, clear sanctions for breaking rules, close supervision), combined with high levels of warmth, helps poor, inner-city children resist forces in their extra-familial environments that in ordinary circumstances contribute to low levels of achievement and poor-quality schooling" (p. 194).

JUVENILE AGGRESSION

This book began with an example of child violence, which is an emergent societal problem. Loeber and Stouthamer-Loeber (1998) comment that "juvenile aggression and violence affect society in a wide and penetrating manner. The victimization and the distress caused by these behaviors are staggering; the numbers of perpetrators and victims have gradually increased over the past decade" (p. 242). These authors summarize the research and conclude that "there is a body of research results that indicate some familial processes are related to overt problem behavior and violence whereas other familial processes are associated with covert problem behavior and property" (p. 251).

DIVORCE AND ADJUSTMENT

There has been a rapid rise in the divorce rate in the United States and a significant decline in two-parent families (Hetherington, Bridges, & Insabella, 1998). "Although there is considerable consensus that, on average, offspring from divorced and remarried families exhibit more problems in adjustment than do those in nondivorced, two-parent families, there is less agreement on the size of these effects" (p. 169). Well-adjusted children cope better with divorce and the associated stress of remarriage. "Dysfunctional family relationships, such as conflict, negativity, lack of support, and nonauthoritative parenting, exacerbate the effects of divorce and remarriage on children's adjustment" (p. 179). "Children, because of individual characteristics such as gender, temperament, personality, age, and intelligence, vary in their influence on family process and their vulnerability or resilience in dealing with their parents' divorce and remarriage and concomitant changes in family roles, relationships, and process" (p. 180).

DRUG AND ALCOHOL ABUSE

Another factor that has major impact on the dysfunctional personologic system is the widespread abuse of psychoactive substances. The use of alcohol and drugs is a major contributor to the level of pathology in the dysfunctional system. Drug and alcohol abuse is associated with increased familial violence and crime. Untreated alcoholic and drug-addicted systems are highly disruptive to the developmental progression of offspring and create an environment conducive to the development of personality pathology.

RESILIENCE

Seminar participants often ask about resilience: Why do some individuals from severely dysfunctional systems do well in spite of abuse, neglect, and so forth? Over the past 25 years researchers have been trying to understand this concept of children at risk and to determine the favorable and unfavorable factors (Matsen & Coatsworth, 1998). In summarizing the research, Matsen and Coatsworth, identify the following factors:

Individual

Good intellectual functioning; Appealing, sociable, easygoing disposition; Self-efficacy, self-confidence, high self-esteem

Family

Close relationship to caring parent figure; Authoritative parenting: warmth, structure, high expectations; Socioeconomic advantages; Connections to extended supportive family networks

Extrafamilial context

Bonds to prosocial adults outside the family; Connections to prosocial organizations; Attending effective schools (p. 212)

The strongest resiliency factors were a strong relationship with caring prosocial adults and intelligence. "The study of competence and resilience offers hope and guidance for those who seek to improve the odds of good developmental outcomes through policy and prevention" (p. 216).

PROGRAMMATIC CONSIDERATIONS AND FOCI OF ATTENTION

QUALITY CHILD CARE

Quality child care is an important issue in developmental science (Hetherington, 1998; Scarr, 1998) and may be another method to mitigate some of the damage sustained in the dysfunctional personologic system. The research has demonstrated that high-quality day care can offset the effects of poor mothering (Scarr). The quality of child care is related to the cost. The lower the cost, the lower the quality of care is. The United States has a two-tier system; poor families and affluent families have access to higher quality day care whereas lower class and middle-class families cannot afford high-quality care. This dilemma is particularly crucial in the case of children from dysfunctional personologic systems in which high-quality care is a mitigating factor that can have a protective effect in the development of more severe psychopathology.

EARLY INTERVENTION

Ramey and Ramey (1998) state that *"early intervention* is a term that refers to a broad array of activities designed to enhance a young child's development" (p. 110). Early intervention for children of poverty and developmental disabilities "can yield significant improvements in cognitive, academic, and social outcomes" (p. 109). Early intervention begins with "a comprehensive assessment of the child's and the family's strengths and needs and extends through the provision of appropriate supports and services to active monitoring and revaluation as the child develops" (p. 110). The effect that early intervention has on personality development has not yet been a focus of researchers' attention, but it is likely that early intervention is better, because personality becomes more entrenched with the passing of time. Families must be taught to emphasize *priming mechanisms* critical to normal development, such as "(a) encouragement to explore the environment, (b) mentoring in basic cognitive and social skills, (c) celebrating new skills, (d) rehearsing and expanding new skills, (e) protection from inappropriate punishment or ridicule for development advances, and (f) stimulation in language and symbolic communication" (p. 115).

Enhancing Emotional Intelligence

In his groundbreaking book, Goleman (1994) makes the case that emotional intelligence is the cornerstone on which character rests. He states that "the bedrock of character is self-discipline; the virtuous life, as philosophers since Aristotle have observed, is based on self-control" (p. 285). Goleman summarizes Salovey's five domains of emotional intelligence: (1) knowing one's emotions; (2) managing emotions; (3) motivating oneself; (4) recognizing emotions in others; and (5) handling relationships. These skills must be taught to members of society so that they are able to function in this complex society. Dysfunctional personologic systems tend to produce individuals who are not well developed emotionally and who require remediation to enable them to progress to a higher level of maturity. Affective education should occur in school systems and should be a required curriculum that families can be involved with.

Ready Access to Drug and Alcohol Treatment

Major strides have been made in the treatment of substance use disorders, but unfortunately many people in need of such service do not receive adequate treatment. Society must strengthen its delivery of care so that individuals suffering from substance use disorders have access to treatment. The current system of punishment and incarceration does little to stem the tide of this social epidemic.

ENCOURAGING A PARADIGMATIC SHIFT

Clinicians and family researchers are well aware of the high prevalence of dysfunctional families and the effects that they have on the personality development of their members. As clinicians and researchers, we need to foster a paradigmatic shift in diagnosis and treatment of these systems. We can no longer view personality pathology as residing only in the individual; we must expand our theories to include the systems in which these pathologies occur. It is imperative that the work to develop an empirically based relational diagnostic system be continued.

INCREASED AWARENESS

Clinicians and policy makers must increase the professional and public awareness of the impact and pervasiveness of disorders of personality and the systems in which they are generated and maintained. Public awareness needs to be fostered in a way that does not stigmatize individuals and families in which dysfunction exists. Mental health professionals need to be able to increase awareness without blaming individuals for their problems and at the same time hold people accountable for their behavior. Perhaps in the near future a Personality Awareness Week will give individuals and families the opportunity to consider the impact that their personality— their strengths and limitations—has on themselves and those in their family and communities. Therapists who are met with the frequent, demoralizing responses heard in this field can remind those patients that behavior changes often lead to personality changes.

DEVELOPING MODEL PROGRAMS OF CLINICAL TREATMENT

We as therapists need to consider delivering treatment in different ways. New and comprehensive model treatment centers that combine state-of-the-art clinical service, including assessment and treatment, can be combined with research and training. Aggressive intervention in the dysfunctional personologic system would probably result in cost savings, considering the amount of emergency room service utilization and general medical overutilization. In my observation, these dysfunctional personologic systems use a disproportionate level of medical, legal, and social services. Model treatment programs, for example, have been developed for the treatment of mood disorders, and outcome findings are highly impressive (McMaster Regional Mood Disorders Program, 1998). An important aspect of programs like the McMaster program is community education, which is critical in identifying the families that require intervention. Model programs should be interdisciplinary in nature and have researchers who are interested in various levels of the biopsychosocial model. Intensive, systemically informed, multimodal treatment could be offered to families on inpatient and outpatient bases with a relapse prevention plan. Vocational rehabilitation and other services could also be offered.

CONCLUSIONS

The societal and economic factors that contribute to the development and maintenance of the dysfunctional personologic system need to be addressed through informed policy decisions and increased awareness. Reduction in the prevalence of personality disorders in the population is an important public health issue. Much research documents the importance of a stable family with enough resources to provide for the enhancement of its members. Society has a responsibility to provide early intervention, treatment, and enhancement so that the multigenerational transmission pattern evident in the dysfunctional personologic system can be modified.

In her seminal article *The Greening of Relationship Science*, Berscheid (1999) writes:

> If public opinion leaders and policy makers really believe that the family as we know it is threatened with extinction, and if they view this constellation of close relationships to be as precious and vital to human welfare and to the future of our culture as they obviously believe endangered species of wildlife are, then they will put their money and their influence alongside their beliefs and support the further development of relationship science. For example, they might well consider investing in a far-ranging big science initiative for the social, behavioral, and biological sciences focused on close relationships, especially marital and parent-child relationships. (p. 265)

References

Ackerman, N. W. (1958). *The Psychoadynamics of family life: Diagnosis and treatment of family relationships.* New York: Basic Books.

Ackerman, N. W. (1966). *Treating the troubled family.* New York: Basic Books.

Alexander, F. G., & French, T. M. (1946). *Psychoanalytic therapy: Principles and applications.* New York: Ronald Press.

Alexander, J. F., & Pugh, C. A. (1996). Oppositional behavior and conduct disorders of children and youth. In F. W. Kaslow (Ed.), *Handbook of relational diagnosis and dysfunctional family patterns* (pp. 210–224). New York: John Wiley & Sons.

Alper, G. (1992). *Portrait of the artist as a young patient: Psychodynamic studies of the creative personality.* New York: Plenum Press/Insight Books.

Alpert, M. C. (1996). Videotaping Psychotherapy. *Journal of Psychotheraphy Practice and Research, 5*(2), 93–105.

American Psychiatric Association. (1994). *Diagnostic and statistical manual of mental disorders* (4th ed.). Washington DC: Author.

Anderson, T. (1996). Language is not innocent. In F. W. Kaslow (Ed.), *Handbook of relational diagnosis and dysfunctional family patterns* (pp. 119–125). New York: John Wiley & Sons.

Arkowitz, H. (Ed.). (1996). Resistance to change in psychotherapy. *In Session: Psychotherapy in Practice, 2*(1), 1–105.

Auerswald, E. H. (1968). Interdisciplinary versus ecological approach. *Family Process, 7*, 202–215.

Ball, S. A., Tennen, H., Poling, J. G., Kranzler, H. R., & Rounsaville, B. J. (1997). Personality disorder, temperament, and character dimensions and the *DSM-IV* Personality disorders in substance abusers. *Journal of Abnormal Psychology, 106*(4), 545–553.

Bandler, R., & Grinder, J. (1975). *The structure of magic: Vol. I.* Palo Alto, CA: Science and Behavior Books.

Barber, J. P., Morse, J. Q., Krakauer, I. D., Chittams, J., & Crits-Chistoph, K. (1997). Change in obsessive-compulsive and avoidant personality disorders following time-limited supportive-expressive therapy. *Psychotherapy, 34*(2), 133–143.

Barlow, D. H. (1996). Health care policy, psychotherapy research, and the future of psychotherapy. *American Psychologist, 51*(10), 1050–1058.

Barth, J. C. (1996). Chronic illness and the family. In F. W. Kaslow (Ed.). *Handbook of relational diagnosis and dysfunctional family patterns* (pp. 496–508). New York: John Wiley & Sons.

Bartholemew, K., & Horowitz, L. M. (1991). Attachment styles among young adults: A test of a four category model. *Journal of Personality and Social Psychology, 61,* 226–244.

Beck, A. T., & Freeman, A., & Associates. (1990). *Cognitive therapy of personality disorders.* New York: Guilford Press.

Beck, A. T., Rush, A. J., Shaw, B. F., & Emery, G. (1979). *Cognitive therapy of depression.* New York: Guilford Press.

Beeder, A. B., & Millman, R. B. (1995). Treatment strategies for comorbid disorders: Psychopathology and substance abuse. In A. M. Washton. *Psychotherapy and substance abuse: A practitioner's handbook* (pp. 76–102). New York: Guilford Press.

Benjamin, L. S. (1993a). Every psychopathology is a gift of love. *Psychotherapy Research, 3*(1), 1–24.

Benjamin, L. S. (1993b). *Interpersonal diagnosis and treatment of personality disorders.* New York: Guilford Press.

Benjamin, L. S. (1997). Personality disorders: Models for treatment and strategies for treatment development. *Journal of Personality Disorders, 11*(4), 307–324.

Beren, P. (Ed.). (1998). *Narcissistic disorders in children and adolescents: Diagnosis and treatment.* New York: Jason Aronson.

Bergantino, L. (1993). *Making impact in therapy: How master clinicians intervene.* New York: Jason Aronson.

Bergantino, L. (1994, Summer). Brief psychotherapy—Family therapy and the pursuit of excellence in a world that only tolerates the illusion of safety! *Voices,* 62–69.

Berkowitz, D. A., Shapiro, R. L., Zinner, J., & Shapiro, E. R. (1974). Family contributions to narcissistic disturbances in adolescents. *International Review of Psychoanalysis, 1,* 353–362.

Berscheid, E. (1999). The greening of relationship science. *American Psychologist, 54*(4), 260–266.

Blatt, S. J., Quinlan, D. M., Zuroff, D. C., & Pilkonis, P. A. (1996). Interpersonal factors in brief treatment of depression: Further analyses of the National Institute of Mental Health treatment of depression collaborative research program. *Journal of Consulting and Clinical Psychology, 64*(1), 162–171.

Borden, E. S. (1979). The generalizability of the psychoanalytic concept of the working alliance. *Psychotherapy, 16,* 252–260.

Boszormenyi-Nagy, I., & Spark, G. M. (1973). *Invisible Loyalties: Reciprocity in intergenerational family therapy.* New York: Harper & Row.

Bowen, M. (1976). Theory in the practice of family therapy. In P. J. Guerin, Jr. (Ed.). *Family therapy: Theory and practice.* (pp. 42–90). New York: Gardner Press.

Bowen, M. (1978). *Family therapy in clinical practice.* New York: Jason Aronson.

Bowlby, J. (1977). The making and breaking of affectional bonds. I. Aetiology and psychopathology in light of attachment theory. *British Journal of Psychiatry, 130,* 201–210.

Bradt, J. O. (1980). The family with young children. In E. A. Carter & M. McGoldrick (Eds.). *The family life cycle: A framework for family therapy* (pp. 121–146). New York: Gardner Press.

Bray, J. H. (1995). Systems-oriented therapy with stepfamilies. In R. H. Mikesell, D. Lusterman, & S. H. McDaniel (Eds.). *Integrating family therapy: Handbook of family psychology and systems theory* (pp. 125–140). Washington, DC: American Psychological Association.

Breunlin, D. C., Rampage, C., & Eovaldi, M. L. (1995). Family therapy supervision: Toward an integrative perspective. In R. H. Mikesell, D. Lusterman, & S. H. McDaniel (Eds.), *Integrating family therapy: Handbook of family psychology and systems theory* (pp. 547–560). Washington, DC: American Psychological Association.

Brody, J. E. (1998a, March 3). Personal health: Depressed parent's children at risk. *The New York Times,* p. F7.

Brody, J. E. (1998b, January 6). Personal health: Trying to cope when a partner or a loved one is chronically depressed. *The New York Times,* p. F9.

Brown, G. W., Birley, J. L. T., & Wing, J. K. (1972). Influence of family life on the course of schizophrenic disorders: A replication. *British Journal of Psychiatry, 121,* 241–258.

Brownell, K. D., Marlatt, G. A., Lichtenstein, E., & Wilson, G. T. (1986). Understanding and preventing relapse. *American Psychologist, 41*(7), 765–782.

Budman, S. H., & Gurman, A. S. (1988). *Theory and practice of brief therapy.* New York: Guilford Press.

Buss, A. J., & Plomin, R. (1975). *A temperament theory of personality development.* New York: John Wiley & Sons.

Buss, A. J., & Plomin, R. (1984). *Temperament: Early developing personality traits.* Hillsdale, NJ: Erlbaum.

Carter, E. A., & McGoldrick, M. (Eds.). (1980). *The family life cycle: A framework for family therapy.* New York: Gardner Press.

Charney, I. W. (1996). Evil in human personality: Disorders of doing harm to others in family relationships. In F. W. Kaslow (Ed.), *Handbook of relational diagnosis and dysfunctional family patterns* (pp. 477–495). New York: John Wiley & Sons.

Cicchetti, D., & Toth, S. L. (1998). The development of depression in children and adolescents. *American Psychologist, 53*(2), 221–241.

Clark, L. A., Livesly, J., & Morey, L. (1997). Personality disorders assessment: The challenge of construct validity. *Journal of Personality Disorders, 11*(3), 205–231.

Clarkin, J. F., & Lenzenweger, M. F. (1996). *Major theories of personality disorder.* New York: Guilford Press.

Cloninger, C. R. (1986). A unified biosocial theory of personality and its role in the development of anxiety states. *Psychiatric Developments, 3*, 167–226.

Cloninger, C. R. (1987). A systematic method for clinical description and classification of personality variables. *Archives of General Psychiatry, 44*, 573–588.

Coley, R. L., & Chase-Lansdale, P. L. (1998). Adolescent pregnancy and parenthood. *American Psychologist, 53*(2), 152–166.

Costa, P. T., & McCrae, R. R. (1992). The five-factor model of personality and its relevance to personality disorders. *Journal of Personality Disorders, 6*, 343–359.

Crittendon, P. M. (1988). Relationships at risk. In J. Belsky & T. Nezworski (Eds.). *Clinical implications of attachment theory* (pp. 136–174). Hillsdale, NJ: Erlbaum.

Daley, D. C., & Lis, J. A. (1995). Relapse prevention: Intervention strategies for mental health clients with comorbid addictive disorders. In A. M. Washton (Ed.), *Psychotherapy and substance abuse: A practitioner's handbook.* New York: Guilford Press.

Davanloo, H. (Ed.). (1980). *Short-term dynamic psychotherapy.* New York: Jason Aronson.

Davanloo, H. (1990). *Unlocking the unconscious: Selected papers of Habib Davanloo, M.D.* New York: John Wiley & Sons.

Denton, W. H. (1996). Problems encountered in reconciling individual and relational diagnosis. In F. W. Kaslow (Ed.), *Handbook of relational diagnosis and dysfunctional family patterns* (pp. 35–45). New York: John Wiley & Sons.

Deutsch, H. (1965). *Neuroses and character types: Clinical psychoanalytic studies.* New York: International Universities Press.

Doane, J. A., & Diamond, D. (1994). *Affect and attachment in the family: A family-based treatment of major psychiatric disorders.* New York: Basic Books.

Donaldson-Pressman, S., & Pressman, R. M. (1994). *The narcissistic family: Diagnosis and treatment.* New York: Lexington Books.

Dutton, D. G., & Starzomski, A. J. (1993). Borderline personality in perpetrators of psychological and physical abuse. *Violence and Victims, 8,* 327–337.

Ekman, P., & Davidson, R. J. (Eds.). (1994). *The nature of emotions: Fundamental questions.* New York: Oxford Press.

Emory, R. E., & Laumann-Billings, L. (1998). An overview of the nature, causes, and consequences of abusive family relationships. *American Psychologist, 53*(2), 121–135.

Engel, G. L. (1977). The need for a new medical model: A challenge for biomedicine. *Science, 196,* 129–136.

Engel, G. L. (1980). The clinical application of the biopsychosocial model. *American Journal of Psychiatry, 137,* 535–544.

Feldman, L. B., & Feldman, S. L. (Eds.). (1997). Integrating psychotherapy and pharmacotherapy. *In Session: Psychotherapy in Practice, 3*(2) 1–109.

Fenichel, O. (1945). *The psychoanalytic theory of the neurosis.* New York: Norton.

Ferenczi, S., & Rank, O. (1925). *The development of psychoanalysis.* New York: Nervous and Mental Diseases Publishing.

Figely, C. R. (1995). Systemic traumatization: Secondary traumatic stress disorder in family therapists. In R. H. Mikesell, D. Lusterman, & S. H. McDaniel (Eds.), *Integrating family therapy: Handbook of family psychology and systems theory* (pp. 571–581). New York: John Wiley & Sons.

Firestone, R. W. (1997). *Combating destructive thought processes: Voice therapy and separation theory.* Thousand Oaks, CA: Sage Publications.

Florsheim, P., Henry, W. P., & Benjamin, L. S. (1996). Integrating individual and interpersonal approaches to diagnosis: The structural analysis of social behavior and attachment theory. In F. W. Kaslow (Ed.), *Handbook of relational diagnosis and dysfunctional patterns* (pp. 81–101). New York: John Wiley & Sons.

Fogarty, T. F. (1975). Triangles. *The Family*, 2, 11–20.

Fogarty, T. F. (1976). System concepts and the dimensions of self. In P. J. Guerin, Jr. (Ed.), *Family Therapy* (pp. 144–153). New York: John Wiley & Sons.

Fosha, D. (1995). Technique and taboo in three short-term dynamic psychotherapies. *Journal of Psychotherapy Practice and Research*, 4, 297–318.

Frances, A. (1987). *DSM-III personality disorders: Diagnosis and treatment.* New York: BMA Audio Cassette—Division of Guilford Press.

Frances, A., Clarkin, J., & Perry, S. (1984). *Differential therapeutics in psychiatry: The art and science of treatment selection.* New York: Brunner/Mazel.

Frankl, V. E. (1959). *Man's search for meaning* (Rev ed.). New York: Washington Square Press.

Freud, S. (1914). Further recommendations in the technique of psychoanalysis: Recollection, repetition, and working through. In *Collected papers* (Vol. 2). London: Hogarth Press.

Freud, S. (1925). Character and anal eroticism. In *Collected papers* (Vol. 2). London: Hogarth Press. (Original work published 1908)

Geffner, R., Barrett, M. J., & Rossman, B. B. R. (1995). Domestic violence and sexual abuse: Multiple systems perspectives. In R. H. Mikesell, D. Lusterman, & S. D. McDaniel (Eds.), *Integrating family therapy: Handbook of family psychology and systems theory* (pp. 501–517). Washington, DC: American Psychological Association.

Gergen, K. J., Hoffman, L., & Anderson, H. (1996). Is diagnosis a disaster? A constructionistic trialogue. In F. W. Kaslow (Ed.) *Handbook of relational diagnosis and dysfunctional family patterns* (pp. 102–118). New York: John Wiley & Sons.

Gerson, R. (1995). The family life cycle: Phases, stages, and crises. In R. H. Mikesell, D. Lusterman, & S. H. McDaniel (Eds.), *Integrating family therapy: Handbook of family psychology and systems theory* (pp. 91–111). Washington, DC: American Psychological Association.

Glick, P. C. (1989). Remarried families, stepfamilies, and stepchildren: A brief demographic profile. *Family Relations, 38*, 2427.

Glickauf-Hughes, C. (1996). Sadomasochistic interactions. In F. W. Kaslow (Ed.), *Handbook of relational diagnosis and dysfunctional family patterns* (pp. 270–286). New York: John Wiley & Sons.

Goldfried, M. R., & Wolfe, B. E. (1996). Psychotherapy practice and research: Repairing a strained alliance. *American Psychologist, 51*(10), 1007–1016.

Goleman, D. (1994). *Emotional intelligence.* New York: Bantam Books.

References   255

Gollan, J. K., Gortner, E. T., & Jacobson, N. S. (1996). Partner relational problems and affective disorders. In F. W. Kaslow (Ed.), *Handbook of relational diagnosis and dystructional family patterns* (pp. 322–337). New York: John Wiley & Sons.

Goreau, A. (1997, December 21). Ménage à cinq: The life and times of violet gordon woodhouse. *The New York Times Book Review*, p. 5.

Greenspan, S. I. (with Benderly, B. L.) (1997). *The growth of the mind and the endangered origins of intelligence.* Reading, MA: Addison-Wesley Publishing.

Grinder, J., & Bandler, R. (1976). *The structure of magic: Vol. II.* Palo Alto, CA: Science and Behavior Books.

Gross, J. (1997, December 18). Fleeing abuse to the streets. *New York Times*, p. B1.

Guerin, P. J., Fogarty, T. F., Fay, L. F., & Kautto, J. G. (1996). *Working with relationship triangles: The one-two-three of psychotherapy.* New York: Guilford Press.

Gustafson, J. P. (1990). The great simplifying conventions of brief individual psychotherapy. In J. K. Zeig & S. G. Gilligan (Eds.), *Brief therapy: Myths, methods, and metaphors* (pp. 407–425). New York: Brunner/Mazel.

Gustafson, J. P. (1997). *The complex secret of brief psychotherapy.* New York: Norton.

Haley, J. (1997). *Leaving home: The therapy of disturbed young people.* New York: Brunner/Mazel.

Hanna, F. J. (1996). Precursors of change: Pivotal points of involvement and resistance in psychotherapy. *Journal of Psychoterapy Integration, 6*(3), 227–264.

Herman, J. L. (1992). *Trauma and recovery.* New York: Basic Books.

Hetherington, E. M. (Ed.). (1998). Applications of developmental science [Special Issue]. *American Psychologist, 53*(2), 93–272.

Hetherington, E. M., Bridges, M., & Insabella, G. M. (1998). What matters? What does not? Five perspectives on the association between marital transitions and children's adjustment. *American Psychologist, 53*(2), 167–184.

Hoffman, L. (1980). The family life cycle and discontinuous change. In E. A. Carter & M. McGoldrick (Eds.), *The family life cycle: A framework for family therapy* (pp. 53–68). New York: Gardner Press.

Holden, G. W., Geffner, R. A., & Jouriles, E. N. (1998). *Children exposed to marital violence: Theories, research and applied issues.* Washington, DC: American Psychological Association.

Horney, K. (1937). *The neurotic personality of our time.* New York: Norton.

Hovarth, A. O. (1995). The therapeutic relationship: From transference to alliance. *In Sessions: Psychotherapy in Practice, 1*(1), 7–17.

Hovarth, A. O., & Symonds, D. D. (1991). Relation between working alliance and outcome in psychotherapy: A meta-analysis. *Journal of Counseling Psychology, 38,* 139–149.

Humphrey, F. (1987). Treating extramarital sexual relationships in sex and couples therapy. In G. Weeks & L. Hof (Eds.), *Integrating sex and marital therapy: A clinical guide* (pp. 149–170). New York: Brunner/Mazel.

Imber-Black, E. (Ed.). (1993). Secrets in families and family therapy. New York: Norton.

Izard, C. E. (1994). Intersystem connections. In P. Ekman & R. J. Davidson (Eds.), *The nature of emotion: Fundamental questions* (pp. 356–361). New York: Oxford University Press.

Jackson, D. D. (1957). The question of family homeostasis. Psychiatric Quarterly Supplement, 31, 79–90.

Jackson, D. D. (1959). Family interaction, family homeostasis, and some implications for cojoint family psychotherapy. In J. Masserman (Ed.), *Individual and familial dynamics* (pp. 122–141). New York: Grune & Statton.

Jacobson, N. S., Gottman, J. M. (1998). *When men batter women: New insights into ending abusive relationships.* New York: Simon & Schuster.

Johnson, J. G., Quigley, J. F., & Sherman, M. F. (1997). Adolescent personality disorder symptoms mediate the relationship between perceived parental behavior and axis I symptomatology. *Journal of Personality Disorders, 11*(4), 381–390.

Joseph, S. (1997). *Personality disorders: New symptom-focused drug therapy.* New York: Haworth Press.

Josephs, L. (1997). The view from the tip of the iceberg. *Journal of the American Psychoanalytic Association, 45* (2), 425–463.

Kagan, J. (1994). *Galen's Prophecy.* New York: Basic Books.

Kaslow, F. W. (1995). The dynamics of divorce therapy. In R. H. Mikesell, D. Lusterman, & S. McDaniel (Eds.), *Integrating family therapy: Handbook of family psychology and systems theory* (pp. 271–283). Washington DC: American Psychological Association.

Kaslow, F. W. (Ed.). (1996). *Handbook of relational diagnosis and dysfunctional family patterns.* New York: John Wiley & Sons.

Kaslow, N. J., Deering, C. G., & Ash, P. (1996). Relational diagnosis of child and adolescent depression. In F. W. Kaslow (Ed.), *Handbook of relational diagnosis and dysfunctional family patterns* (pp. 171–185). New York: John Wiley & Sons.

Kernberg, O. (1984). *Severe personality disorders: Psychotherapeutic strategies.* New Haven, CT: Yale University Press.

Kernberg, O. F. (1996). A psychoanalytic theory of personality disorders. In J. F. Clarkin & M. F. Lenzenweger (Eds.), *Major theories of personality disorder* (pp. 106–140). New York: Guilford Press.

Kirschner, S., & Kirschner, D. A. (1996). Relational components of the incest survivor syndrome. In F. W. Kaslow (Ed.), *Handbook of relational diagnosis and dysfunctional family patterns* (pp. 407–419). New York: John Wiley & Sons.

Koedam, W. S. (1996). Dissociative identity disorder in relational contexts. In F. W. Kaslow (Ed.), *Handbook of relational diagnosis and dysfunctional family patterns* (pp. 420–433). New York: John Wiley & Sons.

Koenigsberg, H. W. (1997). Integrating psychotherapy in the treatment of borderline personality disorder. *In Session; Psychotherapy in Practice, 3*(2), 39–56.

Kohut, H. (1977). *The restoration of the self.* New York: International Universities Press.

Kramer, P. D. (1993). *Listening to Prozac.* New York: Viking.

Lambert, M. J. (1992). Psychotherapy outcome research: Implications for integrative and eclectic therapists. In J. C. Norcross & M. R. Goldfried (Eds.), *Handbook of psychotherapy integration* (pp. 94–129). New York: Basic Books.

Lambert, M. J., Shapiro, D. A., & Bergin, A. E. (1986). The effectiveness of psychotherapy. In S. L. Garfield & A. E. Bergin (Eds.), *Handbook of psychotherapy and behavior change* (3rd ed., pp. 157–212). New York: John Wiley & Sons.

Laporte, L., & Guttman, H. (1996). Traumatic childhood experiences as risk factors for borderline and other personality disorders. *Journal of Personality Disorders, 10*(3), 247–259.

Levitan, R. D., Parikh, S. V., Lesage, A. D., Hegadoren, K. M., Adams, M., Kennedy, S. H., & Goering, P. N. (1998). Major depression in individuals with a history of childhood physical or sexual abuse: Relationship to neurovegetative features, mania, and gender. *American Journal of Psychiatry, 155*(12), 1747–1752.

Lewis, J., Beaver, W. R., Gossett, J. T., & Phillips, V. A. (1976). *No single thread: Psychological health and the family system.* New York: Brunner/Mazel.

Lidz, T. (1973). *The origin and treatment of schizophrenic disorders.* New York: Basic Books.

Linehan, M. M. (1993). *Cognitive-behavioral treatment of borderline personality disorder*. New York: Guilford Press.

Livesly, W. J. (1995). *The DSM-IV personality disorders*. New York: Guilford Press.

Little criminals (episode 1513). (1997). In *Frontline*. Boston, MA: WGBH Educational Foundation.

Loeber, R., & Stouthamer-Loeber, M. (1998). Development of juvenile aggression and violence: Some common misconceptions and controversies. *American Psychologist, 53*(2), 242–259.

Lusterman, D. (1995). Treating marital infidelity. In R. H., Mikesell, D. Lusterman, & S. H. McDaniel (Eds.), *Integrating family therapy: Handbook of family psychology and systems theory* (pp. 259–269). Washington, DC: American Psychological Association.

Lynam, D. R. (1998). Early identification of the fledgling psychopath: Locating the psychopathic child in the current nomenclature. *Journal of Abnormal Psychology, 107*(4), 566–575.

Lyons, M. J., Tyrer, P., Gunderson, J., & Tohen, M. (1998). Special feature: Heuristic models of comorbidity of axis I and axis II disorders. *Journal of Personality Disorders, 11*(3), 206–269.

Madanes, C., & Haley, J. (1977). Dimensions of family therapy. *Journal of Mental and Nervous Disease, 165*(2), 88–98.

Magnavita, J. J. (1993a). The evolution of short-term dynamic psychotherapy: Treatment of the future? *Professional Psychology: Research and Practice, 24*(3), 360–365.

Magnavita, J. J. (1993b). The treatment of passive-aggressive personality disorder. Part I. *International Journal of Short-Term Psychotherapy, 8*(1), 29–41.

Magnavita, J. J. (1993c). The treatment of passive-aggressive personality disorder. Part II. *International Journal of Short-Term Psychotherapy, 8*(2), 109–110.

Magnavita, J. J. (1994a). Premature termination of short-term dynamic psychotherapy. *International Journal of Short-Term Psychotherapy, 9*(4), 213–228.

Magnavita, J. J. (1994b). The process of working through and outcome: The treatment of the passive-aggressive personality disorder. Part III. *International Journal of Short-Term Psychotherapy, 9*(1), 1–17.

Magnavita, J. J. (1996, September 1 & 27). Understanding and changing personality. *Self-Health Networker*

Magnavita, J. J. (1997a). Accelerated methods for treating personality disorders: Upgrading your clinical toolbox. *Psychotherapy in Private Practice, 16*(4), 17–34.

Magnavita, J. J. (1997b). *Restructuring personality disorders: A short-term dynamic approach.* New York: Guilford Press.

Magnavita, J. J. (1997c). Treating personality disorders. Psychotherapy's frontier. *Psychotherapy Bulletin, 32*(1), 23–28.

Magnavita, J. J. (Ed.) (1998a). Advancements in the treatment of personality disorders: Introduction. *In Session: Psychotherapy in Practice, 4*(4), 1–4.

Magnavita, J. J. (1998b). Challenges in the treatment of personality disorders: When the disorder demands comprehensive integration. *In Session: Psychotherapy in Private Practice, 4*(4), 5–17.

Magnavita, J. J. (1998c). Methods of restructuring personality disorders with comorbid syndromes. *In Session: Psychotherapy in Practice, 4*(4), 73–89.

Mahrer, A. R. (1997). What are the "breakthrough problems" in the field of psychotherapy? *Psychotherapy, 34*(1), 81–85.

Main, M. & Goldwyn, R. (1985). *An adult attachment classification system.* Unpublished manuscript, University of California Department of Psychology.

Main, M., & Solomon, J. (1990). Procedures for indentifying infants as disorganized/disoriented during the strange situation. In M. T. Greenberg, D. Cicchetti, & E. M. Cummings (Eds.). *Attachment in the preschool years: Theory, research and intervention* (pp. 121–160). Chicago: University of Chicago Press.

Maine, M. (1991). *Father hunger: Fathers, daughters, & food.* Carlsbad, CA: Gürze Books.

Malan, D. (1963). *Brief study of psychotherapy.* New York: Plenum Press.

Malan, D. M. (1976). *The frontier of brief psychotherapy.* New York: Plenum Press.

Malan, D. M. (1979). *Individual psychotherapy and the science of psychodynamics.* London: Butterworth.

Marlatt, G. A., & Gordon, J. R. (1985). *Relapse prevention: Maintenance strategies in the treatment of addictive behavior.* New York: Guilford Press.

Masterson, J. F. (1988). *The search for the real self: Unmasking the personality disorders of our age.* New York: Free Press.

Matsen, A. S., & Coatsworth, J. D. (1998). The development of competence in favorable and unfavorable environments. *American Psychologist, 53*(2), 205–220.

Maxmen, J. S., & Ward, N. G. (1995). *Essential psychopathology and its treatment* (2nd ed., Rev. for *DSM-IV*). New York: Norton.

McCormack, C. C. (1989). The borderline/schizoid marriage: The holding environment as an essential construct. *Journal of Marital and Family Therapy, 15*(3), 299–309.

McCrae, R. R., & Costa, P. T., Jr. (1997). Personality trait structure as a human universal. *American Psychologist, 52*(5), 509–516.

McCullough Vaillant, L. (1997). *Changing character: Short-term anxiety-regulating psychotherapy for restructuring defenses, affects, and attachments.* New York: Basic Books.

McDaniel, S. H., Hepworth, J., & Doherty, W. (1992). *Medical family therapy: A biopsychosocial approach to families with health problems.* New York: Basic Books.

McDaniel, S. H., Hepworth, J., & Doherty, W. (1995). Medical family therapy with somatizing patients: The co-creation of therapeutic stories. In R. H. Mikesell, D. Lusterman, & S. H. McDaniel (Eds.), *Integrating family therapy: Handbook of family psychology and systems theory* (pp. 377–388). New York: John Wiley & Sons.

McGoldrick, M., & Gerson, R. (1985). *Genograms in family assessment.* New York: Norton.

McLoyd, V. C. (1998). Socioeconomic disadvantage and child development. *American Psychologist, 53*(2), 185–204.

McMaster Regional Mood Disorders Program (1998). Confronting mood disorders through clinical care, research, and education. *Psychiatric Services, 49*(10), 1341–1343.

McWilliams, N. (1994). *Psychoanalytic diagnosis: Understanding personality structure in the clinical process.* New York: Guilford Press.

Messer, S. (1996). A psychodynamic perspective on resistance in psychotherapy: Vive la resistance. *In Session: Psychotherapy in Practice, 2*(1), 25–32.

Messer S. B., & Woolfolk, R. L. (in press). Philosophical issues in psychotherapy. *Clinical Psychology: Science and Practice.*

Mikesell, R. H., Lusterman, D. D., & McDaniel, S. H. (Eds.). (1995). *Integrating family therapy: Handbook of family psychology and systems theory.* Washington, DC: American Psychological Association.

Miklowitz, D. J. (1995). The evolution of family-based psychopathology. In R. H. Mikesell, D. D. Lusterman, & S. H. McDaniel (Eds.), *Integrating family therapy: Handbook of family psychology and systems theory* (pp. 183–197). Washington, DC: American Psychological Association.

Miller, A. (1983). *The drama of the gifted child.* New York: Noonday Press.

Miller, W. R., & Brown, S. A. (1997). Why psychologists should treat alcohol and drug problems. *American Psychologist, 52*(12), 1269–1279.

Miller, W. R., & C'deBaca, J. (1994). Quantum change: Toward a psychology of transformation. In T. F. Heatherton & J. L. Weinberger (Eds.), *Can personality change?* (pp. 253–280). Washington, DC: American Psychological Association.

Miller, W. R., & Rollnick, S. (1991). *Motivational interviewing: Preparing people to change addictive behavior.* New York: Guilford Press.

Millon, T. (1990). *Toward a new personology: An evolutionary model.* New York: John Wiley & Sons.

Millon, T., & Davis, R. D. (1996). *Disorders of personality: DSM-IV and beyond* (2nd ed.). New York: John Wiley & Sons.

Millon, T., Everly, G., & Davis, R. D. (1993). How can knowledge of psychopathology facilitate psychotherapy integration? A view from the personality disorders. *Journal of Psychotherapy Integration, 3*(4), 331–352.

Minuchin, S., & Fishman, H. (1981). *Family therapy techniques.* Cambridge, MA: Harvard University Press.

Morrel, A. (1998). Attention deficit disorder and its relationship to narcissistic pathology. In P. Beren (Ed.), *Narcissistic disorders in children and adolescents: Diagnosis and treatment.* New York: Jason Aronson.

Moultrup, D. (1990). *Husbands, wives, and lovers: The emotional system of the extramarital affair.* New York: Guilford Press.

Murphy, S. L., & Khantzian, E. J. (1995). Addiction as a "self-medication" disorder: Application of ego psychology to the treatment of substance abuse. In A. M. Washton (Ed.), *Psychotherapy and substance abuse: A practitioner's handbook* (pp. 161–175). New York: Guilford Press.

Napier, A. Y., & Whitaker, C. A. (1978). *The family crucible: The intense experience of family therapy.* New York: Harper & Row.

National Center for Infant Clinical Programs (1994). *Diagnostic classification of mental health and developmental disorders of infancy and early childhood.* Arlington, VA: Author.

Nichols, W. C. (1988). *Marital therapy: an integrative approach.* New York: Guilford Press.

Nichols, W. C. (1996). Persons with antisocial and histrionic personality disorders in relationships. In F. W. Kaslow (Ed.), *Handbook of relational diagnosis and dysfunctional family patterns* (pp. 287–299). New York: John Wiley & Sons.

Norcross, J., & Goldfried, M. (Eds.). (1992). *Handbook of psychotherapy integration.* New York: Basic Books.

Norcross, J. C., & Newman, C. F. (1992). Psychotherapy integration: Setting the context. In J. C. Norcross & M. R. Goldfried (Eds.), *Handbook of psychotherapy integration* (pp. 3–45). New York: Basic Books.

Olson, D. H. (1996). Clinical assessment of treatment interventions using the family circumplex model. In F. W. Kaslow (Ed.), *Handbook of relational diagnosis and dysfunctional family patterns* (pp. 59–101). New York: John Wiley & Sons.

Ornish, D. (1998). *Love and survival: The scientific basis for the healing power of intimacy.* New York: HarperCollins.

Pankseep, J. (1994). The basics of basic emotions. In P. Ekman & R. J. Davidson (Eds.), *The nature of emotion: Fundamental questions* (pp. 20–24). New York: Oxford University Press.

Paris, J. (1994). The etiology of borderline personality disorder: A biopsychosocial approach. *Psychiatry, 57,* 316–325.

Parker, G. (1997). The etiology of personality disorders: A review and consideration of research models. *Journal of Personality Disorders, 11*(4), 345–369.

Patterson, T. E., & Lusterman, D. D. (1996). The relational reimbursement dilemma. In F. W. Kaslow (Ed.), *Handbook of relational diagnosis and dysfunctional family patterns* (pp. 46–58). New York: John Wiley & Sons.

Pearlman, L. A., & Saakvitne, K. W. (1995). *Trauma and the therapist: Countertransference and vicarious traumatization in psychotherapy with incest survivors.* New York: Norton.

Peck, M. S. (1983). *People of the lie: The hope for healing human evil.* New York: Simon & Schuster.

Perlmutter, R. A. (1996). *A family approach to psychiatric disorders.* Washington, DC: American Psychiatric Press.

Pianta, R. B., Egeland, B., & Erickson, M. F. (1989). The antecedents of maltreatment: Results of the Mother-Child Interaction Research Project. In D. Cicchetti & V. Carlson (Eds.), *Child maltreatment: Theory and research on the causes and consequences of child abuse and neglect* (pp. 203–253). New York: Cambridge University Press.

Pilkonis, P. (1988). Personality prototypes among depressives: Themes of dependency and autonomy. *Journal of Personality Disorders, 2* (2), 144–152.

Pinsof, W. M. (1995). *Integrative problem-centered therapy: A synthesis of family, individual, and biological therapies.* New York: Basic Books.

Piper, W. E., & Rosie, J. S. (1998). Group treatment of personality disorders: The power of the group in the intensive treatment of personality disorders. *In Session: Psychotherapy in Practice, 4*(4), 19–34.

Pitta, P. (1998). Child centered family: An integrated systemic and psychodynamic approach. *Psychotherapy Bulletin, 23*(2), 24–30.

Pretzer, J. L., & Beck, A. T. (1996). A cognitive theory of personality disorders. In J. F. Clarkin & M. E. Lenzenweger (Eds.). *Major theories of personality disorders* (pp. 36–105). New York: Guilford Press.

Prochaska, J. O., DiClemente, C. C., & Norcross, J. C. (1992). In search of how people change: Applications to addictive behaviors. *American Psychologist, 47*(9), 1102–1114.

Rachman, A. W. (1997). *Sandor Ferenczi: The psychotherapist of tenderness and passion.* New York: Jason Aronson.

Rait, D. S. (1995). The therapeutic alliance in couples and family therapy: Theory in practice. *In Session: Psychotherapy in Practice, 1*(1), 59–72.

Ramey, C. T., & Ramey S. L. (1998). Early intervention and early experience. *American Psychologist, 53*(2), 109–120.

Reich, W. (1945). *Character analysis* (3rd ed.). New York: Noonday Press.

Reiss, D. (1996). Foreword. In F. W. Kaslow (Ed.), *Handbook of relational diagnosis and dysfunctional patterns* (pp. ix–xv). New York: John Wiley & Sons.

Rogers, C. R. (1957). The necessary and sufficient conditions of therapeutic personality change. *Journal of Consulting Psychology, 21*, 95–103.

Rueveni, U. (1975). Network intervention with a family in crisis. *Family Process, 14*, 193–203.

Safran, J. (1993). The therapeutic alliance rupture as a transtheoretical phenomenon: Definitional and conceptual issues. *Journal of Psychotherapy Integration, 3*, 33–49.

Safran, J. D., & Messer, S. B. (1997). Psychotherapy integration: A postmodern critique. *Clinical Psychology: Science and Practice, 4*, 140–154.

Sameroff, M. A., & Emde, R. M. (1989). *Relationship disturbances in early childhood: A developmental approach.* New York: Basic Books.

Sauber, S. R., Beiner, S. F. & Meddoff, G. S. (1995). Divorce Mediation: A new system for dealing with the family in transition. In R. H. Mikesell, D. Lusterman, & S. H. McDaniel (Eds.), *Integrating family therapy: Handbook of family psychology and systems theory* (pp. 285–297). Washington, DC: American Psychological Association.

Scarr, S. (1998). American child care today. *American Psychologist, 53*(2), 95–108.

Schnarch, D. M. (1991). *Constructing the sexual crucible: An integration of sexual and marital therapy.* New York: Norton.

Schnarch, D. M. (1995). *A family systems approach to sex therapy and intimacy.* In R. H. Mikesell, D. Lusterman, & S. H. McDaniel (Eds.), *Integrating family therapy: Handbook of family psychology and systems theory* (pp. 239–257). Washington, DC: American Psychological Association.

Schneewind, K. A., & Ruppert, S. (1998). *Personality and family development: An intergenerational longitudinal comparison.* Hillsdale, NJ: Erlbaum.

Schorer, L. R., Friedman, J. M., Weiler, S. J., Heiman, J. R., & LoPiccolo, J. (1980). *A multi-axial descriptive system for the sexual dysfunctions: Categories and manual.* Stony Brook, NY: Sex Therapy Center.

Seaburn, D., Landau-Stanton, J., & Horowitz, S. (1995). Core techniques in family therapy. In R. H. Mikesell, D. D. Lusterman, & S. H. McDaniel

(Eds.), *Integrating family therapy: Handbook of family psychology and systems theory* (pp. 5–26). Washington, DC: American Psychological Association.

Seligman, M. E. P. (1996). Science as an ally of practice. *American Psychologist, 51*(10), 1072–1079.

Selvini-Palazzoli, M. (1985). The problem of the sibling as the referring person. *Journal of Marital and Family Therapy, 11,* 21–34.

Selvini-Palazzoli, M., Boscolo, L., Cecchin, G. F., & Prata, G. (1978). *Paradox and counterparadox: A new model in the therapy of the family in schizophrenic transaction.* New York: Jason Aronson.

Shapiro, D. (1965). *Neurotic Styles.* New York: Basic Books.

Shapiro, D. (1996). Character and psychotherapy. *American Journal of Psychotherapy, 50*(1), 3–13.

Shapiro, E. R., & Carr, A. W. (1991). *Lost in familiar places: Creating new connections between the individual and society.* New Haven, CT: Yale University Press.

Shapiro, E. R., Zinner, J., Shapiro, R. L., & Berkowitz, D. A. (1975). The influence of family experience on borderline personality development. *International Review of Psychoanalysis, 2,* 399–411.

Sifneos, P. E. (1987). *Short-term dynamic psychotherapy: Evaluation and technique* (2nd ed.). New York: Plenum Medical.

Skynner, A. C. R. (1976). *Systems of family and marital psychotherapy.* New York: Brunner/Mazel.

Slavik, S., Carlson, J., & Sperry, L. (1992). Adlerian marital therapy with the passive-aggressive partner. *The American Journal of Family Therapy, 20*(1), 25–35.

Soloff, P. (1997). Psychobiologic perspectives on treatment of personality disorders. *Journal of Personality Disorders, 11*(4), 336–344.

Solomon, M. F. (1996). Understanding and treating couples with borderline disorders. In F. W. Kaslow (Ed.), *Handbook of relational diagnosis and dysfunctional family patterns* (pp. 251–269). New York: John Wiley & Sons.

Sperry, L. (1995). *Handbook of diagnosis and treatment of DSM-IV personality disorders.* New York: Brunner/Mazel.

Stader, M. (1996). *Object relations brief therapy: The therapeutic relationship in short-term work.* New York: Jason Aronson.

Stanton, M. D., & Heath, A. W. (1995). Family treatment of alcohol and drug abuse. In R. H. Mikesell, D. Lusterman, & S. H. McDaniel (Eds.), *Integrating family therapy: Handbook of family psychology and systems theory* (pp. 529–541). Washington DC: American Psychological Association.

Stanton, M. D., & Todd, T. C. (1979). Structural family therapy with drug addicts. In E. Kaufman & P. Kaufmann (Eds.), *Family therapy of drug and alcohol abuse* (pp. 55–69). New York: Gardner Press.

Stein, J. (Ed.). (1975). *The Random House College Dictionary.* New York: Random House.

Stellato-Kabat, D., Stellato-Kabat, J., & Garrett, J. (1995). Treating chemical-dependent couples and families. In A. M. Washton (Ed.), *Psychotherapy and substance abuse: A practitioner's handbook* (pp. 314–336). New York: Guilford Press.

Stone, M. (1993). *Abnormalities of personality: Beyond and within the realm of treatment.* New York: Norton.

Strack, S., & Lorr, M. (1997). Invited essay: The challenge of differentiating normal and disordered personality. *Journal of Personality Disorders, 1*(2), 105–122.

Stricker, G., & Gold, J. (Eds.). (1993). *Comprehensive handbook of psychotherapy integration.* New York: Plenum Medical.

Sullivan, H. S. (1953). *The interpersonal theory of psychiatry.* New York: Norton.

Sullivan, H. S. (1954). *The psychiatric interview.* New York: Norton.

Synder, D. K., Cavell, T. A., Heffer, R. W., & Mangrum, L. F. (1995). Marital and family assessment: A multifaceted, multilevel approach. In R. H. Mikesell, D. Lusterman, & S. H. McDaniel (Eds.), *Integrating family therapy: Handbook of family psychology and systems theory* (pp. 163–197). Washington, DC: American Psychological Association.

Terkelsen, K. G. (1980). Toward a theory of the family life cycle. In E. A. Carter & M. McGoldrick (Eds.), *The family life cycle: A framework for family therapy* (pp. 21–52). New York: Gardner Press.

Thomas, A., & Chess, S. (1977). *Temperament and development.* New York: Brunner/Mazel.

Trepper, T. S., & Niedner, D. M. (1996). Intrafamily child sexual abuse. In F. W. Kaslow (Ed.), *Handbook of relational diagnosis and dysfunctional family patterns* (pp. 394–406). New York: John Wiley & Sons.

Tyrer, P. (1988). *Personality disorders: Diagnosis, management, and course.* Boston: Wright.

Tyrer, P. (1995). Are personality disorders well classified in *DSM-IV?* In W. J. Lively (Ed.); *The DSM-IV personality disorders* (pp. 29–42). New York: Guilford Press.

Tyrer, P., Gunderson, J., Lyons, M., & Tohen M. (1997). Extent of comorbidity between mental states and personality disorders. *Journal of Personality Disorders, 11*(3) 242–259.

van der Kolk, B. A., McFarlane, A. C., & Weisaeth, L. (Eds.). (1996). *Traumatic stress: The effects of overwhelming experience on mind, body, and society.* New York: Guilford Press.

Vaughn, C. E., & Leff, J. P. (1976). The influence of family and social factors on the course of psychiatric illness: A comparison of schizophrenic and depressed neurotic patients. *British Journal of Psychiatry, 129*, 125–137.

Wachtel, P. L., & McKinney, M. K. (1992). Cyclical psychodynamics and integrative psychodynamic tharapy. In J. C. Norcross & M. R. Goldried (Eds.), *Handbook of Psychotherapy Integration* (pp. 335–370). New York: Basic Books.

Walker, L. (1996). Assessment of abusive spousal relationships. In F. W. Kaslow (Ed.), *Handbook of relational diagnosis and dysfunctional family patterns* (pp. 338–356). New York: John Wiley & Sons.

Watson, J. C., & Greenberg, L. S. (1995). Alliance ruptures and repairs in experiential psychotherapy. *In Session: Psychotherapy in Practice, 1*(1), 19–31.

Watzlawick, P., Beavin, J. H., & Jackson, D. D. (1967). *Pragmatics of human communication: A study of interactional patterns, pathologies, and paradoxes,* New York: Norton.

Watzlawick, P., Weakland, J., & Fisch, R. (1974). *Change—Principles of problem formation and problem resolution.* New York: Norton.

Weil, A. (1995). *Spontaneous Healing.* New York: Fawcett Columbine.

West, M. & Sheldon, A. (1988). Classification of pathological attachment patterns in adults. *Journal of Personality Disorders, 2* (2), 153–159.

Weston, D., & Arkowitz-Weston, L. (1998). Limitations of Axis II in diagnosing personality pathology in clinical practice. *American Journal of Psychiatry, 155*(12), 1767–1771.

Whitaker, C. A., & Keith, D. V. (1980). Symbolic-experiential family therapy. In A. S. Gurman & D. S. Kniskern (Eds.), *Handbook of family therapy* (pp. 187–225). New York: Brunner/Mazel.

Williams, T. G. (1996). Substance abuse and addictive personality disorders. In F. W. Kaslow (Ed.), *Handbook of relational diagnosis and dysfunctional family patterns* (pp. 448–462). New York: John Wiley & Sons.

Wynne, L. C., (1996). Foreword. In R. A. Perlmutter, *A family approach to psychiatric disorders* (pp. ix–xii) Washington, DC: American Psychiatric Press.

Wynne, L. C., & Singer, M. T. (1963). Thought disorder and family relations of schizophrenics: I. A research strategy. *Archives of General Psychiatry, 9*, 191–198.

Yalom, I. D. (1980). *Existential psychotherapy.* New York: Basic Books.

Young, J. E. (1990). *Cognitive therapy for personality disorders: A schema-focused approach* (Rev. ed.). Sarasota, FL: Professional Resource Press.

Young J. E., & Gluhoski, V. L. (1996). Schema-focused diagnosis for personality disorders. In F. W. Kaslow (Ed.), *Handbook of relational diagnosis and dysfunctional family patterns* (pp. 300–321). New York: John Wiley & Sons.

Zanarini, M. C., Frankenburg, F. R., Dubo, E. D., Sickel, A. E., Trikha, A., Levin, A., & Reynolds, V. (1998). Axis I comorbidity of borderline personality disorder. *American Journal of Psychiatry, 155*(12), 1733–1739.

Zucker, R. A., & Lisansky Gomberg, E. S. (1986). Etiology of alcoholism reconsidered: The case for a biopsychosocial process. *American Psychologist, 41*(7), 783–793.

Author Index

Ackerman, N. W., 26, 32, 42, 225
Ainsworth, 38
Alder, W., xii
Alexander, F. G., 8, 10, 83
Alexander, J. F., 210
Alper, G., 79
Alpert, M. C., 15
Ameen, L., xii
Anderson, H., 89–90
Anderson, T., 185, 187
Arkowitz, H., 232
Ash, P., 148
Auerswald, E. H., 81

Ball, S. A., 92
Bandler, R., 185, 194, 196
Barlow, D. H., 5
Barlow, J. P., 90
Barrett, M. J., 144
Barth, J. C., 67
Bartholomew, 38, 39
Beaver, W. R., 54
Beavin, J. H., 187
Beck, A. T., 52, 71, 73–74
Beeder, A. B., 132
Beiner, S. F., 212
Benjamin, L. S., 9, 10, 21, 52, 71, 74, 170, 171
Beren, P., 210
Bergantino, L., 160, 197
Bergin, A. E., 15
Berkowitz, D. A., 62, 161

Berman, L., xii
Berne, E., 191
Berscheid, E., vi, 248
Birley, J. L. T., 196
Blatt, S. J., 11
Bordin, E. S., 222
Boscolo, L., 190
Boszormenyi-Nagy, I., 51
Bowen, M., 20, 22, 24, 29, 31, 53, 55, 64, 101, 205
Bowlby, J., 9, 38, 39
Bradt, J. O., 25
Bray, J. H., 213
Breunlin, D. C., 19–20
Bridges, M., 243
Brody, J. E., 52, 67
Browen, 64
Brown, G. W., 196
Brown, S. A., 133
Brownell, K. D., 7
Budman, S. H., 142, 163, 164
Buss, A. J., 36

Carlson, J., 202
Carr, A. W., 51
Carter, E. A., 50, 51, 101, 112, 203
Cavell, T. A., 101
C'deBaca, J., 12, 110
Cecchin, G. F., 190
Charney, I. W., 65
Chase-Lansdale, P. L., 242

Chess, S., 36
Cicchetti, D., 241
Clark, L. A., 92
Clarkin, J. F., 15, 71
Cloninger, C. R., 34
Coatsworth, J. D., 241, 244
Coley, R. L., 242
Costa, P. T., Jr., 42–43, 92
Crittendon, 38

Daley, D. C., 7, 132
Davanloo, H., xii, 8, 14, 20, 84, 99, 110
Davidson, R. J., 195
Davis, R. D., 4, 7, 9, 13, 14, 16, 20, 33, 37,
    46, 75, 85, 90, 92, 100
Deering, C. G., 148
Denton, W. H., 11, 33, 43, 53, 89, 91, 94
Deutsch, H., 72
Diamond, D., 63
DiClemente, C. C., 12
Doane, J. A., 63
Doherty, W., 153
Donaldson-Pressman, S., 50, 54, 62, 63
Dorman, K., xiii
Dutton, D. G., 146, 218

Egeland, B., 242
Ekman, P., 195
Emde, R. M., 9
Emde, S. B., 106
Emery, G., 73–74
Emory, R. E., 186, 242
Engel, G. L., 33
Eovaldi, M. L., 19–20
Erickson, M. F., 190, 242
Everly, G., 13

Fay, L. F., 13, 23
Feldman, L. B., 161
Feldman, S. L., 161
Fenichel, O., 72
Ferenczi, S., 7, 14, 77–79
Ferrante, A., xii
Firemen, L., xii
Firestone, R. W., 25, 30, 41
Fisch, R., 189
Fishman, H., 119, 190
Florsheim, P., 9, 10, 37
Fogarty, T. F., 13, 20, 23–24, 25
Fosha, D., 7
Frances, A., 15, 46, 80, 95, 158
Frankl, V. E., 30
Franklin, K., xiii
Freeman, A., 52, 71, 74

French, T. M., 10, 83
Freud, S., 72, 123
Friedman, J. M., 146

Garrett, J., 132
Geffner, R. A., 144, 145, 146, 184
Gergen, K. J., 89–90, 187
Gerson, R., 2, 12, 31, 43, 101, 102, 166, 202, 203
Glick, P. C., 213
Glickauf-Hughes, C., 65, 66, 201
Gold, J., 13
Goldfried, M., xi, 5, 7, 13
Goldwyn, 39
Goleman, D., 41, 194, 246
Gollan, J. K., 67, 148
Gordon, J. R., 7
Goreau, A., 2
Gortner, E. T., 67, 148
Gossett, J. T., 54
Gottman, J. M., 66
Greenberg, L. S., 223
Greenspan, S. I., 9, 35–36, 37, 40
Grinder, J., 185, 194, 196
Gross, J., 1
Guerin, P. J., 13, 20, 23, 24, 27, 31, 32–33,
    202, 204, 205, 206, 207, 209, 217
Gunderson, J., 61
Gurman, A. S., 142, 163, 164
Gustafson, J. P., 13, 77, 128, 129
Guttman, H., 144

Haley, J., 119, 203
Hanna, F. J., 12, 114, 115, 116, 118
Heath, A. W., 130, 132
Heffer, R. W., 101
Heiman, J. R., 146
Henry, W. P., 9
Hepworth, J., xii, 153
Herman, J. L., 15, 144
Hetherington, E. M., 241, 243, 245
Hoffman, L., 32, 89–90, 110, 113
Holden, G. W., 184
Horowitz, 38, 39
Horowitz, S., 80
Hovarth, A. O., 221–222, 234
Humphrey, F., 207

Imber-Black, E., 54
Insabella, G. M., 243
Izard, C. E., 195

Jackson, D. D., 188
Jacobson, N. S., 66, 67, 148
Joseph, S., 34, 161

Josephs, L., 84
Jouriles, E. N., 184

Kagan, 36
Kaslow, F. W., viii, xi, 8, 9, 19, 20, 50, 75, 94, 211, 212
Kaslow, N. J., 148
Kautto, J. G., 13, 23
Keith, D. V., 86, 197, 227
Kernberg, O. F., 36, 40–41, 71, 72, 99
Khantzian, E. J., 132
Kirschner, D. A., 144, 146
Kirschner, S., 144, 146
Knoblauch, F., xii
Koenigsberg, H. W., 161
Kohut, H., 137
Kramer, P. D., 34
Kranzler, H. R., 92

Lambert, M. J., 15, 80
Landau-Stanton, J., 80
Laporte, L., 144
Laumann-Billings, L., 186, 242
Leff, J. P., 196
Lenzenweger, M. F., 71
Levitan, R. D., 169
Lewis, J., 54
Lichtenstein, E., 7
Linehan, M. M., 74, 84, 160
Lis, J. A., 7, 132
Lisansky Gomberg, E. S., 33
Livesly, J., 92
Livesly, W. J., 9, 34, 91
Loeber, R., 243
LoPiccolo, J., 146
Lorr, M., x
Lusterman, D. D., 21, 75, 135, 207, 208
Lynam, D. R., 36
Lyons, M., 61

Madanes, C., 119
Magnavita, A. G., xiii
Magnavita, E., E., and C., xiii
Magnavita, J. J., 7, 8, 13, 15, 16, 25, 32, 52, 55, 83, 90, 110, 123, 163, 168, 206
Mahrer, A. R., 5
Main, M., 38, 39
Maine, M., 57
Malan, D. M., 8, 20, 110
Mangrum, L. F., 101
Marlatt, G. A., 7
Masterson, J. F., 201, 208, 213, 214
Matsen, A. S., 241, 244
Maxmen, J. S., 6, 99

McCormick, C. C., 201, 202
McCrae, R. R., 42–43, 92
McCullough Vaillant, L., 32, 52, 73, 83, 85, 123
McDaniel, D. D., 153
McDaniel, S. H., 75, 154
McFarlane, A. C., 15
McGoldrick, M., 2, 31, 43, 50, 51, 101, 102, 112, 203
McKinney, M. K., 77
McLoyd, V. C., 243
McWilliams, N., 93, 100
Meddoff, G. S., 212
Messer, S. B., xii, 13, 42, 232
Mikesell, R. H., 75, 153
Miklowitz, D. J., 81, 140, 196
Miller, A., 63, 137
Miller, W. R., 7, 12, 109, 110, 133
Millman, R. B., 132
Millon, T., ix, xi, 4, 7, 9, 13, 14, 16, 20, 33, 37, 46, 75, 85, 90, 92, 100
Minuchin, S., xii, 119, 190
Morey, L., 92
Moultrup, D., 207
Murphy, S. L., 132

Newman, C. F., 77
Nichols, W. C., 11, 104, 127, 201
Niedner, D., 146
Niedner, D. M., 65, 144
Norcross, J. C., 12, 13, 77

Olson, D. H., 42, 89, 96
Ornish, D., 11

Pankseep, J., 195
Paris, J., 33
Patterson, T. E., 21
Pearlman, L. A., 65, 146
Peck, M. S., 65, 207
Perlmutter, R. A., 20, 31, 53, 57, 91, 127, 140, 147, 148, 152
Perry, S., 15
Phillips, V. A., 54
Pianta, R. B., 242
Pilkonis, 40
Pilkonis, P. A., 11
Pinsof, W. M., 13, 15, 19, 162, 165, 166, 184, 221, 222, 224, 227, 231, 233
Piper, W. E., 160
Pitta, P., 210
Plomin, R., 36
Poling, J. G., 92
Prata, G., 190

Pressman, R. M., 50, 54, 62, 63
Prochaska, J. O., 12, 110
Pugh, C. A., 210

Quinlan, D. M., 11

Rachman, W., 77, 78
Rait, D. S., 221, 227, 228
Ramey, C. T., 245
Ramey, S. L., 245
Rampage, C., 19–20
Rank, O., 7, 14
Reich, W., 8, 72, 85–86
Reiss, D., 8
Rogers, C., 10, 79
Rollnick, S., 7
Rosie, J. S., 160
Rossman, B. B. R., 144
Rounsaville, B. J., 92
Rueveni, U., 81
Ruppert, S., 52, 123, 201
Rush, A. J., 73–74

Saakvitne, K. W., 65, 146
Safran, J. D., 13, 234
Sameroff, M. A., 9, 106
Sauber, S. R., 212
Scarr, S., 245
Schnarch, D. M., 160, 208, 209
Schneewind, K. A., 52, 123, 201
Schorer, L. R., 146
Seaburn, D., 80, 190
Seligman, M. E. P., 6
Selvini-Palazzoli, M., 128, 190
Shapiro, D., 4, 73
Shapiro, D. A., 15
Shapiro, E. R., 51, 62, 161
Shapiro, R. L., 62, 161
Shaw, B. F., 73–74
Sheldon, 39, 40
Sifneos, P. E., 14, 84, 87
Singer, M. T., 196
Skynner, A. C. R., 63
Slavik, S., 201
Solomon, 38
Solomon, M. F., 24, 201
Spark, G. M., 51
Sperry, L., 4, 16, 33, 202
Stader, M., 52
Stanton, M. D., 130, 132, 190
Starzomski, A. J., 146, 218
Stein, J., 128, 223

Stellato-Kabat, D., 132, 133
Stellato-Kabat, J., 132
Stephens, V., xii
Stone, M., 46
Stouthamer-Loeber, M., 243
Strack, S., x
Stricker, G., 13
Sullivan, H. S., 74, 128
Symonds, D. D., 221
Synder, D. K., 101, 106

Tennen, H., 92
Terkelsen, K. G., 21–22, 50, 51, 57–58, 112, 113, 122
Thomas, A., 36
Tiepper, 146
Todd, T. C., 190
Tohen, M., 61
Toth, S. L., 241
Trepper, T. S., 65, 144
Tyrer, P., 33, 61, 67, 94, 169

Van der Kolk, B. A., 15, 144
Vaughn, C. E., 196

Wachtel, P. L., 77
Walker, L., 144, 145, 218
Ward, N. G., 6, 99
Watson, J. C., 223
Watzlawick, P., 187, 189, 190, 191, 192, 193
Weakland, J., 189
Weil, A., 11, 80, 186
Weiler, S. J., 146
Weisaeth, L., 15
West, 39, 40
Whitaker, C. A., xii, 86–87, 197, 225, 227
Williams, T. G., 104
Wilson, G. T., 7
Wing, J. K., 196
Wolfe, B. E., 5, 7
Woolfolk, R. L., 42
Wynne, L. C., 20, 196

Yalom, I. D., 30
Young, J. E., 123

Zanarini, M. C., 168
Zinner, J., 62, 161
Zucker, R. A., 33
Zuroff, D. C., 11

Subject Index

Abuse
case study of severely abused male,
95–96, 98
in couple treatment, 218
of drugs and alcohol, 244
Ferenczi on, 78–79
Abusive family relationships, 242–243
Acculturation problems, in addictive
dysfunctional personologic
systems, 133
Achievement, and narcissistic
dysfunctional personologic system
(NarDps), 62
Action, 12
Action stage of change, 111
Activation, of therapeutic alliance, 223–224
AdcDps. *See* Addictive dysfunctional
personologic system (AdcDps)
Addiction, 244
"hitting rock bottom" in, 114
Addictive disorders, transtheoretical
model and, 12
Addictive dysfunctional personologic
system (AdcDps), 61–62
assessment of, 133
case study of, 134
intervention in, 134
themes, communications, and relational
issues of, 131
treatment protocols for, 172–173
Adolescent-centered triangles, 22

Adolescents
families with, 204
pregnancy of, 241–242
Adult children, in developmentally
arrested dysfunctional personologic
system (DevDps), 142–143
Adults, launching children from family,
203–205
Adult to adult attachment, 39–41
Affective illness, and depressigenic
dysfunctional personologic system
(DepDps), 147
Affective matrix, 40–41
Affective restructuring, 123–124
Affective science, emotional language
and, 195–196
Aggression, 144
juvenile, 243
Alcohol abuse, 244
access to treatment for, 246
addictive dysfunctional personologic
system and, 130–134
Alexithymic patient, 41
Alliance with therapist. *See* Therapeutic
alliance
American Psychiatric Association
(APA). *See Diagnostic and Statistical
Manual* (DSM)
Analysis. *See* Psychotherapy; Therapy
Anger, sexual dysfunction and,
209–210

Angry-withdrawn attachment, 40
Antisocial Relational Disorder (Nichols), 104
Anxiety
  associated with change, 87–88
  attachment and intimacy disturbances
    and, 25–26
  and battered woman syndrome, 145
  clinical guidelines for shifting and
    regulating, 87–88
  conflictual, 30–31
  existential, 30
  exploring catastrophic fears, 86–87
  genetics and, 34–35
  individual and systemic roots of,
    29–30
  management of, 31–32
  and personologic system, 29
  as precursor to change, 115–116
  shifting from one subsystem to
    another, 86
  shifting to another member of system,
    85–86
  systemic, 31
  systemic management and regulation
    of, 85–87
  vertical and horizontal, 31
Anxiety-arousing maneuvers, 14
Anxiety level, emotional growth, defense
  restructuring, and, 84–85
Anxious-ambivalent attachment, 38
Anxious-avoidant attachment, 9–10, 38
Approach/avoidance paradox, intimacy
  and, 25
Assessment. *See also* Diagnostic labeling;
  Integrative relational assessment
  of addictive dysfunctional personologic
    systems, 133
  based on type of dysfunctional
    personologic system, 130–155
  categories of procedures, 99–106
  of chronically medically ill
    dysfunctional personologic system
    (MedDps), 150–151
  clinical interviewing and, 99–100
  conceptual model for assessing family
    from systems perspective, 103
  of couples, 104
  of covertly narcissistic dysfunctional
    personologic system (CNrDps), 138
  of depressigenic dysfunctional
    personologic system (DepDps), 148

  of developmentally arrested
    dysfunctional personologic system
    (DevDps), 142–143
  and diagnostic labels, 89–91
  of family process, 105
  methods of, 98–99
  multilevel approach to, 102–106
  multisystem assessment of personality
    pathology, 94–97
  of narcissistic dysfunctional personologic
    system (NarDps), 136
  of paranoid dysfunctional personologic
    system (ParDps), 152
  of parent-child relationships, 106
  of physically/sexually traumatizing
    dysfunctional personologic system
    (TraDps), 144–146
  psychological tests and, 100
  of psychotic dysfunctional personologic
    system (PscDps), 140
  relevance of, 89–91
  of somatic dysfunctional personologic
    system (SomDps), 154
Assumptions, cognitive restructuring
  and, 124
Attachment
  adult to adult, 39–41
  child to parent, 39
  classifications of, 38–40
  disturbances in, 25–26
  maladaptive, 9
  personality and, 9
  process of, 74
  shifting in family, 205
  styles of, 36–37
  system of, 241
  in therapeutic alliance, 223–224
Attention deficit disorders, genetic
  component of, 36
Audiovisual technology, 15
Auditory paramessages, 196–197
Authority vs. authoritarianism, of
  therapist, 230–231
Automatic thoughts, 74
Awareness, as precursor to change, 116
Axis I disorder, 34–35

Battered woman syndrome, 145
Batterers
  and couple therapy, 218
  profile of, 66

Behavior, pathology and deficit model of, 186–187
Behavior patterns
  cultural and family systems and, 11
  of infants, 35–36
Beliefs, cognitive restructuring and, 124
Biological factors in personality development. *See also* Biopsychosocial model
  attachment styles and, 36–37, 38–40
  development processes and, 37
  genetics and, 34–36
  temperament styles and, 36
Biopsychosocial factors, 11
Biopsychosocial model, 20
  aspects and assumptions for personality pathology, 43–44
  in assessment and case conceptualization, 44–47
  biological factors in, 34–40
  general system model, 43
  matrix of, 34–47
  psychological factors in, 40–41
  in relational field, 32–34
Bipolar disorder, genetic component of, 36
Blending systems, 212–213
Body morphology, personality and, 36
Borderline and narcissistic couple, 215–216
Borderline personality disorder, cognitive-behavior model for, 74
Boundary problems
  impermeable or weak external boundaries, 54
  poor boundaries within family system, 55
Breakthrough problem
  bridging gap between research and practice, 5–7
  defined, 5
  for psychotherapy, 5

Caretaking roles, reversal of, 205
Case study
  of addictive dysfunctional personologic systems, 134
  of chronically medically ill dysfunctional personologic system (MedDps), 151
  of couples, 217
  of covertly narcissistic dysfunctional personologic system (CNrDps), 138–139
  of depressigenic dysfunctional personologic system (DepDps), 125–126, 149–150, 199
  of developmentally arrested dysfunctional personologic system (DevDps), 143–144
  of dysfunctional personologic family system, 28–29
  of family held hostage, 2–3
  on locating fulcrum point for treatment, 128–129
  man with chronic pain, 58
  of narcissistic dysfunctional personologic system (NarDps), 137, 193–194
  of NarDps in precontemplative stage of change, 229
  of paranoid dysfunctional personologic system (ParDps), 152–153
  of passive-dependent personality, 45–46
  of physically/sexually traumatizing dysfunctional personologic system (TraDps), 147, 182–184, 198
  of psychotic dysfunctional personologic system (PscDps), 141
  of severely abused 28-year-old male, 95–96, 97
  of somatic dysfunctional personologic system (SomDps), 154
  substance abuse and, 231–232
  of therapeutic misalliance, 236
Categorical classification of personality, 91–92, 95
Change
  anxiety associated with, 87–88
  assumptions about, 188
  discontinuous transformational experiences and, 109–110
  first- and second-order, 112–114
  framing reasons for, 191–192
  individual quantum change episodes, 109–110
  natural, due to development and passage of time, 112
  nonverbal communication and, 196
  precursors to, 114, 115–118
  process and types of, 12, 109–114
  quantum change episodes, 12
  research demonstrating active ingredients of, 15

Change (Continued)
    resistance to, 114–118, 214–215,
        232–233
    restructuring dysfunctional
        personologic system and, 118–121
    spiral pattern of, 110–112
    at system fulcrum points, 127–155
    transtheoretical model of, 111
Changing Character: Short-Term Anxiety-
    Regulating Psychotherapy for
    Restructuring Defenses, Affects, and
    Attachments (Vaillant), 83
Character and Anal Eroticism (Freud), 72
Character neurosis, 72
Characterological transformation, 7–8
Character pathology, 7
Chemical dependence. See Addictive
    dysfunctional personologic system
    (AdcDps)
Child care, access to, 245
Child-centered triangles, 22
Childrearing behavior, generational
    passage of, 51–52
Children
    arrival of, 204
    in narcissistic dysfunctional
        personologic system, 62
    restructuring parent-child relations,
        120–121
    and reversal of parent-child
        relationship, 56
Child to parent attachment, 39
Chronically medically ill dysfunctional
    personologic system (MedDps), 67,
    150–152
    assessment of, 150–151
    case study of, 151
    themes, communications, and relational
        issues of, 31
    treatment of, 151
    treatment protocols for, 177–178
Chronic pain, case study of, 58
Classification. See also Classification
    systems for personality disorders
    of dysfunctional personologic
        systems, 4–5
    of personality disorders, 8, 9
    and therapeutic alliance, 224–225
Classification systems for personality
    disorders, 91–94
    categorical, 91–92
    cognitive, 93

    dimensional, 92
    interpersonal, 93–94
    relational, 94
    structural, 92–93
Clinical interviewing, 99–100
Clinical practice, gap with research, 5–7
Clinical treatment. See Treatment
Clinical utility of concepts, 6
Clinicians
    characteristics of, 79
    Ferenczi on, 79
    process issues for, 84–88
    requirements of, 46–47
Cluster A Personality Disorders, 53
Cluster C (dependent, avoidant,
    obsessive-compulsive) spouse, 216
CNrDps. See Covertly narcissistic
    dysfunctional personologic system
    (CNrDps)
Cobras, as type of batterer, 66
Codependency, couples therapy and, 214
Cognitive/affective matrix, 40–41
Cognitive classification of personality,
    91–92, 95
Cognitive disturbance, and battered
    woman syndrome, 145
Cognitive matrix, 41–42
Cognitive restructuring, 123–124
Cognitive theory, 73–74
Cognitive theory—cognitive domain, 72
Cohesion, of family, 96
Common factors, 15
Communication
    auditory paramessages, 196
    in family system, 55–56, 96–97
    language of emotions and, 194–196
    language of therapeutic alliance and,
        185–200
    metacommunication and, 187–189,
        197–198
    miscommunication and, 235
    in narcissistic dysfunctional
        personologic system (NarDps),
        193–194
    nonverbal, 196–197
    in psychotic dysfunctional personologic
        system (PscDps), 139–140
    scripts and, 198
    symptomatic presentation as, 193
    visual paramessages, 196
Community, assessing families from
    perspective of, 103

Community aspects of divorce, 212
Comorbidity, 168–169
  personality disorders and, 169
Comprehensive treatment protocols,
    163–164
Compulsive caregiving attachment, 39
Compulsive care-seeking attachment, 39
Compulsive self-reliant attachment, 39
Computer technology, 14–15
Concurrent treatment, 165
Conflict
  displacement of, 206
  triangle of, 26–27
Conflict pathology, 73
Conflictual anxiety, 30–31
Confronting problem, as precursor to
    change, 116
Confusion, as precursor of reframing, 190
*Constructing the Sexual Crucible: An
    Integration of Sexual and Marital
    Therapy* (Schnarch), 209
Contemplation, 12
Contemplation stage of change, 111
Control issues, in couple treatment, 218
Coparenting issues, 212
Core techniques of family systems
    interventions, 81–84
  corrective emotional experiencing,
    83–84
  ecosystem, 84
  multigenerational, 81
  psychoeducational, 81–82
  restructuring, 82–83
Corrective emotional experiencing, 81,
    83–84
Cost/benefit analysis, defensive
    restructuring and, 123, 158–159
Cost containment, 13–14
Countertransference
  and narcissistic dysfunctional
    personologic families, 62
  therapeutic alliance and, 233
Couples. *See also* Dysfunctional
    personologic family system; Family
    life cycle
  abuse and, 218
  borderline and narcissistic, 215–216
  case study of, 217
  clinical assessment of, 102–105
  containment of tension in, 206
  control in, 218
  crisis points of, 206–213

defense against intimacy in, 206
displacement of conflict in, 206
divorce and, 211–212
domination in, 218
joining of families through marriage
    and, 204
maladaptive parenting, conflicting
    parenting styles, and, 210
  marital infidelity and, 207–208
personality modification in system
    members and, 118–119
personality pathology in, 25–26
and physically/sexually traumatizing
    dysfunctional personologic
    system, 65
remarriage, blending systems, and,
    212–213
resistant, 214–215
separation and, 210–211
sexual dysfunction and, 208–210
technical issues in treatment of,
    217–218
treating with integrative relational
    approach, 201–219
treatment-engaged spouse in, 214–215
treatment of, 213–218
Couples assessment, for TraDps family, 183
Couples therapy, 8
  as treatment modality, 160–161
Covertly narcissistic dysfunctional
    personologic system (CNrDps), 63,
    137–139
  assessment of, 138
  case study of, 138–139
  intervention in, 138–139
  themes, communications, and relational
    issues of, 131
  treatment protocols for, 174–175
Crisis points of couples from
    dysfunctional personologic systems,
    206–213
  maladaptive parenting and conflicting
    parenting styles as, 210
  marital infidelity as, 207–208
  remarriage, blending systems, and,
    212–213
  separation and divorce as, 210–211
  sexual dysfunction and, 208–210
  stages and dynamics of divorce and,
    211–212
Cultural/societal factors, in personality
    development, 42

Cultural systems, assessing families from perspective of, 103
Custody issues, 212
Cycles of change. *See* Spiral pattern of change

Death anxiety, 30
Death themes, in addictive dysfunctional personologic systems, 133
Deep structure, 194–198
Defeat, language of possibility and, 188–189
Defense-challenging maneuvers, 13
Defenses, against intimacy and closeness, 10
Defensive restructuring, 123
Defensive system, 41
Deficit pathology, 73
Denial, by health professionals and educators, 240
DepDps. *See* Depressigenic dysfunctional personologic system (DepDps)
Depressigenic dysfunctional personologic system (DepDps), 66–67, 147–150
   assessment of, 148–149
   case study of, 125–126, 149–150, 199
   intervention in, 149
   themes, communications, and relational issues of, 131
Depression. *See also* Depressigenic dysfunctional personologic system (DepDps)
   as family matter, 52
   genetics and, 34–35
   and psychotic dysfunctional personologic system, 140
Depressive disorders, 21
Depressotypic developmental organization, 241
Detriangulation. *See also* Triangles/triangulation
   couple therapy and, 217–218
   functioning of child and, 121
   restructuring interventions and, 82
DevDps. *See* Developmentally arrested dysfunctional personologic system (DevDps)
Development
   of couple, 213
   natural change through, 111

Developmentally arrested dysfunctional personologic system (DevDps), 64–65, 142–144
   assessment of, 142–143
   case study of, 143–144
   intervention in, 143
   themes, communications, and relational issues of, 131
   treatment protocols for, 175–176
Developmental processes, biopsychosocial matrix and, 37
Developmental stages, of family, 97
Diagnosis. *See also* Assessment
   assessment procedure categories and, 99–106
   of starting point for treatment, 128–130
Diagnostic and Statistical Manual (DSM)
   Axis VI and, 95
   categorical classification of personality and, 91–92
   DSM-IV and, 8, 53
   personality pathology classified in, 19, 20
Diagnostic labeling, 82. *See also* Classification systems for personality disorders
   relevance of, 89–91
   using clinical judgment about, 90–91
Diagnostic taxonomy, relational and *DSM* formulations, 95
Differential therapeutics, for dysfunctional personologic system, 158–159
Differentiation, 205–206
   process of, 24, 74
Dimensional classification of personality, 91–92, 95
Disadvantaged. *See* Socioeconomic disadvantage
Discontinuous transformational experiences, 109–110
   family change episodes, 110
   quantum change episodes, 109–110
Dismissive attachment, 39
Disorders of Personality DSM-IV and Beyond (Millon and Davis), 33
Disorganized/disoriented attachment, 38
Dissociative identity disorders, and battered woman syndrome, 145
Divorce
   adjustment and, 243–244
   mediation during, 212

stages and dynamics of, 211–212
therapy and, 210–211
Domestic violence, 144
Domination issues, in couple treatment, 218
Drug abuse, addictive dysfunctional
    personologic system and, 130–134
Drugs, 244
Drug treatment, access to, 246
*DSM. See Diagnostic and Statistical Manual
    (DSM)*
Dyadic relationships, 22, 73. *See also*
    Couples
assessing families from perspective of,
    103, 201
Dynamic system, defined, 53
Dysfunctional, use of term, 59
Dysfunctional personologic family
    system, 1–2, 54. *See also* Couples;
    Personality disorder(s); Personality
    pathology; Subtypes of dysfunctional
    personologic family system
anxiety and, 29–32
attachment and intimacy disturbances
    in, 25–26
biopsychosocial matrix of personality
    development and, 34–47
boundary problems in, 54–55
classification and diagnosis issues,
    53–59
classification of, 59–70
common features of, 69–70
communication levels in, 55–56
with conflict pathology, 87
crisis points of couples from, 206–213
with deficit pathology, 87
degree of pathology in, 60
description of, 50–51
differential therapeutics for, 158–159
emotional differentiation and
    regulation in, 56–57
emotional malnourishment in, 57
financial instability in, 57
goal attainment in restructuring, 122
individual variation in, 58–59
mitigating factors in, 59
multigenerational transmission effects
    in, 49, 57–58
multiple level assessment of, 102–106
narcissistic parent in, 56
normalizing anxiety associated with
    change, 87–88

paradigmatic shift in, 246–247
politicization of societal factors and, 240
relational mechanisms in, 20–21
resilient individuals in, 244–245
restructuring, 107–126, 118–121
reversal of parent-child relationship
    in, 56
signs of personality disorders and, 98–99
societal factors and, 241–244
treating couple in, 201–219
understanding and treating, 20
Dysfunctional relationships, psychometric
    assessment instruments for, 14

Early intervention, 245–246
prevention and, 239–248
Economic divorce, 212
Ecosystem interventions, 80, 81, 84
Ecotherapy, as treatment modality, 162
Educators, denial by, 240
Effort, as precursor to change, 117
Ego, undifferentiated, 24
Ego functions, personality and, 73
Ego-syntonicity, 86
Emotion(s)
affective restructuring and, 123–124
experiencing of, 41
language of, 194–196
Emotional abuse, 50, 78
Emotional development, emotional
    language and, 195–196
Emotional differentiation, 24
in family system, 56–57
Emotional intelligence, 246. *See also*
    Emotion(s)
Emotional malnourishment, in family
    system, 57
Emotional regulation, in family system,
    56–57
Empathic failures, of parents, 78
Engagement, in therapeutic alliance, 223
Enmeshment, 24
in developmentally arrested
    dysfunctional personologic system
    (DevDps), 142
Equilibrium, 24
Essential Psychopathology and Its Treatment
    (Maxmen and Ward), 99
Evil subtype system, of
    physically/sexually traumatizing
    dysfunctional personologic system, 65

Existential anxiety, 30
Existential structures, 41
Expectancy (placebo effect), 15, 80
  in spontaneous healing, 186
Extended family, assessing families from
    perspective of, 103
Extramarital affairs, 22, 207–208
  restructuring triangles and, 208
Extratherapeutic factors, 15, 79–80
Eye contact, intimacy and, 26

Factor analytic approaches, 92
Family
  abuse relationships in, 242
  with adolescents, 204
  adult children separation from,
      203–204
  blended, 212–213
  cohesion of, 96
  communication in, 96–97
  and context in personality disorders, 127
  defined, 50
  developmental stages of, 97
  differentiation and, 205–206
  flexibility of, 96
  in later life, 205
  maltreatment vs. violence in, 242
  rationalizations in, 70
  realignment of hierarchy in, 119–120
  restructuring of, 81
  restructuring parent-child relational
      subsystem in, 120–121
  shifting of attachment in, 205
  with young children, 204
Family aspects of divorce, 212
Family discontinuous change episodes, 110
Family history, 3
  genogram and, 101–102
Family life cycle
  individual in, 167–168
  second-order change and, 112–113
  stages of, 203–206
Family Life Cycle, The: A Framework for
    Family Therapy (Carter &
    McGoldrick), 50
Family life cycle transitions, intervention
    selection and, 167
Family process relational assessment, 105
Family secrets, 54
Family system. See also Dysfunctional
    personologic family system
  benefits of support, 11

  differentiation in, 24
  dysfunctional personologic, 1–2
  fusion/enmeshment in, 24
  genogram of, 2
  homeostasis in, 24
  modifying structure of, 119–120
  operating system in, 23–24
  personality development within, 10
  relational psychodynamics in, 78
  systemic factors in, 42
  triangle/triangulation in, 22–23
Family systems approach
  to personality pathology, 19
  theory of, 8
Family therapy
  core techniques in, 80–81
  family systems theory and, 8
Father hunger, 57, 129
Fearful-avoidant attachment, 39
Feelings. See Emotion(s)
Ferenczi's technical developments, 77–79
Financial instability, in family
    system, 57
First-order change, 112
Five-factor model, 92
Flexibility. See also Flexible treatment
    formats
  of family, 96
  in therapeutic stance, 225
Flexible treatment formats, 162–164
  length of sessions, 163
  length of treatment, 163–164
  scheduling of sessions, 163
Fourth stage of integration, 19–20
Freudian theory. See Psychoanalytic
    theory
Fulcrum, identifying for treatment,
    128–129
Functional family, 51, 53–54
Fusion/enmeshment, 24

General systems theory, 11
Generational issues
  multigenerational dysfunctional
      system, 57–58
  passage of childrearing behavior, 51–52
  shifting dysfunctional personologic
      system, 69
Genetics, personality development and,
    34–36
Genogram, 2, 3
  family history and, 101–102

Goals
    basic restructuring, 124–125
    in restructuring interventions, 121–122
    of treatment in integrative relational
        psychotherapy, 88
Greening of Relationship Science
    (Berscheid), 248
Group psychotherapy. *See also* Support
    groups
    as treatment modality, 160
Growth factors
    expectancy (placebo effect), 80
    extratherapeutic, 79–80

*Handbook of Relational Diagnosis and
    Dysfunctional Family Patterns*
    (Reiss), 8
Health care delivery system, treatment
    duration and, 13–14
Health professionals, denial by, 240
Health schemes, 6
Here and now interventions, 80
    corrective emotional experiencing as,
        83–84
Heredity. *See* Genetics
Hidden triangles, 22
Hierarchy. *See* Family
Histrionic and passive-aggressive
    couple, 216
Histrionic individual
    intimacy and, 25
    and schizoid or cluster spouse, 216
Histrionic Relationship Disorder (Nichols), 104
Holidays, negative reactions to, 69
Homeostasis, 24
    intervention selection and, 167
Hope, as precursor to change, 117
Horizontal anxiety, 31

Id-ego-supergo, conflictual anxiety
    and, 20
Illness. *See* Chronically medically ill
    dysfunctional personologic system
    (MedDps)
Impermeable external family
    boundaries, 54
Incompetent subtype, of
    physically/sexually traumatizing
    dysfunctional personologic system, 65
Individual
    assessing families from perspective
        of, 103

in family life cycle, 167–168
personality pathology within, 7–8
variation in dysfunctional personologic
    system, 58–59
Individual dysfunction triangles, 22
Individual psychotherapy, as treatment
    modality, 160
Individual treatment protocols, 170–172
    intermittent interventions and, 171–172
    long-term intervention and, 171
    maintenance intervention and, 172
    short-term intervention and, 171
Individuation issues
    in developmentally arrested
        dysfunctional personologic system
        (DevDps), 142–143
    developmentally arrested dysfunctional
        personologic system and, 64
Infants
    behavior patterns of, 35–36
    development of, 9
Infidelity. *See* Marital infidelity
Information-processing model of
    psychopathology, 74
In Session: Psychotherapy in Practice,
    "Resistance to Change in
    Psychotherapy" (Arkowitz), 232
Integration
    of practice and research, 6
    relevance and types of, 76–79
    technical eclecticism and, 77
    theoretical, 77
Integrative, use of term, 20
Integrative psychotherapy. *See also*
    Dysfunctional personologic family
    system; Integrative relational
    psychotherapy
    evolution of, 13
    model of, 20
    for personality disorders, 8
Integrative relational approach, couple
    therapy with, 202–219
Integrative relational assessment
    categories of procedures, 99–106
    classification systems for personality
        disorders, 91–94
    combining classifications: multisystem
        assessment of personality
        pathology, 94–97
    methods of, 98–99
    relevance of assessment and diagnostic
        labels, 89–91

Integrative relational model of personality disorders, 11–17
advancements to treating disorders and dysfunctional personologic systems, 12–16
recommendations for broadening effectiveness, 16–17
Integrative relational psychotherapy
adopting orientation of, 76–80
core techniques of family systems intervention, 80–84
personality theories and, 71–76
process issues in, 84–88
systemic and psychodynamic constructs of, 26–32
theory of, 19–47
treatment goals of, 88
Integrative theory, 75
Intensive short-term dynamic psychotherapy, 14
Intergenerational transfer. See also Generational issues
of childrearing patterns, 52
Intermittent interventions, 171–172
Interpersonal classification of personality, 91–92, 95
Interpersonal insensitivity, 40
Interpersonal matrix, 42, 84
Interpersonal relationships, role of, 8–9
Interpersonal structures, 41
Interpersonal systems, 20
Interpersonal theory, 74–75
Interpersonal theory—interpersonal-Dyadic domain, 72
Intervention. See also Therapy; Treatment
in addictive dysfunctional personologic systems, 134
based on type of dysfunctional personologic system, 130–155
categories of, 81
in covertly narcissistic dysfunctional personologic system (CNrDps), 138–139
in depressigenic dysfunctional personologic system (DepDps), 149
in developmentally arrested dysfunctional personologic system (DevDps), 143
early, 239–248
ecosystem, 81
family restructuring, 81

frameworks for, 170–172
here and now, 80
intermittent, 171–172
long-term, 171
maintenance, 172
multigenerational, 81
in narcissistic dysfunctional personologic system (NarDps), 136
in paranoid dysfunctional personologic system (ParDps), 152–153
in physically/sexually traumatizing dysfunctional personologic system (TraDps), 146–147
psychoeducational, 81
in psychotic dysfunctional personologic system (PscDps), 140
selecting type of, 166–168
short-term, 171
in somatic dysfunctional personologic system (SomDps), 154
system fulcrum point and, 128–129
targeting, 3, 165–168
transgenerational, 80, 81
Interviewing
clinical, 99–100
structural, 99–100
Intimacy, 10
couple treatment and, 213–214
defense against, 206
disturbances in, 25–26
sexual dysfunction within couple and, 208–210
in therapeutic alliance, 224
Intrapersonal structures, in personality development, 40–41
Intrapsychic matrix
cognitive, 74
restructuring, 123–124
Intrapsychic systems, 20
I-You relationship, 24

Judo technique, 192–193
Juvenile aggression, 243

Labeling. See also Diagnostic labeling
language of, 186–187
pejorative use of, 90
Language. See also Communication
of emotions, 194–196
finding system for treatment, 229
of labeling, 186–187

metaphor and, 198–199
of paradox, 189–194
of possibility, 188–189
power of, 185–186
of resistance, 191
of therapeutic alliance, 185–200
Learning disabilities, genetic component
of, 36
Legal aspects of divorce, 212
Libido (sexual expression), personality
and, 73
Life cycle changes
in family life cycle, 203–206
second-order change and,
112–113
triangles and, 22
Life events, capitalizing on, 168
Lineage of pathology, 49
Long-term intervention, 171
Low self-esteem, among family
members, 70
Loyalty issues, in developmentally
arrested dysfunctional personologic
system (DevDps), 142

Maintenance, 12
Maintenance intervention, 172
Maintenance stage of change, 111
Major Theories of Personality Disorder
(Clarkin and Lenzenweger), 71
Maladaptive attachment, 9
Maladaptive parenting, and conflicting
parenting styles, 210
Managed care movement, treatment
duration and, 13–14
Marital disorders, 21
and narcissistic dysfunctional
personologic system
(NarDps), 135
Marital infidelity, 207–208
restructuring extramarital triangles
and, 208
Marital triangles, 22
Marriage. *See also* Marital infidelity
differentiation and, 205–206
divorce and, 210–211
joining of families through, 204
Matrix, biopsychosocial and relational,
34–47
Maturation, developmentally arrested
dysfunctional personologic system
and, 64

McMater Regional Mood Disorders
Program, 247
MedDps. *See* Chronically medically ill
dysfunctional personologic system
(MedDps)
Mediation, in divorce, 212
Medical paradigm, of personality
disorders, 16
Medication. *See* Pharmacotherapy
Memory disturbance, and battered
woman syndrome, 145
Metacommunication, 197–198
language of, 187–189
Metaphors, 198–199
therapeutic, 82
Midrange family, 54
Millon Clinical Multiaxial Inventory-III
(MCMI-III), 100
Mind-body dichotomy, in somatic
dysfunctional personologic system
(SomDps), 155
Minnesota Multiphasic Personality
Inventory (MMPI), 100
Misalliance, in therapy, 234, 235–237
MMPI. *See* Minnesota Multiphasic
Personality Inventory (MMPI)
Modalities of treatment. *See* Treatment
modalities
Models. *See also* specific models
for treatment, 247–248
Modification of personality, in key
members of system, 118–119
Monitoring, of anxiety, 32
Mood disorder, and depressigenic
dysfunctional personologic system
(DepDps), 148
Morphology. *See* Body morphology
Motivation, intervention selection and,
166–167
Motivational interviewing, 7
Multidimensional restructuring process,
123–125
basic goals of, 124–125
triangle of conflict and, 123–124
triangle of persons and, 124
triangle of relationships and, 124
Multigenerational dysfunctional system,
49. *See also* specific systems
transmission effects in, 57–58
Multigenerational interventions, 81
Multilevel approach, to marital and
family assessment, 102

Multimodal treatment programs, 3, 247–248
Multisystem assessment of personality pathology, 94–97

Naming. *See* Diagnostic labeling; Labeling
Narcissistic dysfunctional personologic system (NarDps), 62, 135–137
  assessment of, 136
  case study of, 137, 193–194
  case study of patient in precontemplative stage of change, 229
  intervention in, 136
  marital dysfunction in, 135
  themes, communications, and relational issues of, 131
  treatment protocols for, 173–174
Narcissistic parent, in dysfunctional personologic family system, 56
Narcissistic spouse
  borderline spouse and, 215–216
  Cluster C spouse and, 216
NarDps. *See* Narcissistic dysfunctional personologic system (NarDps)
Natural change, due to development and passage of time, 111
Nature of Emotion, The (Ekman and Davidson), 195
Necessity, as precursor to change, 115
Neglect, 50
Network sessions, 81
Neurobiological system, 34
Neurosis, 72
Neurotic character, 73
Noble ascription, 191
Nonverbal communication, 196–197
Normal anxiety, 32
Nuclear family, assessing families from perspective of, 103
Nurturance, by therapist, 226

Object relations, personality theory and, 73
Object representation system, 41
Obsessive-compulsive personality, 40
  intimacy and, 25
Operating system, in relational framework, 23–24
Opposing systems, therapeutic alliance and, 233

Pain, in triangle, 22
Paradigm
  encouraging paradigmatic shift and, 246–247
  replacing medical, 16
Paradox, language of, 189–194
Paramessages, 196–197
Paranoid dysfunctional personologic system (ParDps), 68, 152–153
  assessment of, 152
  case study of, 152–153
  intervention in, 152
  themes, communications, and relational issues of, 131
ParDps. *See* Paranoid dysfunctional personologic system (ParDps)
Parental psychopathology, Ferenczi on, 78
Parent-child relations
  assessment of, 105–106
  in narcissistic dysfunctional personologic system, 135
  restructuring of, 120–121
  reversal of relationship in, 56, 135
  triangle of, 22
Parents and parenting. *See also* Dysfunctional personologic family system; Personality disorders; Subtypes of dysfunctional personologic family system
  biological dispositions and, 37
  maladaptive and conflicting, 210
  treatment of pathology in, 120
  treatment of relational differences in styles, 120–121
Passage of time
  change and, 114
  natural change through, 111
Passive-aggressive individual
  histrionic spouse and, 216
  intimacy and, 25
Passive-dependent personality, case study of, 45–46
Passivity, in developmentally arrested dysfunctional personologic system (DevDps), 142
Pathological themes, dysfunctional personologic systems and, 3–4
Pathology. *See* Dysfunctional personologic family system
Pathology and deficit model, of human behavior, 186–187
Patient system, 222

Patterned sequence of behaviors
 determining deep structure and,
  194–198
 family structure unit and, 21–22
Pejorative use of labels, 90
People of the Lie (Peck), 207
Personality
 of couple, 213
 family and, 2
 formation of, 9–10
 history of study of, 9
 modification in key members of system,
  118–119
 organization and shaping within
  family, 10
 psychometric assessment instruments
  for, 14
 restructuring of, 113–114
 in systemic therapy, 198–199
 treatment to restructure, 7
Personality development
 biopsychosocial model in relational
  field, 32–34
 body morphology and, 36
Personality disorder(s)
 as adaptive response to dysfunctional
  family system, 51–52
 from addictive dysfunctional
  personologic system (AdcDps),
  61–62
 change processes and, 113–114
 from chronically medically ill
  dysfunctional personologic system
  (MedDps), 67–68
 classification of, 8, 91–94
 clinical requirements for treating,
  46–47
 and comorbid clinical syndromes, 169
 couples treatment and, 201–219
 from covertly narcissistic dysfunctional
  personologic system (CNrDps), 63
 from depressigenic dysfunctional
  personologic system (DepDps), 67
 from developmentally arrested
  dysfunctional personologic system
  (DevDps), 65
 diagnosing treatment starting point,
  128–130
 family context of, 127
 inoculating child against, 120
 integrative relational model of,
  11–17

integrative therapy for, 8
 as maladaptive developmental
  sequence, 44
 multidetermination of, 44
 from narcissistic dysfunctional
  personologic system, 62
 new attitudes toward, 16
 organic nature of personality and, 44
 from paranoid dysfunctional
  personologic system (ParDps), 68
 from physically/sexually traumatizing
  dysfunctional personologic system
  (TraDps), 66
 from psychotic dysfunctional
  personologic system (PscDps), 64
 signs of, 98–99
 from somatic dysfunctional
  personologic system
  (SomDps), 68
 systems theory and, 44
 use of term, 9
Personality-disordered individuals. *See
 also* Personologic therapy; Therapy
 clinician reasons for not
  treating, 108
 intimacy, closeness, and, 10
 relational disturbances and, 10
 therapeutic alliance and, 10
Personality modification, language
  of, 185
Personality pathology. *See also*
  Dysfunctional personologic family
  system
 biopsychosocial model of personality
  development and, 43–44
 biopsychosocial perspective on, 20
 breakthrough problems for
  psychotherapy, 5–7
 conceptual shift toward, 8–9
 DSM classification of, 19
 frequency of disturbances, 4
 within individual, 7–8
 limitations of models, 52–53
 lineage of, 49
 multisystem assessment of, 94–97
 paradigmatic shift in treating, 4–9
 quantum change episodes, 12
 relational context of, 11
 relational perspective on, 9–11
 seen as existing within the
  individual, 7–8
 triangles and, 23

Personality theories, 71–76
   cognitive, 74–75
   integrative, 75
   interpersonal, 74–86
   psychoanalytic, 72–73
   systemic, 75–76
Personality traits, assessing, 100
Personologic disturbance, Ferenczi on, 78
Personologic system. *See* Dysfunctional
   personologic family system
Personologic therapy. *See also* Change
   attitudes toward, 107–109
   beliefs and reasons undermining, 108
   goals in restructuring process, 121–122
   multidimensional restructuring process
      and, 123–125
Persons, triangle of, 27, 124
Persuasion, as precursor to change, 118
Pharmacotherapy, 35
   as treatment modality, 161
Physical abuse, 78
Physically/sexually traumatizing
   dysfunctional personologic system
      (TraDps), 65–66, 144–147
   assessment of, 144–146
   batterers and, 65–66
   case study of, 147, 182–184, 198
   couples dynamics in, 65–66
   evil subtype of, 65
   incompetent subtype of, 65
   intervention for, 146–147, 183–184
   themes, communications, and relational
      issues of, 131
   treatment protocols for, 176–177
Physiological arousal, and battered
   woman syndrome, 145
Pit Bulls, as type of batterer, 66
Placebo effect. *See* Expectancy (placebo
   effect)
Politicization of societal factors, 240–241
Popeye Syndrome, 85
Positive connotation, reframing and,
   190–191
Possibility, language of, 188–189
Power struggles, in therapy, 234–235
Practice, gap with research, 5–7
Pragmatics of Human Communication
   (Watzlawick, Beavin, and Jackson),
      187–188
Precontemplation, 12
   as stage of change, 111
Predivorce, 212

Pregnancy, adolescent, 241–242
Preoccupied attachment, 39
Preparation stage of change, 111
Prevention, and early intervention,
   239–248
Primary etiological model, and
   psychopathology, 140
Priming mechanisms, 245–246
Problem-centered therapy, 165–166
Problem-maintenance structures, 15, 158
Programmatic considerations
   access to drug and alcohol treatment
      as, 246
   early intervention as, 245–246
   enhancing emotional intelligence as, 246
   quality child care as, 245
Projective techniques, 100
Protocols. *See* Comprehensive treatment
   protocols; Treatment protocols;
   individual treatment protocols
PscDps. *See* Psychotic dysfunctional
   personologic system (PscDps)
Pseudoindividuation, in addictive
   dysfunctional personologic
   systems, 133
Psychic divorce, 212
Psychoanalytically oriented therapists, 7
Psychoanalytic diagnostic formulations,
   structural classification of personality
   and, 92–93
Psychoanalytic theory, 72–73
Psychoanalytic theory—affective
   domain, 72
Psychodynamic and systemic constructs,
   27–32
Psychoeducational intervention, 81–82
   as treatment modality, 161–162
Psychological factors in personality
   development, intrapersonal
   structures in, 40–41
Psychological tests, 100
   Millon Clinical Multiaxial Inventory-III
      (MCMI-III), 100
   Minnesota Multiphasic Personality
      Inventory (MMPI), 100
   projective techniques and, 100
   Rorschach Inkblot Test, 100
   Thematic Apperception Test, 100
Psychometric instruments. *See also*
   Psychological tests
   for assessing personality and
      dysfunctional relationships, 14

Psychopathology, Ferenczi on, 78
Psychopharmacological approaches. *See also* Pharmacotherapy
curative aspect of, 10–11
Psychotherapists, as clinical researchers, 6
Psychotherapy
breakthrough problems for, 5–7
curative aspect of, 10–11
duration of, 13–14
health schemes and, 6
individual, 160
integrative relational, 19–47
intensive short-term, 14
treatment-matching models and technology, 15
Psychotic dysfunctional personologic system (PscDps), 63–64, 139–142
assessment of, 140
case study of, 141
intervention in, 140
judo technique in, 192–193
themes, communications, and relational issues of, 131
treatment protocols for, 175
Psychotropic medication. *See* Pharmacotherapy
Public, increasing awareness of personality disorders in, 247
Public vs. family persona, 70

Quantum change episodes, 12, 109–110

Rapport, 14
Rationalizations, family, 70
Reactivity model, and psychopathology, 140
Reframing
confusion as precursor of, 190
language of paradox and, 189–194
and language of resistance, 191
technique of, 190–191
Regulation, of anxiety, 32, 85–87
Relapse
prediction of, 193
prevention of, 7
Relatedness, in therapeutic alliance, 225
Relational classification of personality, 91–92, 95
Relational disturbances, 169–170
Relational framework, 9. *See also* Integrative relational approach
benefits of support, 11
biopsychosocial model and, 32–34

differentiation in, 24
disturbances in, 10
DSM classification and, 20
fusion/enmeshment in, 24
homeostasis in, 24
operating system in, 23–24
personality pathology and, 9–11
in personologic dysfunctional family system, 20–21
triangle/triangulation in, 22–23
Relational matrix, 84
assessing, 96
maximizing therapeutic relationship in, 221–237
personality development within, 50–53
prevention and early intervention with, 239–248
Relations, triangle of, 27
Religious aspects of divorce, 212
Remarriage, 212–213
Replacement, as goal, 122
Research
demonstrating active ingredients of change, 15
gap with practice, 5–7
relevance to clinical treatment, 5–6
Resilience, 244–245
Resistance
to change, 114–118, 191–192, 232–233
by couples, 214–215
judo technique and, 192–193
language of, 191
of unmotivated patient, 7
Restoration, as goal, 122
Restructuring, of depressigenic dysfunctional personologic system, 125–126
Restructuring interventions, 82–83
affective, 123–124
cognitive, 124
defensive, 123
detriangulation as, 82
extramarital triangles and, 208
initial goals in, 121–122
modification of member personality as, 83
Restructuring Personality Disorders: A Short-Term Dynamic Approach (Magnavita), 83
Rorschach Inkblot Test, 100

Sadomasochistic interactions, 65–66
Safety, in therapeutic alliance, 229–230
Scheduling of sessions, 163
Schema
    cognitive, 93
    interpersonal strategies and, 74
    for personality disorders, 74
Schizoid and cluster C or histrionic
        couple, 216
Schizophrenia
    communication and, 196
    family psychoeducational interventions
        and, 81–82
    genetic component of, 36
    and psychotic dysfunctional
        personologic system, 63–64, 142
Scripts, 198
Second-order change, 112–113, 190
Secure attachment, 38
Self, family context of, 50
Self-disclosure, by therapist, 227
Self-other differentiation, 24
Separation issues
    in developmentally arrested
        dysfunctional personologic system
        (DevDps), 142–143
    young adult and, 203–204
Sequential treatment, 3, 165
Sessions
    length of, 163
    scheduling of, 163
Sex and sexuality. See also
        Physically/sexually traumatizing
        dysfunctional personologic system
        (TraDps)
    libido and, 73
Sexual abuse, 78, 144. See also
        Physically/sexually traumatizing
        dysfunctional personologic system
        (TraDps)
Sexual dysfunction
    and battered woman syndrome, 145
    and depressigenic dysfunctional
        personologic system (DepDps), 148
    and marital dissatisfaction, 208–210
    medical specialists and, 209
    personality pathology and, 209
Shared vulnerability model, and
        psychopathology, 140
Short-Term Dynamic Psychotherapy:
        Evaluation and Technique (Sifneos), 87
Short-term intervention, 171

Social factors in personality development,
        42–43
    cultural/societal factors, 42–43
    interpersonal matrix, 42
    systemic factors, 42
Social support, as precursor to change,
        117–118
Social welfare programs, politics and, 240
Societal factors
    abusive family relationships and, 242
    adolescent pregnancy as, 241–242
    divorce, adjustment, and, 243–244
    drugs, alcohol abuse, and, 244
    and dysfunctional personologic system,
        241–244
    dysfunctional personologic system
        and, 241
    juvenile aggression and, 243
    in personality development, 42
    politicization of, 240–241
    socioeconomic disadvantage and,
        242–243
Socioeconomic disadvantage, societal
        factors and, 242–243
Somatic dysfunctional personologic
        system (SomDps), 68, 153–155
    assessment of, 153–154
    case study of, 154
    intervention in, 154
    themes, communications, and relational
        issues of, 131
    treatment protocols for, 179
Spiral pattern of change, 110–112
Split alliances, 233
Spontaneous healing, expectancy and, 186
Spousal subsystem. See also Couples;
        Family
    and depressigenic dysfunctional
        personologic system
        (DepDps), 148
Stepfamilies, 212–213
Structural Analysis of Social Behavior
        (SASB), 75
Structural classification of personality,
        91–92, 95
Structural interviewing, 99–100
Structure
    deep, 194–198
    modification of family system,
        119–120
    systemic meaning in family system,
        21–24

Structure of Magic, The (Bandler and Grinder), 185
Substance abuse
  addictive dysfunctional personologic system and, 130–134
  case study of, 231–232
Substance use disorders, and addictive dysfunctional personologic system (AdcDps), 61
Subsystems. *See* Couples; Parent-child relations
Subtypes of dysfunctional personologic family system, 60–70
  addictive dysfunctional personologic system (AdcDps), 61–62
  blends of, 68–70
  chronically medically ill dysfunctional personologic system (MedDps), 67–68
  covertly narcissistic dysfunctional personologic system (CnrDps), 63
  depressigenic dysfunctional personologic system (DepDps), 67
  developmentally arrested dysfunctional personologic system (DevDps), 64–65
  narcissistic dysfunctional personologic system (NarDps), 62
  paranoid dysfunctional personologic system (ParDps), 68
  physically/sexually traumatizing dysfunctional personologic system (TraDps), 65–66
  psychotic dysfunctional personologic system (PscDps), 63–64
  somatic dysfunctional personologic system (SomDps), 68
Supplementation, as goal, 122
Support groups, as treatment modality, 162
Symbiotic relationships, in addictive dysfunctional personologic systems, 133
Symbolic-Experiential Family Therapy, 86–87
Symptoms
  presentation of, 193
  in triangle, 22
System(s)
  for assessing families, 103
  defined, 53
  goals in restructuring of dysfunctional personologic, 121–122

  opposing, 233
  therapeutic alliance and, 222
  understanding dynamics of, 228
Systemically oriented therapist, complexity for, 227–228
Systemic and psychodynamic constructs, 26–32
  anxiety and personologic system, 29
  anxiety management, 31–32
  blending of, 28
  case study of, 28–29
  individual and systemic roots of anxiety, 29–30
  types of anxiety, 30–31
Systemic anxiety, 31
  management and regulation of, 85–87
Systemic constructs, meaning of structure, 21–24
Systemic factors, in personality development, 42
Systemic model, 20
Systemic modification, language of, 185
Systemic theory, of personality disorders, 75–76
Systemic theory—relational domain, 72
Systemic therapy. *See also* Systemic theory; Therapy
  metaphor and personality in, 198–199

Targeted intervention strategies, 3, 165–168
Team approach
  conditions of, 7
  treatment and, 163
Technical eclecticism, 77
  Ferenczi's technical developments, 77–79
Techniques, process issues, 84–88
Technological advancements, clinical practitioners and, 14–15
Teenage pregnancy. *See* Adolescents
Temperament
  defined, 73
  genetics and, 35–36
Temperamental styles, 36
Tension, containment of, 206
Thematic Apperception Test, 100
Theoretical integration, 77
Therapeutic alliance, 10
  activation and, 223–224
  bond in, 222
  building and strengthening, 228–233

Therapeutic alliance (Continued)
  case study of, 231–232
  characteristics of good, 226–228
  classification and, 224–225
  collaboration in, 222
  conditions necessary for, 223–225
  defined, 222
  direct system in, 222
  engagement and, 223
  free expression in, 229–230
  indirect system in, 222
  language of, 185–200
  limits of, 231
  maintaining, 6–7
  maximizing in relational matrix,
      221–237
  mutual goals in, 222
  patient system in, 222
  relatedness and, 225
  resistance as counterforce to, 232–233
  safety in, 229–230
  split alliance and, 233
  therapeutic holding in, 230
  therapeutic stance and, 225
  therapist system in, 222
  transferences, countertransference, and
      opposing systems in, 233
Therapeutic alliances, ruptures in, 234–237
Therapeutic field, 179–182
  broadening, 180
  deepening, 179–180
  narrowing, 180
Therapeutic metaphors, 82
Therapeutic stance, and therapeutic
    alliance, 225
Therapists. See also Clinicians
  as authority, 230–231
  belief in capacity to change by, 227
  and characteristics of good therapeutic
      alliance, 226–228
  complexity for, 227–228
  enjoyment of process by, 226
  individual responses to, 233
  movement in and out of frame by,
      226–227
  nurturance by, 226
  self-disclosure by, 227
Therapist system, 222
Therapy. See also Change; Intervention;
    Personologic therapy
  case study of misalliance in, 236

divorce stage and, 210–211
  duration of, 7, 13–14
  flexibility needed in, 221
  misalliance in, 234, 235–237
  miscommunication in, 235
  power struggles in, 234–235
  problem-centered, 165–166
  restorative/healing aspect of, 10
  restructuring, 7–8
Threesomes, vs. triangles, 22–23
TraDps. See Physically/sexually
    traumatizing dysfunctional
    personologic system (TraDps)
Traits. See Personality traits
Transactional analysis, scripts and, 198
Transference, therapeutic alliance
    and, 233
Transference/countertransference
    processes, interpersonal classification
    of personality and, 93–94
Transference neurosis, 7
Transformation, characterological, 7–8
Transformational experiences, 12, 113
  discontinuous, 109–110
Transformational psychotherapy, impact
    on family, 83
Transgenerational interventions, 80, 81
Transtheoretical model of change, 12, 111
Trauma, and battered woman
    syndrome, 145
Trauma theory, 15–16
  Ferenczi on, 78–79
Treatment. See also Intervention;
    Personologic therapy; Psychotherapy;
    Therapy; Treatment modalities
  of addictive dysfunctional personologic
      systems, 133
  broadening spectrum of effectiveness,
      16–17
  of chronically medically ill
      dysfunctional personologic system
      (MedDps), 151
  clinician requirements, 46–47
  comprehensive protocol for, 164–165
  of couples, 213–218
  developing model programs of,
      247–248
  diagnosing starting point for, 128–130
  differential therapeutics concept and,
      158–159
  for drug and alcohol abuse, 246

duration of, 13–14
of dysfunctional personologic
    systems, 4–5
factors in developing program of, 168–170
flexible formats for, 162–164
goals based on integrative relational
    model, 88
individual protocols for, 170–172
intervention strategies for TraDps,
    183–184
length of, 163–164
models of change, 12
of personality pathology, 4–9
program components, 159–164
shifting frame of, 180–182
suggested protocols for, 172–179
symptoms, personality, family
    dynamics, and, 157–158
targeted intervention strategies and,
    165–168
therapeutic field and, 179–182
Treatment-matching models, 15
Treatment modalities, 159–162
couples therapy, 160–161
ecotherapy, 162
group psychotherapy, 160
individual psychotherapy, 160
pharmacotherapy, 161
psychoeducational intervention,
    161–162
recommendation for no treatment, 162
support groups, 162
Treatment protocols
for addictive dysfunctional
    personologic system (AdcDps),
    172–173
for chronically medically ill
    dysfunctional personologic system
    (MedDps), 177–178
comprehensive, 163–164
for covertly narcissistic dysfunctional
    personologic system (CNrDps),
    174–175
for developmentally arrested
    dysfunctional personologic system
    (DevDps), 175–176
individual, 170–172

for narcissistic dysfunctional
    personologic system (NarDps),
    173–174
for physically/sexually traumatizing
    dysfunctional personologic system
    (TraDps), 176–177
for psychotic dysfunctional
    personologic system (PscDps), 175
for somatic dysfunctional personologic
    system (SomDps), 179
Treatment team approach, 163
Triangles/triangulation, 22–23
child- or adolescent-centered, 22
of conflict, 26–27, 123–124
in couple relationships, 202–203
couples therapy and, 217–218
family case study and, 28–29
in family system, 22–23
individual dysfunction and hidden, 22
for intrapsychic, interpersonal, and
    relational systems, 20
marital, 22
and multidimensional restructuring
    process, 123–125
operating system and, 24
for orienting clinician, 84
of persons, 27, 124
of relationships, 27–28, 124
structure of, 22
threesomes compared with, 22–23
Two-person system, 23

Unconscious process, 7
Undifferentiated ego, 24

Vertical anxiety, 31
Victimization. *See* Physically/sexually
    traumatizing dysfunctional
    personologic system (TraDps)
Violence, 144
family, 242
Visual paramessages, 196

Weak external family boundaries, 54–55
*Working with Relationship Triangles: The
    One-Two-Three of Psychotherapy*
    (Guerin et al.), 22